THE REPUTATION OF JONATHAN SWIFT

1781-1882

BY

DONALD M. BERWICK

HASKELL HOUSE
Publishers of Scholarly Books
NEW YORK
1965

published by

HASKELL HOUSE

Publishers of Scholarly Books

30 East 10th Street • New York, N. Y. 10003

Library of Congress Catalog Card Number: 65-21096

PRINTED IN UNITED STATES OF AMERICA

PREFACE

The reader will notice that this study is divided into four parts according to chronology, and he may wonder why I have chosen certain dates for certain sections. Actually, though the several phases of the development of Swift criticism can be roughly distinguished from each other, my choice of terminal dates has been virtually an arbitrary one. For this I can offer no apology beyond the fact that I had to decide upon some way of organizing my material; and the chronological system, whatever its imperfections, seemed the best method for facilitating the reader's work. It must, however, be borne in mind that I have no intention of implying a sharp distinction between the criticism treated in one part and that of the next. In the same way, I have discussed opinions of separate works under various headings, respectively alike in each of the four large sections. For example, the reader will find such diverse pieces as the _Modest Proposal_ and the _Polite Conversations_ grouped together, along with several others, as Bagatelles and Miscellaneous Works; and the sole test of this somewhat arbitrary system must be the pragmatic one. I am aware of its limitations, but I think it will work.

This monograph is a briefer reworking of a doctoral dissertation completed at Princeton University in 1937. For assistance in its preparation I am indebted to Mr. J. R. Fredland for his sympathetic interest and often valuable suggestions; to Dr. J. F. A. Taylor for his willing drudgery in verifying the manuscript; to Mr. Malcolm O. Young of the Princeton University Library; and especially to Professor Robert Kilburn Root, under whose careful and instructive guidance my work took shape.

I sincerely wish this were a better book; if it were, I should feel justified in dedicating it to the memory of my cherished friend Josiah Marshall Linton, Jr.

TABLE OF CONTENTS

INTRODUCTION

I

Conceptions of art change with the changing moods of succeeding ages, and the standards of yesterday often become the misinformed prejudices of today. The reputation of an accepted classic of the English language does not, therefore, develop in a vacuum. It lives and grows and varies according to some appreciable pattern of thought or feeling, whether well or ill-defined; and an attempt to trace that pattern becomes an interesting and not entirely fruitless task.

Though it is nearly two hundred years since Jonathan Swift passed on "ubi saeva indignatio ulterius cor lacerare nequit," the story of that "saeva indignatio" has persisted through the centuries. The problems of Swift's life and personality have captured the fancy and enslaved the pens of men from his day to our own, and the study of his mind and art has grown increasingly thorough with successive ages. He has been despised as a man and idolized as a writer; he has been admired as a man, and his abilities as a writer have been questioned. On no single problem of Swift criticism has there ever been unanimity of opinion. "The catalogue of Swift's literary enemies," says a writer in the Saturday Review of 1883, "if it were drawn up, would include some of the most apparently remarkable inconsistencies, and would offer to a classifier some of the most curious difficulties, to be found in or suggested by any list of the kind."[1] And the same thing might be said with equal truth of the catalogue of Swift's literary friends. His biographers have in general been either passionately adverse or passionately sympathetic; but it is difficult to find a common bond between the members of each respective group beyond the inevitable fascination which grips every student of Swift, whether repelled or invigorated by the personality and life story of the man. In studying the history of successive attitudes toward Swift the writer, we are, indeed, confronted with a real problem. Although, except for a few short poems and a journal not intended for the public eye, he wrote almost nothing of an intensely personal nature, his works have seldom been discussed without strong biographical overtones. Many critics have, in short, been unable to see the writings for the man behind them.

A survey of Swift criticism, then, which would attempt to deal only with the works, much as such a limited study might be desirable, would be virtually impossible

[1] LV, 51-52. A review of Craik's *The Life of Jonathan Swift.*

of execution. A recent biographer has suggested that a thorough study of Gulliver's Travels as it has appeared to critics since Swift's time "would throw a great deal of light upon the formation of standard attitudes towards well-known works of art and the manner in which these attitudes are perpetuated."[1] This is at first glance an attractive idea; but judgments of Gulliver's Travels have so frequently depended upon judgments of Jonathan Swift himself that the task of separating the chaff from the wheat might vex even the most expert of winnowers. A discussion of the biographical material alone would be simpler, and there have been several such, the most nearly complete of which can be found in M. Pons' excellent biography of the early years of Swift.[2] M. Pons has, however, treated the subject only as it relates to the accumulation of factual material about the life and has merely touched upon Swift's reputation as an author. My object, then, has been to make a survey of critical opinion as it has dealt with the writings of Swift, but I have included such biographical discussion as seems to have affected literary judgments.[3]

The dual purpose of my study is to attempt to gain not only a picture of Swift's reputation as such but also an understanding of the temper of the years during which that reputation developed. I have, therefore, limited my major discussion to a period of about a century--from 1781, when Johnson brought out his Lives of the English Poets, to 1882, the date of Craik's monumental biography of Swift. Johnson, the first important critic to write at length upon Swift, published his essay at the end of a period marked by literary gossip and ostensibly eye-witness reports of various phases of the manifold Swiftian problems. During the century which followed, a new kind of criticism slowly evolved, a sympathetic, truth-seeking scholarship, which bases its judgments, whenever possible, upon a more solid foundation than that of mere prejudice. And that type of criticism reached its full flowering toward the end of the nineteenth century, with the works of such men as Forster and Craik. Between Johnson and Craik, however, intervened a hundred years which, from the historical and ideological point of view, are of unique interest to the student of English literature. The wide-eyed Romantic and the stern-voiced early Victorian--what could they have had to say about the rationalistic age of Queen Anne, and especially about Jonathan Swift, who was so typical a product of that age?

[1] Ricardo Quintana, *The Mind and Art of Jonathan Swift*, New York, 1936, p. 306.

[2] *Swift. Les Annees de Jeunesse et Le "Conte du Tonneau"*, Strasbourg, 1925, 1-105.

[3] Maxwell B. Gold's study of the marriage question, *Swift's Marriage to Stella*, Cambridge, 1937, though somewhat suspect in its conclusions, makes so complete a chronological survey of that field that a similar attempt is unnecessary. Thus I shall treat discussions of the marriage only as they have some effect upon broader judgments.

One other limitation I have made: for the sake of unity--and, too, brevity--I have not tried to incorporate any non-British material in this work, though Swift has, of course, been studied widely both on the continent and in America. Nor have I searched frantically for every scattered reference to Swift; I have, rather, sought to discover the important trends in biographical and literary criticism; and toward that end I have considered divergent opinions with an attempt at classification wherever possible.

In order to begin, however, we must glance at the true beginnings. Let us, then, turn to a necessarily brief survey of Swift criticism in the eighteenth century before Johnson.

II

The history of Swift criticism and controversy really begins with the Earl of Orrery's Remarks, published in 1751.[1] Three years earlier the notorious Mrs. Letitia Pilkington had given the world the first volume of her memoirs, some of which touched upon Dean Swift as she had known him in the latter part of his life. Though it later became the style to impugn her integrity as a writer,[2] Mrs. Pilkington's stories of the Dean sound authentic--possibly because of their very unpretentiousness. She makes, for example, no claim to omniscience. On controversial matters she maintains discreet silence and is content with describing him as she saw him. Her work is the ultimate source of many of the least equivocal Swiftian anecdotes,[3] and the most militantly antagonistic of her accusers have not been above pillaging their veracious material from her suspect pages. She can hardly, however, be called a critic. That honor belongs, as I have said, to John Boyle, fifth Earl of Orrery.

Orrery and Swift had been friends in Ireland, but no affection for the Dean brightens the pages of Orrery's book. Whatever its cause,[4] Orrery's animosity toward the memory of Swift marks even the few laudatory passages of his work. In a series of long letters ostensibly directed

[1] *Remarks on the Life and Writings of Dr. Jonathan Swift*, London. The first edition is dated 1752, but seems to have been printed in 1751.

[2] Probably in great part because of her reputation as a loose woman. Monck Berkeley, in 1789, dismissed her from his list of Swift's biographers as a "lying gossip," and the appellation seems to have stuck.

[3] For example, the story of Lady Burlington's refusal to sing for the Dean; Swift's strenuous method of taking indoor exercise; his treatment of the cook who served the beef over-roasted, *etc.*

[4] George-Monck Berkeley, *Literary Relics*, was the first to explain Orrery's coldness to Swift by the now well-known story of the unopened letter from the Earl, labeled by the Dean, "This will keep cold."

to his son as a rather peculiar means of improving his mind, but obviously intended for publication, he paints a most unflattering portrait of Swift. Smugly insisting upon his unbounded admiration for his friend, he none the less seizes the slightest opportunity for dwelling on and magnifying such natural faults as that friend may have had; and Swift emerges from the pages of the Remarks as sour, envious, vain, depraved, cruel, stupidly ambitious, and so mad that his giddiness at last rendered him "the exact image of one of his own Struldbruggs, a miserable spectacle." (p. 19)

What was later to become the great mystery of Swift's life held no mystery for the self-confident Orrery. Stella, he tells us, was "the concealed, but undoubted wife of Dr. SWIFT." (p. 22) Since she was, however, the daughter of Sir William Temple's steward, Swift's pride kept him from acknowledging his marriage into a family of menials. The prevalent rumor that both Stella and Swift were natural children of Sir William Temple he denies in a few words. To us, of course, his denial is chiefly interesting because it proves that there were well-credited rumors in existence even before 1752. We cannot hope to learn whence those potential legends ultimately arose, but we can, I think, acquit Orrery of the charge of conscious falsification which has sometimes been leveled against him. He took such facts as he knew to be true and added others on the authority of certain friends and relations of Swift's; for the recital of those facts he can hardly be held morally reprehensible. It is for his interpretation of them alone that he must assume full responsibility.

Certainly the Vanessa story, fantastically passionate ending and all, appears in full bloom in the Remarks; but in this case, perhaps to prove his impartiality, Orrery casts most of the blame upon the woman. Vanessa was weak, vain, and flighty. Preferring wit to religion, she suffered accordingly. Swift's sole cruelty beyond the final tragic gesture lay in his incorporating one short passage into that otherwise excellent poem, Cadenus and Vanessa:

> But what success Vanessa met,
> Is to the world a secret yet.
> Whether the nymph, to please her swain,
> Talks in a high romantic strain;
> Or whether he at last descends
> To act with less seraphic ends;
> Or to compound the business, whether
> They temper love and books together;
> Must never to mankind be told,
> Nor shall the conscious Muse unfold.[1]

---

[1]Jonathan Smedley originally called attention to this passage in his *Gulliveriana*, London, 1728, p. xxx.

Those lines infuriate Orrery, who seems to forget that they were, after all, written for the eyes of Vanessa alone. Much as he disapproves of Miss Vanhomrigh, he sees no reason for ungentlemanly insinuations--especially from a man whose cold temper probably proceeded "from defects in nature." (p. 113) And in those words, of course, we hear the opening note of another important motif in the symphony of biographical criticism: the question of Swift's physical impotence.

Obviously Orrery does not approve of Swift as a man. Toward the works his attitude is mixed. The Dean wrote with masterly conciseness, humor, and perspicuity; his style was clear and strong, excelling in "elegance and propriety of language." (p. 234) But an inexcusable want of delicacy and decorum, both in the poems, which are also lacking in imagination and engaging qualities, and in a great part of the prose, necessarily repels the well-bred reader. Instead of applying the faculties of his mind to one great and useful subject and working toward the moral betterment of mankind, Swift preferred wit to sentiment; and therein he failed as a writer. Nothing, says Orrery in all sincerity, could be more shocking than his ridicule of Robert Boyle, who "will always remain invulnerable," (p. 95) in the Meditation upon a Broomstick. Too much given to such vicious trifling, Swift would have done better to play at "push-pin" instead of composing "nonsense."

Despite his stern disapproval of the "bagatelles" on moral grounds, the Remarker, however, defends Swift warmly against those who censure him for irreligion in such pieces as the Tale of a Tub and the Argument against Abolishing Christianity. The Dean's ungovernable irony may have carried him into unwarranted flights of wit, but in these works there is no intended insult to Christianity, but rather a serious effort to laugh people into religion and to satirize wild errors of worship. Curiously enough though, these and the Proposal for Correcting...the English Tongue are the only works upon which the Earl looks with an unjaundiced eye. The chasms in The Battle of the Books and its rancor toward Dryden puzzle and annoy him; the politician outweighs the divine in the sermons; the minor efforts abound in "low" humor; even the epitaph is composed in harsh Latin and is "scarce intelligible." (p. 263) The judicial tone which strikes the keynote of most early criticism of Swift is perhaps best stated in the Remarks:

> A man of SWIFT's exalted genius ought constantly to have soared into higher regions. He ought to have looked upon persons of inferior abilities as children whom nature had appointed him to instruct, encourage, and improve. (p. 283)

Tirelessly, then, Orrery searches through Gulliver's Travels for the morally elevated and sublime, and he never recovers from the shock of not always finding them. The work remains, to his mind, a moral-political romance of delightful imagination and wit--but of over-venomous and splenetic satire. Swift's fine "irregular" genius never indeed appeared to better advantage than in his account of the voyages to Lilliput and Brobdingnag, where he observes such great exactness in proportions; but he tires the mind with too much dwelling upon these "optical deceptions," especially since "he points out no beauty, nor use in such amazing discoveries, which might have been so continued as to have afforded improvement, at the same time that they gave astonishment." (p. 135) And especially disappointing to Orrery's constant expectation of noble things is the cursory manner in which Gulliver calls up and dispenses with the various famous dead during his stay in Glubbdubdrib.

Even those critics who have been sympathetic toward Swift and his "misanthropy" have often found the fourth voyage of Gulliver's Travels a stumbling block to complete appreciation of the work. It palpably fails in its purpose if, as so many have assumed, its creator intended it as a representation of a Utopia; but there is possible another interpretation of the voyage--an interpretation which, from our knowledge of Swift, who was not given to systematic philosophy, must seem infinitely more acceptable. The Brobdingnagian King avers, after he has wrung from Gulliver an account of his world, that Gulliver's fellow-men must be a "pernicious race of little odious vermin." And this incident, elaborated upon and made concrete, has grown into the fourth voyage. The odious vermin have been given human shape; and the author, his fund of queer, man-like creatures now exhausted, has created a new race of superior beings called Houyhnhnms, differing in no essential respect except their horsehood from the Brobdingnagians. If this is the correct explanation of the voyage to the Houyhnhnms, its didactic and philosophical implications must to some extent give way to the picturesque and expository; but the type of eighteenth-century mind of which Orrery's is so splendid an example sought the moralistic at any cost. In most of the early commentators on Gulliver's Travels we see an identical reaction to the last voyage. Even those who defend it argue from the didactic and Utopian point of view.

I have indulged in this digression in order to clarify much that will follow, for the voyage to the Houyhnhnms has been a major battle-field of Swift controversy. Orrery carries on his discussion of it querulously and, as he admits, with reluctance, for in this last part of his imaginary travels "SWIFT has indulged a misanthropy that is intolerable." (p. 184) The fable disgusts instead of entertaining; instead of instructing, it shocks! It is an insult to mankind--and incidentally to God, since He is responsible for mankind. Therefore, as the self-appointed champion of God, Orrery expends much energy in vindicating human nature and proclaiming it good.

As for the author of Gulliver, his picture of the Houyhnhnms is "cold and insipid"; and in painting Yahoos, "he becomes one himself." (p. 188)

And so on a scene of utter darkness, brightened only occasionally by a casual reference to the fact that we are after all dealing with the life and works of a great--if faulty--man, the history of Swift criticism begins. The Remarks gained immediate fame. It went into several editions before the end of 1752, and it has exerted a real influence upon the work of later critics, no matter how much they have, as in the case of Macaulay, scorned the author. It is indeed a question whether a prevalent nineteenth-century conception of Swift as an inhuman monster--an impression which persists faintly even today--could have arisen had some other work than Orrery's been first in the field. At any rate, the popularity of his book is attested not merely by the number of its editions, but by numerous contemporary references to it, most of them definitely favorable. Samuel Richardson, for example, in a letter dated February 23, 1752, spoke approvingly of the Remarks and seconded Orrery's observation that Swift's eventual madness seemed a punishment "that had terrible justice in it."[1] And another critic found the Remarks, if not satisfactory in every particular, at least of extreme value as a portrait of Swift and as judicious criticism of his art; he could not help observing, however, that the noble author's charity has somewhat biased him in favor of the Dean![2] Orrery had conceded to Swift a modicum of true religious feeling; now even this was challenged.

But it was inevitable that many would disapprove of Orrery and that some one of these should spring to Swift's defense. This was the task to which Patrick Delany rose, if anonymously and somewhat timidly, in 1754.[3]

Delany, like Orrery, had known Swift personally, had, in fact, been one of his intimate friends during his years in Ireland as Dean of St. Patrick's. Of a sensitive nature, one of his chief quarrels with the author of

[1]*The Correspondence of Samuel Richardson*, London, 1804, VI, 153. In a letter of April 22, 1752, also addressed to Lady Bradshaigh, Richardson again commends Orrery for his impartiality and tells for the first time the famous story of Swift as *Terrae Filius* at Dublin University--a story which was to serve as the basis for Barrett's study of the early life of Swift.

[2]Ralph Griffiths, *Monthly Review*, V, 407-24; 475-87 (1751).

[3]William Monck Mason, *History of St. Patrick*, p. 436, note b., mentions also a series of letters which appeared in 1752, "From a Gentleman in the Country, to his Son in the College of Dublin, relating to the Memoirs of the life and Writings of Dr. Swift, Dean of St. Patrick's; ascribed to the Rt. Hon. the Earl of Orrery." I have not seen the work, which seems to have ludicrously burlesqued Orrery in matter and style and to have attempted to show the real greatness of Swift by ironically portraying Orrery as the fool he was.

the Remarks grew from the Earl's statement that Swift's susceptibility to flattery led him to choose his friends from among a group of inferior sycophants. Swift's Irish friends were not fools and flatterers, Delany maintains; they were wise and good men. And with that truth as a spring-board, he dives into the unfamiliar waters of literary criticism, in order to prove their wisdom by his own example. What he does succeed in proving in his diffident[1] effort to defend the reputation of his late friend is the innate gentleness of his own nature as opposed to Orrery's.

Bravely and earnestly Delany considers each point of Orrery's indictment of Swift, and his work is of tremendous biographical value for setting the Dean's actions and personality forth in a very different light from that of the noble Remarker. Later biographers have been compelled, so to speak, to take their choice of the two contemporary impressions; and it is the essential difference between them which is responsible in large measure for the insistence of some critics upon paradox after paradox in the character of Swift. According to Delany he was not cruel, merely outspoken--a hypocrite reversed. He hated flattery and loved true merit, was more open to honest admonition than low adulation. The avarice of which Orrery accuses him appeared only in later life; otherwise he was, though personally frugal, extravagantly generous to others. His cleanliness, his hospitality, the kindness of a heart which only seemed churlish because of his hatred of hypocrisy, his fervent piety--to all these Delany attests by numerous anecdotes, the veracity of each of which is more or less questionable according to its source. One vice alone, overweening pride, slightly darkens the glowing portrait painted by Swift's second biographer.

In his treatment of the works, however, Delany does his subject less justice. He had become Dean of Downs by the time he wrote his Observations, and he felt the responsibility of his position. With the touchstone of what a greater critic has called "high moral seriousness" he searches furiously for pure gold in the writings of Swift--and finds, alas, too much dross. Then too, the innate sentimentality of an over-kindly nature renders him incapable of appreciating the keenly realistic asperities which constitute one of Swift's chief charms for the impartial reader. In general, to be sure, Swift, whom he compares with Addison for his fund of humor and his fine English style, has written nothing which is entirely unworthy of notice. He has stamped his indelible mark upon all that he has written, the trivial as well as the great; for his style, whatever the matter, is always excellent--clear, correct, and terse. And his poetry

[1]The *Observations upon Lord Orrery's Remarks on the Life and Writings of Dr. Jonathan Swift*, London, 1754, was published anonymously; its constant allusions to Lord Orrery are so deferential as to smack of servility.

cannot be praised too highly; even the most offensive poems are after all only "the prescriptions of an able physician, who had, in truth, the health of his patients at heart." (p. 198)

But aside from this inexplicable predisposition toward overlooking the nauseating scatology of the poems, Delany invariably bases his judgments on the visionary criteria of delicacy and morality. For especial praise he singles out the Letter to a Young Gentleman, lately entered into Holy Orders and calls it one of the most masterly of all Swift's performances, abounding in genius, wit, observation, and learning throughout, but more particularly "in his fine account, and high contempt of free-thinkers, and thinking." (p. 104) And for especial opprobrium he chooses Gulliver's Travels!

The reason, obviously, is its indecency: "Swift never could keep his stile clear of offence, when a temptation of wit, came in his way." We are, of course, assured, to the somewhat dubious credit of Swift's better nature, that "the defilement became much more conspicuous, upon his return from his first long visit to Mr. Pope." (p. 74) But the fact remains that the "defilement" did become conspicuous. Thus the exaggerated satire of Gulliver, capable only of shocking and not of doing good, would have been better left unwritten! More concerned for the reputation of mankind than for that of Jonathan Swift, Delany casts reserve to the winds and completes the work of demolishing the voyage to the Houyhnhnms that Orrery had begun.

His attitude toward the work--"a piece more deform, erroneous, and (of consequence) less instructive, and agreeable, than any of his productions" (p. 161)--differs little from Orrery's except in the extent of its passion. He begins his discussion with a naive defense of mankind, expatiating upon the marvelous physical powers of man, who can, for instance, dart himself into the air head over heels, thus "inverting the centre of gravity, with an amazing power." (p. 163) What can Swift's horses do to compare with this?

> The utmost capacity, with which even Swift, with all his wit and invention, was able to endow his Houyhnhnms, was that of carrying a little oats between his hoof and his fetlock: and what a fine figure must he make, even in that action, hobbling aukwardly, upon three legs! (p. 166)

They are lacking in all the tender passions and affections; their supposedly superior powers of unbiased reason confer none of the true blessings of life upon them; no sane person could possibly prefer such a passive, dull existence as theirs to our own. So the argument progresses, until it rises to a grand climax in the posing of one short rhetorical question:

> ...who would not wish rather to be the author of one Arcadia, than fifty Laputa's Lilliputs, (sic) and Houyhnhnms. (p. 171)

At that parallel, we can only gasp and remain silent.

As a fitting conclusion to our discussion of Delany, it might perhaps be well to quote a passage from the Observations which epitomizes the spirit of the age and its twofold approach to the problems of literary criticism. For an age is seldom best represented by its great men; and it is just because Patrick Delany was far from being a great man that his extravagant sentimentality may serve as a key to the period in which he lived. In remarking upon Cadenus and Vanessa then--a poem for which in general he entertains the highest regard--he says:

> And yet, I have something to censure even in this, besides those passages, which you so justly blame. The lines are these.
>
> Where never blush was call'd in aid,
> That spurious virtue in a maid:
> A virtue but at second hand,
> They blush because they understand.
>
> Give me leave to say, my blood boils with indignation against the folly, the vanity, (I had almost said the blasphemy) of these lines.
>
> Here, my Lord, the finest instinct, and noblest power, with which God hath endowed the human frame, is treated with scandalous contempt, and insolent abuse! that great and amazing protector of virtue, and avenger of guilt, that astonishing power by which all the blood in our frame rises, in one instant, to repel every attempt, every approach of vice; is branded, not as the genuine offspring of God, but the spurious offspring of prudery, and affectation: to be called in, and cast off at our pleasure. (p. 118)

Delany's defense of Swift had a curious effect. It called forth one of the most recriminative documents in the history of English literature: Deane Swift's biography of his eminent relation.[1] The Swift family, not notable for its mental balance, produced in Deane Swift almost its culminating specimen of eccentricity. Not a

[1] *An Essay upon the Life, Writings, and Character, of Dr. Jonathan Swift. Interspersed with some occasional Animadversions upon the Remarks of a late critical Author, and upon the Observations of an anonymous Writer on those Remarks.* London, 1755.

genius like his elder cousin, he nevertheless combined in his own nature several of the characteristics most typical of the Dean--combined them in such a way as to make him seem, in the work under discussion at least, like a gross caricature of Jonathan. He addresses his book to the friends of "truth" and, as the sole owner of truth, castigates both Orrery and Delany for their falsifications. He is the last of Swift's biographers who may be said to have known the Dean personally,[1] and his book is therefore of value, since it contains some new biographical material, including Swift's own fragmentary autobiography. But, in his overheated attempt to salvage the reputation of Swift, and especially that of the Swift family, the author's categorical statements tend to be perverse and even self-contradictory; and his antagonism toward the Remarker and the Observator, the latter of whom he considers doubly vicious because his enmity is cloaked in the guise of friendship, carries him to ludicrous lengths. In his lust for veracity, he pounces upon the most innocent statements of the earlier biographers and tears them to shreds. His book overflows with quiblings like the following:

> WE are also told by the Observator, 'that a friend of MRS. WHITEWAY's sometimes marketted for DR. SWIFT, when his infirmities called for a more that ordinary attention to his diet.' It is false: There never was any friend of MRS. WHITEWAY's, that ever once marketted for him; nor anybody else that I know of, except MRS. WORRALL, and his own domestics. (p. 349)

So indignantly intent is he upon proving the antiquity and nobility of his family that he labels every word of reproach leveled upon Swift himself by Orrery and Delany as a malicious slander upon the whole tribe. Swift's rightful pride rose above all tincture of envy; his ambition was noble, exalted, "worthy to be cherished in the breast of an angel." (p. 364) Nor was he at all at fault in his treatment of either Stella or Vanessa. Stella, for example, had followed him to Ireland with the express purpose of winning his heart. It was her own misfortune that her lowly--though definitely legitimate--birth precluded any possibility of an acknowledged marriage with the high-born Jonathan Swift.

Deane Swift's book deals in an equally positive manner with all controversial issues. The author summarily accepts the story of the marriage and of the Dean's great love for Stella, while palliating the offenses of Swift and Miss Vanhomrigh; he defends the questionable lines in Cadenus and Vanessa; he indulges in one panegyric after another upon Swift's generosity and kindness to the Irish

[1]Thomas Sheridan the younger was a mere boy at the time of Swift's death. He wrote from distant recollection of his father's reminiscences.

in spite of their scurrilous treatment of him; he adduces incontestable proof of Swift's legitimacy in the fact of Sir William Temple's residence abroad during the years from 1665 to 1670; he scores Orrery's insinuation of impotence in a bitterly satiric style, not quite so facile as, though much influenced by, that of his maligned cousin.

In all this there is much of sheer bombast, much that springs from irrational prejudice, much ill-tempered carping and tactlessly personal criticism of preceding biographers. Yet, though Deane Swift has not been the "unquestionably authentick" source for Swiftiana he thought himself, his work possesses a real value for later truth-seekers. Somehow his blood told; and far more than Orrery or Delany, he penetrated into motives and causes. His methods of defense are sometimes painful, his inaccuracies glaring; but the defense itself attains occasionally to uncanny heights of perception. In his judgment of the works, for example, though too prone to inordinate enthusiasms, he often shows a remarkable understanding of Swift's genius. First of all, he has no use for literary critics in general. "This race of animals proceed in the course of their observations upon the noblest writers...by several rules of art, which from age to age they have been raking up one from another." (p. 67) But they are worst of all when they presume to venture beyond their bounds, to attack the private character of an author and to judge his works accordingly.

> When you behold the Doctor in his own _writings_, there indeed you find him in a thousand different attitudes, agreeable to the diversity of his character; but when you behold him in the _Remarks_ you see him (as it were through a glass darkly, just as if you were gazing at PHOEBUS in an eclipse) in all the variety of a _caricatura_. (p. 70)

Except for the Pindarics, which he dismisses hastily, Deane Swift has something good to say about all the works. The political pamphlets are not mere occasional journals, but lectures of true, unprejudiced politics, "calculated to expose the enemies of the publick, and to maintain at once the honor of the CROWN, and the liberties of the PEOPLE of _England_." (p. 150) _The Argument against Abolishing Christianity_ is the most "delicate, refined, compleat, unvaried piece of irony, from the beginning to the end, that ever was written since the creation of the world." (p. 135) In short the witty and humorous masterpieces of Swift approach more nearly to perfection than the works of any other genius who has ever lived. But it is when the biographer takes up an extended survey of the "heteroclite" poetry that family pride most tells. Swift's verse, compared favorably with that of Homer, Virgil, Shakespeare, was after all only a minor interest to him; yet his admirers prefer him above all poets of modern times and liken his works to those of Horace, whose whole business was poetry! And Cadenus and Vanessa, especially, "beyond all other pieces, whether of DR. SWIFT, or any Poet that ever writ in English...appears calculated to abide the severest examination of criticks." (p. 241)

In his appreciative discussion of Gulliver's Travels Deane Swift comes closer to truth, however, and succeeds in clarifying much that had offended the beclouded minds of Orrery and Delany. He sees one purpose in the whole work: it plainly and bitterly satirizes folly and corruption in all branches of life; nor is its severity by any means unjustifiable. Never did Swift maliciously castigate any one person; and impersonal vice cannot too frequently be exposed to contempt and ridicule.

Those, then, who censure the fourth voyage simply stamp themselves as depraved Yahoos. Shall we praise Hogarth as an excellent moralist for exposing debauchery in a series of "hieroglyphicks" intended to improve the wild, the gay, the "frolick," the extravagant? And shall we yet condemn a minister of God for embodying the deformity and corruption of Godless vice in the character of a nasty Yahoo?

> Ought a preacher of righteousness...to hold his peace, like a dumb dog that cannot bark, when avarice, fraud, cheating, violence, rapine, extortion, cruelty, oppression, tyranny, rancour, envy, malice, detraction, hatred, revenge, murder, whoredom, adultery, lasciviousness, bribery, corruption, pimping, lying, perjury, subornation, treachery, ingratitude, gaming, flattery, drunkenness, gluttony, luxury, vanity, effeminacy, cowardice, pride, impudence, hypocrisy, infidelity, blasphemy, idolatry, sodomy, and innumerable other vices are as epidemical as the pox, and many of them the notorious characteristicks of the bulk of humankind? (p. 219)

Even this merely partial enumeration of human failings--a delectable example, by the way, of the influence of the elder upon the younger Swift in style and thought--sufficiently points Deane's concluding remarks on the voyage to the Houyhnhnms. If, he says, Swift has painted the brutality of the Yahoos in shocking colors, he has done so because man is deservedly more contemptible than a beast when he flies in the face of his God and enlists under the banners of the Devil. The picture is the more striking, and therefore "more likely to enforce the obligation of religion and virtue upon the souls of men." (p. 225)

Admittedly, I think, this last of the early biographies, for all its faults of naive partiality and unrestrained rhetoric, shows a truer understanding of Swift than that of many later and greater critics. Its most apparent blemish lies in its belligerent assumption of omniscience; but that is a fault it shares with most of the early writers on Swift. Only gentle Patrick Delany admitted his fallibility. In a public letter to Deane Swift[1] called forth by the latter's strictures on his honesty, Delany, his feelings hurt to the quick, defended himself with passionate earnestness. And yet, while claiming rightly to have known Dr. Swift "fifty times better than you did," (p. 16) he candidly owned that a false memory was among his manifold infirmities. Such diffidence is, however, a marked exception to general eighteenth-century practice. In 1757 appeared an article in the Gentleman's Magazine,[2] which, in order to defend Swift against accusations of pride and cruelty, professed to have definite knowledge--authoritative sources unnamed--of the kindred illegitimacy of Swift and Stella, the discovery of which upon the day of their marriage blasted their hopes and embittered their lives. The writer gives just enough detail to lend an air of probability to his thesis and thus to revivify the rumors refuted by the earlier biographers. Thomas Amory promised the world definite knowledge of Swift's character as he alone was capable of portraying it, and fortunately failed to keep his promise.[3] Horace Walpole speaks of Swift with definite knowledge as "that brute, who hated everybody that he hoped would get him a mitre, and did not" and is convinced from a casual reading of his correspondence that he and Vanessa had carnal intercourse, "notwithstanding his supposed incapacity, yet not doing much honour to that capacity, for he says he can drink coffee but once a week, and I think you will see very clearly what he means by coffee."[4]

Horace Walpole had, to be sure, more real cause for hatred of Swift than most of his contemporaries. Yet when he speaks of the Dean as "a wild beast, who baited and worried all mankind almost, because his intolerable arrogance, vanity, pride, and ambition were disappointed,"[5] we are encountering only a sample of the personal criticism which flourished at the time and was to continue for decades.

Of the several biographical problems which have confronted students of Swift, almost all were at least

[1]*A Letter to Dean Swift, Esq; on His Essay upon the Life, Writings, and Character of Dr. J. Swift*, London, 1755.

[2]XXVII, 488-91. Initialed C.M.P.G.N.S.T.N.S.

[3]In the Introduction to his *Memoirs of several ladies of Great Britain*, 1755, Amory promises to include a portrait of Swift among those of the ladies. Only two volumes of the projected work appeared. A brief characterization of the Dean, from the Introduction, is quoted *in toto* by Pons, *op. cit.*, p. 33.

[4]*The Letters of Horace Walpole*, ed. Paget Toynbee, Oxford, 1904. No. 1118, to George Montague, June 20, 1766.

[5]*ibid.* No. 2018, to Sir Horace Mann, Jan. 13, 1780.

touched upon by Orrery, Delany, Deane Swift, and their contemporaries. Swift's misanthropy, his friendships and enmities, his sexual propensities, his relationship with Stella and Vanessa, his religious principles or lack of them, his avarice, his attitude toward Ireland--by some or all of the earliest commentators each of these tangled threads was given a twist; and from the confusion brought about first by Swift's own curious life and personality, and secondly by the uncritical critical efforts of his original biographers, the Swift mystery developed in all its glory. One strand alone seems to have been left hanging for later writers to join to the tangled skein: the charge of political apostasy. Early critics, much as they might accuse him of overambition, remained blind to the great field for recrimination latent in the fact of Swift's change of party; it was the nineteenth-century which insisted upon party loyalty as a primary moral virtue.

Criticism of the works did not always, as we have seen, depend upon judgments of the man. Delany's harsh strictures of Gulliver's Travels accord poorly with his defense of Swift as a person. But in general we find little attempt at impartiality. Again, it remained for later generations to create, as it were, a bifurcation between the man and his art. In the period at present under consideration those who disliked Swift were apt to dislike his work; those who approved of him tried to find hidden beauties even in his least successful bagatelles.

Meanwhile, whatever their reactions, critics displayed a constant interest in the late Dean of St. Patrick's. Incidental references to him can be found throughout eighteenth-century literature, and two or three of those which occur during the decades before 1780 merit recording. Henry Fielding, for example, speaks of Swift as one of an immortal triumvirate of Wits--Lucian and Cervantes are the others--immortal because, unlike bad humorists like Aristophanes and Rabelais, they used their great powers "to expose and extirpate those Follies and Vices which chiefly prevailed in their several Countries."[1] Fielding's admiration for the Dean, "one of the greatest Enemies that Dulness ever had,"[2] was of course that of one great satirist for another. Only the author of Tom Jones could have been capable of carrying the Modest Proposal one step further, as he did when he affirmed the impossibility of following Swift's excellent advice in England; since English children, unlike their milk-fed Irish cousins, are little better than a composition of gin, and would probably poison anyone who tried eating them.[3]

[1] *The Covent-Garden Journal* (1751-52), ed. G. E. Jensen, New Haven, 1915, I, 194. See also *Amelia,* VIII, Chap. V.

[2] *ibid.* I, 244.

[3] *ibid.* I, 201.

Oliver Goldsmith seems to have admired Swift's poetry rather than his prose.[1] The Dean, he said, simply described nature as it was, with all its deformities, as a revolt against the fashion of seeing only its pleasing side. Therefore he owed his fame "not so much to the greatness of his genius, as to the boldness of it."[2] This is at least an original point of view and shows a grasp of the subject never reached by those who, like Edward Young, recoiled from what they saw only as shocking indecency. Like Orrery, Young castigates Swift for his sordid preoccupation with wit, and accuses him of having so satirized human nature "as to give a demonstration in himself, that it deserves to be satirised." He can only wish that Swift had used his undoubted powers for some other purpose than that of glorifying horses and blaspheming "a nature little lower than that of angels."[3]

On one point, however, most commentators agree. The excellence of Swift's dry, severe, concise style, his superb control of word and tempo, are only once questioned in the pre-Johnsonian era--and then by the Scotchman, David Hume. Hume, in a letter to William Robertson of 1768, rebukes him for using old-fashioned, dangling words, like <u>wherewith</u>, and says:

> I know your affection for <u>wherewith</u> proceeds from your partiality to Dean Swift, whom I can often laugh with, whose style I can even approve, but surely can never admire. It has no harmony, no eloquence, no ornament, and not much correctness, whatever the English may imagine. Were not their literature still in a somewhat barbarous state, that author's place would not be so high among their classics.[4]

That chilling concession to Swift of a place among the classics tells more about the extent of his reputation than could be gained from a more amicable source. Whether or not he was liked, Swift was at least read in the eighteenth-century. Much indeed that was not Swift was read because it was published as his. To Hawkesworth's twelve-volume edition of the Works extra volumes were added from time to time by Bowyer, Deane Swift, Hawkesworth himself, and the indefatigable John Nichols, until by 1779 the world possessed a twenty-five-volume

---

[1]He included three of the poems with appreciative comments in *The Beauties of English Poesy* (1767), an anthology; and one of his imitations of Swift, *The Logicians Refuted*, was long included in editions of Swift's works.

[2]*The Works of Goldsmith*, ed. J. W. M. Gibbs, London, 1886, V, 346.

[3]*Conjectures*, 1759, ed. E. J. Morley, Manchester, 1918, p. 28. Here too Young tells the famous story of Swift's premonition of madness upon seeing a tree withered at the top.

[4]*The Letters of David Hume*, ed. J. Y. T. Greig, Oxford, 1932, II, 424.

collection of the Dean's writings and correspondence--including much, of course, that has since been omitted from the canon.[1]

We have reached the end of the first period of Swift criticism--a period when living witnesses to the life of the Dean had held the stage, with their reminiscences and their vaguely authenticated stories. Samuel Johnson was not, however, the first critic to write a biography of Swift without having known him; as early as 1755 Hawkesworth prefaced his edition of the Works--the first, by the way, to be published after Swift's death--with an account of Swift's life, in which he attempted to consider the facts and opinions of Orrery, Delany, and Deane Swift impartially and to create, as it were, a final synthesis.[2] And three years later W. H. Dilworth, convinced that the time was ripe for a really fair biography, brought out a work which pretended to discuss Swift's merits unclouded by party quibblings.[3] Dilworth's book is based entirely on those of the early biographers. It offers no original contribution to the history of Swift criticism, being in its entirety a pastiche of Orrery, Delany, and Deane, with a final anecdotal portion taken from Mrs. Pilkington. And Hawkesworth, though he sincerely admired the Dean, had little to say that was new and, indeed, avoided all controversial matters as "unprofitable objects of speculation." (p. 26)[4]

It is to Johnson then that we turn for our first example of bold new criticism. And with Johnson's essay on Swift we begin in earnest our study of the reputation of one of Britain's most incomprehensible geniuses.

---

[1]See John Nichols, *Literary Illustrations*, London, 1828, V, 391-96, for a first-hand account of the early editions of Swift.

[2]*An Account of the Life of the Reverend Jonathan Swift, D.D.* In volume I of the *Works*, London, 1755.

[3]*The Life of Jonathan Swift*, London, 1758.

[4]These words refer to inquiries concerning the reasons for Swift's conduct toward Esther Johnson. Hawkesworth, however, takes for granted the fact of the marriage.

PART ONE
(1781-1814)

I

Swift the Man

In 1779 John Nichols added the twenty-fifth and last volume to the Hawkesworth edition of Swift. The world had what must have seemed like a complete collection of the Works; the sharp-tongued controversy between his personal acquaintances had died down; and the time was ripe for impartial criticism. A writer in the Monthly Review found his opinion of Swift confirmed by the Nichols Supplement; and with this article[1] we reach a period during which an attempt to see Swift as a coherent whole is begun. The search for "truth" still goes on--it continues even today--but from an end in itself it has become a means toward an end. And that end is a solid, consistent picture of the Dean and his works. The reviewer finds him a man of great genius, inexhaustible fancy, and excellent common sense, whose odd economies can be overlooked for the sake of his charities, and whose many peculiarities were after all inseparable from his genius. Too much a prey to prejudice, especially against dissenters; wanting in one distinguished virtue, forgiveness; over-proud: these were faults which, when we examine the uniform tenor of his disposition and conduct, detract but slightly from his general greatness.

Clearly this is not a finished picture of Swift, who was something more than merely an eccentric and faulty genius. The reviewer's approach to his subject, however, is worth noting. We shall meet few such matter-of-fact judgments of the Dean in the pages to come. The desire for uniformity and consistency of character in a man of as incomprehensibly subtle a nature as Swift, so simply begun in 1779, was to lead in time to the exquisitely unified, if pathetically factitious, portraits by men like Thackeray and Taine.

Of the early syntheses Dr. Johnson's is naturally one of the more laudably realistic. No figure of mystery stalks furtively through the pages of his Life of Swift,[2] but a man of flesh and blood--withal a most repulsive one. A Scotch lady once asked whether Johnson believed that no man was naturally good. "JOHNSON. 'No, madam, no more than a wolf.' BOSWELL. 'Nor no woman, sir?' JOHNSON. 'No, sir.' Lady MacLeod started, saying.

---

[1]*Month. Rev.* LXI, 356-65 (November, 1779).

[2]In *Lives of the English Poets* (1781), ed. G. B. Hill, Oxford, 1905, vol. III.

low, 'This is worse than Swift.' "[1] Others as well have seen a resemblance between the two great literary Tories; yet it is a fact that Johnson felt little sympathy for his Irish predecessor. Boswell frequently mentions his unaccountable prejudice toward Swift, and, whatever its cause, that prejudice colors all the learned Doctor's judgments.

Johnson's Swift emerges as a three-dimensional but extremely unsubtle figure. From a cursory reading of the essay we are likely to carry away an idea of the Dean as a nasty-minded and petulant grown-up child, who delighted in shrouding himself in a veil of mystery which the maturer mind scorns to attempt to pierce.[2] Contemptuously Johnson attacks Swift for the childish freedom with which he insisted upon treating with the great--a mere sign of saucy servility. And, though sufficiently charitable to his inferiors, so peevish and tyrannical a benefactor must he have been that "those who were fed by him could hardly love him." (p. 58) Discontented, malignant, querulous, his greatest fault, none the less, lay in a depraved intellect which led him to take delight in revolving ideas "from which almost every other mind shrinks with disgust." (p. 63) And Delany's suggestion that Swift had been tainted by his close association with Pope, if true, simply "degrades his hero by making him at fifty-nine the pupil of turpitude....But the truth is that Gulliver had described his Yahoos before the visit, and he that had formed those images had nothing filthy to learn." (p. 63)

In all this Johnson's position is not entirely untenable. Though it wilfully evades mention of the brighter side of Swift's character, it does not accuse him of vices of which he was utterly devoid. When, however, in treating of the insolent letter to Queen Caroline _requiring_ her patronage for Mrs. Barber, it is insisted that the letter was Swift's and that Swift himself never denied it but shuffled "between cowardice and veracity," (p. 39) we are faced with a different matter. In accusing Swift of cowardice Johnson was guilty of either ignorance or misrepresentation. But false as it is, cowardice rightly belongs with the other failings which compose the man Swift as Johnson saw him. It belongs no less than the arrogance and puerile susceptibility to cheap flattery, no less than the licentiousness and the petulant frolicsomeness, to the picture of arrested development Johnson has drawn.

He was not of course alone in his insistence upon the Dean's haughtiness--a characteristic which seems

[1] Boswell, *Tour*, ed. Pottle and Bennett, New York, 1936, (14 September, 1773), p. 170.

[2] Sheridan, *Life of Swift*, p. 497, interprets Johnson's decision to leave the question of Swift's place of birth in obscurity as another way of saying, "It is of very little moment where the fellow was born."

particularly to have enraged most of the unsympathetic eighteenth-century commentators. Joseph Warton says, in a passage which stems from one of similar content in Johnson:

> Pope, Swift, and Bolingbroke, appear... to have formed a kind of haughty triumvirate....And by their own account of themselves, they would have the reader believe, that they had engrossed and monopolized all the genius, and all the honesty of the age, in which, according to their opinion, they had the misfortune to live.[1]

And not long after the publication of Johnson's essay, a writer in the Gentleman's Magazine (October, 1782), who boasts of having known Swift, characterizes him in one paragraph as an ill-humored person, who chiefly delighted in attacking less witty people in order "to assert the superiority of his own talents." (p. 470)

It is a curious fact that, with all his coldness, Johnson judges Swift's treatment of Stella and Vanessa less harshly than do many of the Dean's most valiant defenders. He fails, to be sure, to concur in the general respect for Stella, who, though doubtless virtuous and beautiful, spelled execrably, and whose wit, so loudly vaunted, could hardly have been very great, judging from the specimens collected by Swift himself. Nor can the reader of the Letter to a Young Lady on her Marriage think at all highly of his opinion of female excellence; for if his thoughts on women were such as he exhibits there, "a very little sense in a lady would enrapture and a very little virtue would astonish him." (p. 42) The marriage resulted from Swift's resolve to make sure of Stella and to annex her to himself by secret bonds, thus tasting all the joys of perfect friendship with none of the pains of conjugal restraint; and Johnson, superbly unsentimental, wastes few tears upon the situation. But he handles Swift's treatment of Esther Vanhomrigh--a woman "ignominiously distinguished by the name of Vanessa" (p. 31)--with a delicate understanding which quite transcends the harsh tone of the essay in general. Naturally he makes no effort at palliation. What he says in effect is simply this: Swift was forty-seven when Vanessa fell in love with him, and at forty-seven a man's vanity is easily excited by the attentions of a woman. Men are but men, and Swift could not help being flattered. Perhaps he did not even know his own mind at first; and when, after his marriage, he allowed her still to hope, he may simply have been delaying a disagreeable discovery, "dreading the immediate bursts of distress, and watching for a favorable moment." (p. 32)

Johnson's Life added little new factual material to the existent body of Swiftiana. In 1784, however,

[1] *Essay on Pope*, London, 1782, II, 407.

appeared a seventeen-volume edition of the Works, compiled by Thomas Sheridan, the son of Swift's light-hearted friend--an edition to which the younger Sheridan prefixed a long biographical essay, replete with new anecdotes and "true" facts inherited from Sheridan the elder.[1] This is the first really complete biography after Deane Swift's, and like Deane's it is almost preposterously laudatory in tone. The eighteenth century seems to have been divided into two equal camps, and Swift scarcely lacked champions. Against every Orrery arose a heavily-armed Deane Swift, against every cudgel-wielding Johnson a Sheridan. Even the anonymous writer in the Gentleman's Magazine of 1782 met his match in one "Presto," who, in a letter to Mr. Urban (January, 1783), charged him with malevolence of spirit and vindicated Swift of the accusation of morose arrogance by the simple expedient of calling his accuser an impostor. But Sheridan's biography, with its elaborate glorification of Swift as both man and writer, stands as the greatest pro-Swiftian work of the latter half of the century.

The book has many faults. It is diffuse. It devotes too many pages to a glowing account--forgivable perhaps--of the Swift-Sheridan friendship. It is prone to accept any sort of gossip, especially when creditable to the Dean, as incontrovertible truth. In style it is flat and stilted. Unwaveringly adulatory in tone, the picture it creates wants shadows, for Swift was not an unmitigatedly virtuous person any more than he was the petulant egotist of Johnson's one-sided essay. But Sheridan's is, none the less, a refreshing point of view. With none of Delany's pathetic timidity, with none of Deane Swift's extravagant belligerence, he brings the Dean frankly into the open air; and the sight is good to behold--even through rose-colored glasses.

First of all, he considers Swift's early want of fortune a blessing rather than a curse, for it was his failure at the University that kept him from becoming merely a great scholar and his comparative poverty that compelled him to be a paragon of continence. Early hardship engendered in him great ambition, but it also taught him largeness of soul and inculcated those moral principles to which he was ever after true. So he became one of a race of superior beings--and, rightly, knew it. He refused to pay homage to superiority of birth or fortune; he scorned to purchase the gratification of his natural ambitions at the expense of his principles; he cultivated the acquaintance of men of genius, but he never allowed his inferior brethren to feel the superiority which his intellect gave him over them. Yet such malicious detractors as Orrery dare to attack his character, dare to accuse him of servile flattery to such men as Oxford and Bolingbroke, by whom he was not merely trusted but sincerely loved, dare finally to maintain that in working for the

---

[1]*The Life of Dr. Swift*, in *Works*, ed. J. Nichols, London, 1801, vol. I.

good of the state his intentions were not always completely disinterested. They too, who knew him only in his decline, have insisted upon his morbidity and misanthropy. His true friends, however, could attest to his constant good humor, his tender heart, his unselfishness, his benevolence which soured into acrimony only with the advance of old age. For at the height of his career the Dean was known to all as a good companion, a benefactor, and a lover of virtue.

> Upon the whole, when we consider his character as a man, perfectly free from vice, with few frailties, and such exalted virtues; and as an author, possessed of such uncommon talents, such an original vein of humour, such an inexhaustible fund of wit, joined to so clear and solid an understanding; when we behold these two characters united in one and the same person; perhaps it will not be thought too bold an assertion, to say, that his parallel is not to be found either in the history of ancient or modern times. (p. 517)

It is unfortunate that there should be a blemish upon such a character. But blemish there is; for Sheridan has a new story to tell, on the authority of his father, about the last hours of Stella, and it is a story in surprising contrast to the earlier one. Swift, according to the original tale, offered to acknowledge his marriage in order to brighten Stella's last hours, but she replied, "It is too late." Sheridan's version of the incident, on the other hand, portrays Swift as refusing Stella's death-death-bed request to make the matter public and shows him cruelly quitting the sick-room never to return. It lies not within the province of this work to discuss the possible truth of either account; but the fact of Sheridan's recounting a story so injurious to his hero's reputation is worth noting. Even here, however, he condemns Swift only partially. To have acknowledged the marriage at that late date could have done no good. Stella's vanity might have been gratified, but Swift's reputation would have suffered from the scandalous talk which must have ensued. He had after all agreed to marry her only out of compassion, for his fondness for her had no mixture in it of sexual love, "but was rather the tenderness of a parent to a favourite child." (p. 284) And he had determined never to marry until he had a fortune suitable to provide for a family—a fortune which, of course, he never accumulated.

Toward Vanessa, however, he did experience "that all powerful passion, which the greatest heroes, and most renowned sages, have not been able to withstand, I mean, love." (p. 296) From 1712, when his love for her began,[1] until the end of his life, he could not free his mind from the disturbance thus created. No illicit commerce ever took place between the lovers, partly because Swift governed his conduct strictly, partly because, after the marriage, his ardor cooled, but especially because his power of gratifying his desires had been destroyed by constant suppression. This last is, Sheridan hastens to assure us, merely his opinion of the case; but it is an opinion confirmed by a saying of Swift's:

> "that he never yet saw the woman, for whose sake he would part with the middle of his bed." A saying, which, I believe, all mankind will judge could come from no person, but one incapable of enjoying the highest and most innocent of all gratifications here below, when sanctified by marriage. (p. 326)

Thus, though his biography in the main sets Swift up as an example of all the finer virtues, Sheridan contributes in no small way to later impressionistic studies. Every flattering statement in the book is likely to pale into insignificance when compared with the startling facts of the Dean's sexual impotence and his cruelty to the women who loved him.

Reviews of Sheridan's Life were mixed. A writer in the European Magazine (October, 1784) found it badly written and over-partial.[2] No attempt to draw a veil over Swift's manifold imperfections can blind one to the fact that the Dean's behavior was, from first to last, a strange compound of "pride, artfulness, and what he has so much professed to detest--duplicity." And Sheridan's reluctant relation of the death-bed scene is sufficient to brand Swift as a "monster of inhumanity." (p. 285) The writer pleads finally for an unbiased account, to steer a middle course between Johnsonian condemnation and stupid panegyric. Very different, however, is the opinion expressed in the Critical Review (November, 1784) by one who evidently admired Swift greatly. Sheridan's access to the best information, his freedom from party rancor and prejudice--these have resulted in a work which at last shows Swift in his true light as a great, though peculiar, character, with a capacious mind, clear

[1]Because of the tampering with the original language of the *Journal to Stella* indulged in by Hawkesworth and Deane Swift, its first editors, Sheridan was led erroneously to believe that Swift no longer used the "little language" in his letters after March, 1712, and therefore assumed that that date marked the beginning of his affair with Vanessa. Scott among others blindly accepted his conclusions, thus lending his authority to the false impression that Swift shows less fondness for Stella in the latter part of the *Journal*.

[2]See also *Month. Rev.*, May, 1785.

comprehension, and an unfailing dignity which exalts even his triflings. Though his conduct to Stella and Vanessa admits of little defense, he appears at least not to have been actuated in either situation "by interested and pecuniary motives." (p. 355) And his seeming arrogance, says the writer, arose not from false pride but from a frank indifference to the "approbation" of the world.

Thus the Dean appears a devil to one commentator, little less than an angel to another. Perhaps the most impartial essay in the periodicals of the time can be found in the European Magazine for November, 1790.[1] A short critique written for no special occasion, it treats mainly of Swift the writer; but what it has to say of his character is not without value as an example of a really sane, if slightly intolerant, middle-of-the-road point of view. The author sternly chides Swift for his cruelty, pride, selfishness, parsimony, and all the other vices which had by that time become standard criticism; but he praises him for his charity and excuses him for his occasional lapses into levity on the ground that he was not really a divine at heart. And more forcefully even than Sheridan, he presses the distinction between the two periods of Swift's life, during the first of which he showed few signs of the moroseness and peevishness so characteristic of the latter. That distinction, sometimes ignored even today, has been, it seems to me, too often neglected by critics, who in their desire for consistency have forgotten that Swift was known to his comrades in England as the "laughter-loving dean" and that only in old age did he fall utterly prey to melancholy.[2]

So far we have been dealing primarily with the reputation of the man Swift as it developed during the latter part of the eighteenth-century as a result of various syntheses of already existent biographical material. Some of these syntheses added information to the story of Swift; some were sheer critiques. Sheridan, of course, made revelations unnumbered and searched for truth with only less avidity than had Deane Swift or Orrery. But there were other channels by which new truths--and falsehoods--could be brought to light. One was by word of mouth. Talk about the Dean had never ceased, especially in Ireland, where legends and shamrocks bloom with equal facility. A second outlet, and the one by which most oral tradition eventually sought permanent recording, presented itself in the sea of periodicals which was already beginning to flood the British Isles. Anecdotes without end found their way into print in the journals and magazines of the time; and while most of them were soon forgotten, some attached themselves to the ever-growing body of Swiftiana and have since been shaken off only

[1]Because of differences in style and sentiment this cannot be attributed to the writer in the *European Magazine* already mentioned.

[2]William Alfred Eddy's Introduction to his selection from the *Satires and Personal Writings*, Oxford, 1932, makes much of this point--and with reason.

with great effort.[1] I have mentioned them here because, false though they were, by becoming part of the body of knowledge and pseudo-knowledge about Swift upon which later criticism was to depend they helped to create an impression of the Dean not easily dispelled.[2]

At the same time, research of a sort was being carried on in other quarters. With Monck Berkeley, and with Beddoes and Barrett in the first decade of the nineteenth-century, we see the faint glimmerings of modern scholarly methods. For their interesting attempts to ferret out hidden truths those three men merit at least a brief discussion in this place.

George-Monck Berkeley's Literary Relics (London, 1789), to which was prefixed an Inquiry into the life of Dean Swift, inaugurates a period of what M. Pons calls "romantic elaboration" in the history of Swift criticism. We have now reached an age in which few important discoveries about major problems remain to be made. Specialization must of necessity set in, and with specialization a search for novel attitudes and esoteric information. Enthusiasm for Swift inevitably led to increased interest in everything Swiftian and thence to a kind of minute research which, poorly disciplined as it was during the eighteenth and early nineteenth centuries, too often overstepped its bounds and gave imagination free play. There is nothing, in short, quite so romantic as romantic scholarship.

Berkeley's primary object is to defend Swift against the usual charges of misanthropy, impiety, and cruelty. We shall glance at his treatment of the first two of these in a later section. What occupies him chiefly, however, is that part of Swift's conduct which alone seems to deserve censure--his relations with Stella and Vanessa. And by "candid" investigation he has found the Dean to be "not wholly undeserving of pity." (p. xxviii) His cruelty to Stella sprang from remembrance of Varina's abuse of his love, from his insufficient financial resources, and, finally, from the situation in which he found himself with Vanessa. For all this and the fatal effects of blinding passion he should not be too much blamed.

So far we are still in the realms of judicial criticism. But Berkeley's interest in the Stella problem has led him on into untrodden paths of scholarship. Thus he

[1]The famous story of the rape at Kilroot is one of these. Nichols, in his edition of the *Tatler*, 1786, note to No. 188, lent his authority to the libel, which he afterwards repudiated. The matter is discussed pro and con in various numbers of the *Gent. Mag.* See, for example, LVI, 694; LVII, 194; LX, 157; and LX, 191, in which the legend is controverted with finality as merely a rumor for which no factual evidence can be discovered.

[2]See *European Mag.*, October and December, 1807, for two examples of probably unfounded Swift stories, one suggested by the other.

becomes the first of Swift's biographers to accept Swift's own account of Stella's parentage; thus he gives the marriage story to us on entirely new and seemingly incontestable authority; but thus also, alas, he is prone to grasp at any bit of gossip either for its novelty or for its help in proving a point. Though he does not vouch for it, for instance, he alludes almost wistfully to an anecdote told by Richard Brennan, Swift's servant, of a child who might have been the son of Swift and Stella. This tendency toward what might be called partial scholarship can dangerously mislead the casual observer; and we find a commentator in the English Review (March, 1791) swallowing all Berkeley's conclusions whole, even to the palpably specious Brennan story.

The researches of Thomas Beddoes led him into far different fields of study. Preoccupied with mental disorders in general, his interest in Swift was merely incidental; but his ten-page discussion of Swift's illness[1] created a veritable furore in literary circles. He assumed the fact of sexual impotence in the Dean, ascribing it to early sexual indulgence, but ascribing it in such ambiguous terms that I quote the passage in full:

> I do not conceive that any one can read, without commiseration, of his wretched state of desertion, or of his college solitude, at that dangerous period, without alarm. Who, that is capable of entering into the situation of young men of deep sensibility, shut out in any manner from society, and bereaved of the amusements of their age, can be at a loss in imagining to what means of assuaging desire they may be reduced, and what kinds of solace they may seek under the gloom of discouragement, and in a state of rejection by the world? (loc. cit., 188-89)

Whatever, exactly, these chary euphemisms may mean, they can lend themselves to almost any interpretation; and Scott and others, assuming Beddoes to have meant that Swift's youth had been one of libertinism and profligacy, rose in wrath to the Dean's defense.[2] However, the harm had been done, and a new cause for recrimination invented. Future critics, though cautious in their terminology, will make the most of it.[3]

The third of these early elaborations of minor Swift problems, John Barrett's Essay on the Earlier Part of the Life of Swift (London, 1808), stems from Richardson's

---

[1]In *Hygeia*, Bristol, 1803, III, Essay IX, 186-96.

[2]See Roscoe, *Life of Swift*, p. xv; and Wilde, *Closing Years*, p. 3

[3]See, for example, *Crit. Rev.*, October, 1809, 151-59. In a review of Barrett's essay the writer alludes constantly to Swift's early life as a period of "unnatural" misconduct. Drake, *Essays*, p. 168, also refers to "the excesses of a secret habit."

story of the Terrae Filius episode. Barrett writes with the double intention of disproving that anecdote and showing the real reason for Swift's animosity toward the University of Dublin. In so doing, he involves himself and the reader in much controversial material and provides fertile ground for the lucubrations of future scholars by ascribing a college Tripos, ostensibly written by one Jones, to Swift--and this by means of one criterion alone, indelicacy.[1]

Meanwhile the collection of Swiftian anecdotes has been growing; and in 1804 all the waifs and strays of fact and tradition are gathered together in Wilson's volume of Swiftiana, an utterly worthless miscellany of disconnected stories, some true, some doubtful, many definitely false, acquired in various ways, though mostly, according to the compiler, from the lips of several unnamed "gentlemen." As an appendix to the book we have a letter from the ubiquitous Theophilus Swift, eccentric son of the eccentric Deane, warning the reader against placing any confidence in Mrs. Pilkington and regaling him at the same time with another series of anecdotes so vulgar and ridiculous as to make all former accounts--especially that of poor Mrs. Pilkington--seem like truth incarnate by contrast. The Swiftiana, at any rate, wretched though it was, contributed along with the studies of Berkeley, Beddoes, and Barrett to prevalent nineteenth-century conceptions of the Dean. Therein lies its importance; and therein, for our purpose at least, lies the sole value of all these works.[2]

The first decade of the nineteenth-century brought forth no new biographical criticism of importance; but such incidental remarks on Swift as we find clearly point toward the prevailing tendencies of the new age. With an eye toward pointing a moral and adorning a tale, the critic begins picking and choosing such non-contradictory materials from the abundant store of Swiftiana as will exactly suit his purpose, whatever it may be. Thus Chalmers, in his historical and biographical preface to The Tatler,[3] while allowing the Dean's works to be illustrious ornaments of literature, scores Sheridan for his attempt to "construct a Christian Hero from the materials of an inconsistent Humourist" (p. 57), finds in Swift's character few claims to our esteem, and sees nothing of the problematical or mysterious in his general conduct, which was simply uniformly sinful.

---

[1]For an unsympathetic review of Barrett see *Quart. Rev.*, February, 1809. See also *Month. Rev.*, June, 1810.

[2]Compare John Timbs' "Anecdote" biography of Swift, *Lives of Wits and Humourists*, London, 1862, I, 1-121, for an example of the anecdotal tendency carried far into the nineteenth century. Teerink also mentions L. T. Rede, *Anecdotes and Biography*, London, 1799, which contains ten Swift anecdotes. I have not seen a copy.

[3]*The British Essayists*, 1803. My references are to the Boston edition, 1856, I, 54ff.

Nathan Drake[1] also adds his bit to the trend toward creating a dichotomy between Swift and his works. Though he considers him an incomparable literary artist, he can extend his admiration no further. An eternal stain on the reputation of the Dean, the Stella-Vanessa stories never can be forgotten; the hypothesis of Beddoes, in which he unquestioningly acquiesces, adds one more blot to the 'scutcheon and should be a "lesson of incalculable utility to the rising generation"; (loc. cit., p. 168) and Swift's more estimable qualities--his charity, his frankness, his championship of an oppressed people--were all "sullied and debased by pride, dogmatism, and misanthropy; by a temper harsh, gloomy, and discontented." (p. 171) And so Drake, finding his interest in both the life and the works destroyed, concurs in the poetically just punishment allotted to Swift by William Hayley, who in 1781 had consigned the Dean to Hell:

> The proudest Phantom of the gloomy clan,
> Appointed, by this surly Monarch's grace,
> High-priest of all his Misanthropic race!
> See o'er the crowd a throne of vapours lift
> That strange and motley form, the shade of SWIFT![2]

It is only fair, however, to add that the motley shade of Swift was not condemned to flames by the whole world. In one corner of Great Britain--in a corner newly awakened to a realization of its unique place in the world--the Dean's memory was revered by men who remained obstinately blind to the faults so overwhelmingly apparent to their contemporaries elsewhere. Let us, therefore, close this section of our study with a paragraph or two from the pen of the Irish patriot and historian, John Wilson Croker:

> On this gloom one luminary rose, and Ireland worshipped it with Persian idolatry: Her true patriot--her first, almost her last. Sagacious and intrepid--he saw, he dared; above suspicion he was trusted; above envy, he was beloved; above rivalry, he was obeyed. His wisdom was practical and prophetic--remedial for the present, warning for the future: He first taught Ireland that she might become a nation, and England that she might cease to be a despot. But he was a churchman. His gown impeded his course, and entangled his efforts--guilding (sic) a senate or heading an army he had been more than Cromwell, and Ireland

[1]*Essays...Illustrative of the Tatler...*, London, 1805, III, 138-82.

[2]*The Triumphs of Temper*, London, 1781, Canto III. In the second edition of the poem Hayley appended a note apologizing for his almost too severe censure of Swift, but refused to retract. It is interesting to note, however, that in later editions, while he retained the idea of a misanthropic monster ruling over one portion of Hell, he omitted all specific reference to Swift.

not less than England: As it was, he saved her by his courage--improved her by his authority--adorned her by his talents--and exalted her by his fame. His mission was but of ten years, and for ten years only, did his personal power mitigate the government; but though no longer feared by the great, he was not forgotten by the wise; his influence, like his writings, has survived a century, and the foundations of whatever prosperity we have since erected, are laid in the disinterested and magnanimous patriotism of Swift.

This is not digression--it is instruction; justice to the dead--example to the living;--it is the debt we owe, and the precept we should inculcate;--when he is emulated, his country is redeemed.[1]

---

[1]*A Sketch of the State of Ireland, Past and Present,* Dublin, 1808, 9-11.

II

The Works

During the period from 1781 to 1814 two important editions of the complete works of Swift appeared. The first was Sheridan's in 1784, the second, John Nichols' in nineteen volumes in 1801.[1] This was reprinted (in twenty-four volumes) in 1803, and again, revised and augmented, in 1808. Meanwhile other publications came out--a collection of the poetry in 1806, for instance, and miscellaneous works in prose and verse from time to time.[2] So much was printed, in fact, that one or two critics complained about the surfeit of worthless material beginning to clutter up their Swift libraries. But the number of editions attests to the fact that the Dean was being read; the popularity of his writings was not diminishing in proportion to the ever-growing antipathy toward his personality. Let us turn now to a study of the works as they appeared to critics; and, in seeing how opinion began to crystallize, we shall perhaps also learn what the age wanted in its literature and what it found in Swift to satisfy its tastes.

I

Personal Papers and Political Writings

The Journal to Stella and the correspondence have seldom been extensively discussed as literature. Though referred to frequently, they have not, in general, been read and quoted for such aesthetic value as they may have, but in order to clarify biographical issues; and this is especially true of the thirty-odd years between Johnson and Scott. Of the few criticisms of the Journal, the first appears in the Monthly Review for November, 1779. The writer, censuring Nichols for having published too much in his Supplement, complains particularly of the Journal, which includes so many disgusting passages, and which, not having been intended for the eyes of the world, ought never to have been printed! This is an understandable attitude, fewer than a dozen years having passed since the publication of the last of the letters to Esther Johnson. As readers grew more accustomed to seeing Swift's mind in undress, however, they prized the Journal increasingly;[3] and I have found no other such

[1]See *Month. Rev.*, February, 1802, for a colorless but appreciative review of this.

[2]There were also numerous imitations of *A Tale of a Tub* and *Gulliver's Travels*. See Teerink's *Bibliography* for fuller lists.

[3]See, for example, *European Mag.*, November, 1790; and Mackintosh, *Memoirs*, March 4, 1811. Edmund Burke also praised the *Journal* highly, *Table Talk*, p. 25.

desire for its suppression. It is condemned, if at all, as Drake condemns it, for its display of affectionate language, "which, if he had formed the resolution of never marrying, as hath been asserted by some of his biographers, was deceptive, and, therefore, highly blameable." (loc. cit., p. 165)

Mild approbation is usually vouchsafed to the rest of the correspondence. The letters are "elegant and judicious specimens of epistolary writing."[1] Or, though unaffectedly easy in style, they are over-querulous, splenetic, undignified, deficient in tenderness, dignity, and eloquence.[2] Or, finally, they can be classified in two distinct types: "His writings to his friends have an incomparable beauty of style; but all his epistles to people in an higher sphere were unnatural and laboured."[3] This last statement appears in an unusually hostile "character" of the Dean and is interesting chiefly because, from an a priori judgment of Swift as a flatterer of the great, it insinuates servility into letters written according to eighteenth-century convention--a slyly honest-sounding method of falsification too often indulged in by malicious critics of every age.

The political pamphlets are almost universally admired, though more for the effect they produced upon the public than for their intrinsic merit. Dr. Johnson, however, steadfastly refuses to allow their efficacy as propaganda to influence his judgments. It is on record that he sneered at the Journal to Stella, "for it contains slight topicks, and it might soon be written."[4] And with equal justice he disparaged the Conduct of the Allies as a performance of little ability. At one time, Boswell tells us, Dr. Douglas objected:

> "Surely, Sir, (said Dr. Douglas,) you must allow it has strong facts." JOHNSON. "Why yes, Sir; but what is that to the merit of the composition?... Housebreaking is a strong fact;...and murder is a mighty strong fact; but is great praise due to the historian of those strong facts? No, Sir. Swift has told what he had to tell distinctly enough, but that is all. He had to count ten, and he has counted it right." (II, 65)

Johnson was not simply arguing for victory at this point, nor was his eternal prejudice against Swift at the root of his criticism. He was, rather, unable to appreciate an art which chooses, examines, and advances facts in a seemingly unadorned, though exquisitely patterned, manner.

---

[1] *European Mag.*, November, 1790, p. 332.

[2] Drake, *loc. cit.*

[3] *Gent. Mag.*, October, 1782, p. 218.

[4] Boswell, *Life of Johnson*, IV, 177.

And he repeats his dictum in the Life of Swift:

> Yet, surely, whoever surveys this wonder-working pamphlet with cool perusal will confess that its efficacy was supplied by the passions of its readers; that it operates by the mere weight of facts, with very little assistance from the hand that produced them. (p. 19)

But Johnson stands aloof from the general trend. To most commentators the pamphlets are models of political controversy, and Swift is praised for his adherence to principle and his sincerity. "He acted from conviction and patriotism," says the not entirely sympathetic European Magazine. (loc. cit.) And William Godwin, marveling at the effect produced by the tracts, commends their profound "sagacity."[1] Sheridan, as we should expect, goes even further: Swift's political tracts, in contradistinction to all others, were written for perpetuity and borrow their chief value from immensity of genius rather than from transitory circumstance. Greatest of them all are the Drapier's Letters, for their plain language, intelligible to the meanest capacities, their easy, natural arguments, and their superb appeal to the emotions as well as the understanding.

> (Without) ever appearing to apply at all to the passions, he raises them to the highest pitch, by seemingly casual strokes here and there interspersed.... Yet plain and simple as these writings seem to be at first view, and such as every common reader would imagine he could produce himself, upon a clear inspection they would to be found to be works of the most consummate skill and art. (op. cit., p. 231)

They are compared favorably with the art of Demosthenes; but, Sheridan assures us, Swift had the advantage over Demosthenes in his "admirable vein of wit and humour" (p. 232) and in his brilliant choice of ground both for attack and defense, wherein, steering clear of party, he treated the matter all along "as if there were no parties concerned but William Wood hardwareman, on the one side; and the whole kingdom of Ireland on the other." (p. 233)

Sheridan's favorable statements about the Drapier's Letters were echoed twenty years later by Drake; and with varying turns of expression much the same things have been said by most--but not all--other critics, with occasional qualifications as to Swift's knowledge of economics.

---

[1] *The Enquirer*, London, 1797, Essay XII, p. 443.

2

Bagatelles and Miscellaneous Works

Delany had sorrowfully accused Swift of having been in the end "almost totally engrossed by that detestable maxim, Vive la bagatelle." (op. cit., p. 120) We find that accusation repeated again and again during the age now under discussion. Johnson could be playful on occasion; but to Swift trifles were "a necessary part of life," (op. cit., p. 46) and from the contemplation of such childishness the Doctor passes with disdainful haste to worthier matters. Warton, in his Essay on Pope, speaks of the Dean's old age as a despicable one, misspent "in trifling and in railing; in scribbling paltry riddles and rebusses, and venting his spleen in peevish invectives." (II, 343-44) Another critic blames Swift himself in part for a market glutted with unworthy stuff, because he "gave the most contemptible nonsense to the booksellers with the same readiness as the most admirable and elegant compositions."[1] And in the Monthly Review for January, 1790, we find an early statement of what never ceases to be a problem:

> Must we read every unimportant scrawl because it fell from the pen of Swift? must we witness every irritable and peevish expression of his splenetic and distempered hours? and be pestered with every quibbling conundrum of his gayer moments, when vive la bagatelle was all his conversation? It would be well if editors considered whether they were adding to the reputation of the deceased, or gratifying the wishes of the survivors, by thus turning literary "resurrection-men," and dragging to light what was "quietly in-urned." Will they never add some portion of judgment to their abundant industry? (p. 1)

This was indeed a serious-minded age; and so intent was it upon painting a consistently dark picture of Dean Swift that, when required to credit him with playful moments not consonant with preconceived notions, it either neglected them entirely or treated them with contempt. Even the most sanguine admirer of the works had to justify the trifles by minimizing their frivolous playfulness; and the Critical Review (November, 1784) calls them "the gambols of a lion, who can, in a moment, reassume his majesty, and range the forests with unimpaired vigour." (p. 354)

Swift in dead earnestness, even when ironical, is better understood. Of the more serious lesser pamphlets,

---

[1] *European Mag.*, November, 1790, p. 332. It is interesting to note that even Mason, in the next age, speaks with apparent regret of the "indiscriminate publication of his works." *Hist. St. Pat.*, p. 383.

Johnson himself cannot withhold his approbation of The Sentiments of a Church of England Man, "written with great coolness, moderation, ease, and perspicuity," (p. 12) or of An Argument against Abolishing Christianity, "a very happy and judicious irony." (ibid.) One critic, on the other hand, lumps together with those two pamphlets the papers in defense of the Sacramental Test, and that strangest of bedfellows, "the ridicule of astrology, under the name of Bickerstaff," and says of them:

> In these publications Swift does not rise superior to the prejudices which agitated the contending parties of those days. His principles of toleration may be clearly perceived to have been inimical to a general liberty of conscience. He speaks the language of those days, when bigotry, under the specious name of zeal and orthodoxy, shook the very pillars of the Reformation; and, while it pretended to secure the church from danger, was undermining the best interests of truth, religion, and liberty.[1]

These words were penned by a Scotch Presbyterian. Obviously, Swift appears as a true churchman or a religious bigot according to the sectarian prejudices of most eighteenth-century commentators.

Peculiarly enough, little attention is paid before Scott to some of the Dean's more interesting minor works; the Modest Proposal, for example, is hardly touched upon. Much, on the other hand, is said about the Proposal for Correcting the English Tongue, which, being perhaps Swift's most vulnerable piece, provides an easy target for the critical sharpshooter. Johnson's remark that it was written without sufficient knowledge either of English or of the history of language in general, and that the stability which, contrary to all experience, Swift thought attainable could not and should not come about, is only too well known. And Hugh Blair devoted the whole twenty-fourth section of his Lectures on Rhetoric (London, 1783) to a critical appraisal of the pamphlet's style, finding it full of inaccuracies and, though unaffected and precise in its choice of words, neither elegant nor correct! It became thereafter matter of common knowledge that Swift was ill-qualified for philological discussion, and of ironical truth that the very pamphlet in which he proposed a scheme for bettering the English language was "in point of grammar and style, the most defective and erroneous of any production in his voluminous works."[2]

---

[1]Robert Anderson, Life of Swift, in *Works of the British Poets*, London, 1795, IX, vii.

[2]This is from Drake, *Essays*, p. 146. The same idea is often repeated during the years of Blair's popularity as a rhetorician. See, for example, Chalmers, *British Essayists;* and, in the next period, *Dublin U. Mag.*, XV, 342 (1840).

3

The Battle of the Books and A Tale of a Tub

Two of Swift's greatest productions are the buoyant output of comparative youth, and they are generally linked together. Of the first we shall have little to say at this point. In 1780 men no longer quarreled about the ancients and moderns, nor were they much interested in a contest so recent as to be of small historical importance. There could be little disagreement as to the superbly satirical Battle; and so, beyond calling it excellent and explaining its background, critics neglect it shamelessly.[1] Only Johnson, again, finds food for cavil. Swift had claimed complete originality for the work which, according to Wotton, had been based directly on the French Combat des Livres; and Johnson, following Wotton, sees such a similarity between the two works that the improbability of coincidence is not, in his mind, "balanced by the anonymous protestation prefixed, in which all knowledge of the French book is peremptorily disowned." (p. 11)[2]

But if the ancients-moderns dispute lacked interest, religious questions had lost none of their vitality. The Tale of a Tub, for writing which Jonathan Swift seems to have been denied his cherished mitre, provided fertile field for discussion. On the critic's interpretation of it depended in great part his conclusions as to Swift's highly questionable piety; or, indeed, the proposition could be put with equal justice in reverse order. In all solemnity, the literary judges approached a work renowned today for its wit and color. But Dr. Johnson for once distinguished himself by seeing in the Tale sidelights to which his contemporaries paid slight attention. With characteristic bias, indeed, he doubted the universal attribution of the piece to Swift, whom he considered inferior to both Arbuthnot and Addison as a humorist:

> ...it has so much more thinking, more knowledge, more power, more colour, than any of the works which are indisputably his. If it was his, I shall only say he was impar sibi.[3]

In his Life of Swift he speaks of it as so distinct and peculiar, so superior in vehemence and mental rapidity, in imagery and vivacity of diction, that it must be

[1]See, for example, *European Mag.*, November, 1790, p. 329. The writer simply calls it a "beautiful satire." Sheridan, *op. cit.*, p. 43, does no more than name it.

[2]This is a gross mis-statement. Johnson could hardly have made an actual comparison of the *Battle* with what is now known to have been a non-existent *Combat des Livres*. The book Swift may have seen was de Callières' *Histoire poétique*. For a fuller discussion of this, see below, Part Two.

[3]Boswell, *Tour*, 16 August, 1773, p. 27.

judged apart from the Dean's other writings. Its faults, nevertheless, are such as none can overlook: though charity might persuade one to believe it the work of a man of peculiar character "without ill intention," yet "it is certainly of dangerous example." (p. 10) And the digressions relating to Wotton and Bentley must be confessed to discover either want of knowledge or want of integrity.

> But Wit can stand its ground against Truth only a little while. The honours due to learning have been justly distributed by the decision of posterity. (p. 11)

Thus we see Johnson praising the work for its intelligence and style, while decrying its frivolous treatment of religion and pedantry--a surprisingly advanced type of criticism for an age which was prone to like only what it agreed with.

Johnson alone takes serious notice of the digressions. Others of the time occupy themselves solely with the religious allegory--an allegory condemned as too mean for a truly dignified argument, by James Beattie in his Dissertations (London, 1783). It tends, he thinks, to produce in the mind of the reader "some very disagreeable associations, of the most solemn truths with ludicrous ideas." (p. 516) The habit of laughing at serious matters is a dangerous one; and clergymen, of all people, have least right "to take liberties of this sort with the most awful, and most benign dispensations of Providence." (516-17) And though the compliments paid to the Church of England and part of the satire leveled at Rome may be well-founded, Swift's abuse of Presbyterians is unforgivable. Whatever its merits, finally, the work abounds in "vile images, and obscene allusions; such as no well-bred man could read, or endure to hear read, in polite company." (517-18)

Directly opposed to Beattie's Puritanical animadversions is Sheridan's summary of the virtues of the Tale; and, in a way, the too frequently muddle-headed champion of the Dean cuts deeper than either of his predecessors at this juncture. The contemporary neglect of religion, he says, pained Swift, who purposed in the Tale to revive an interest in it and at the same time to show the excellency of the established church, in a manner both understandable and pleasurable. For some appeal to the fancy was necessary:

> People were quite wearied out with the continual repetition of the same dull arguments; or sore, on account of the ill temper with which the disputes were carried on, and the ill blood which they occasioned. (46-7)

Swift's object then was to make religion once more a general "topick" of conversation, but of such conversation as should give rise to cheerfulness and mirth rather than bigotry and malevolent enthusiasm. The Tale of a Tub rendered the pageantry of Roman Catholicism and the hypocrisy of Calvinism not hateful and formidable, but ridiculous and contemptible--thus showing the beauty of the Church of England in its most obvious light, as the epitome of simplicity and moderation, "the true marks of Christianity." (p. 48)

This, I think, is a rather stimulating apology for the Tale, which, as a matter of fact, finds at this stage of Swift criticism fewer hard-headed opponents than any of the other works. While Berkeley, in his Literary Relics, cannot help wishing away some of its wilder flights of fancy, he confesses himself unable to see the danger implied by Johnson in a work which after all never attacks "the essentials of religion." (p. xxv) That the Dean never swerved from a firm piety Berkeley is convinced; and he even refuses to credit Orrery's stories of "Dearly beloved Roger" and the whimsical "Race Ecclesiastic," the undue levity of which proves them false. As a vigorous and truly Christian book, the Tale discovers new defenders with each new work of criticism. The English Review (March, 1791) ascribes the suspicions cast upon it to the narrowness of the age in which it appeared; everything ridiculed in it is, the writer insists, ridiculed in the highest strain of satire. But there is no ridicule of the truth of revelation or of "the mode of faith which the Dean conceived founded in truth, and which the wisdom of his country authorised." (p. 213) And critics, remarkably close to unanimity in thinking it unobjectionable, often repeat the sentiments just quoted.[1]

They do not always agree, however, upon its two great faults--obscenity and obscurity. In the Enquirer, for example, Godwin, with his interest in rhetoric, censures the negligence and disjointedness of its style and describes it as written in a strange sort of "banter," or, rather, in a "low and anomalous" slang. (p. 444) The European Magazine (November, 1790) is annoyed equally at its obscurities of style and its vulgarity; whereas Nathan Drake, expressing the opinion of many, considers the Tale, in spite of occasional coarse passages, to exceed everything else of Swift's in literary merit, for its imagery, spirit, and original wit, "supported throughout with undiminished vigour." (loc. cit., p. 143)

The Tale of a Tub, unique work that it is, could exert little direct influence upon literary men; but one of the greatest tributes ever paid it came from the pen of William Cobbett, a true Swiftian, who tells us how in 1774, at the age of thirteen, he bought a copy for threepence, and ever afterwards considered it "a sort of birth

[1]See, for example, *Month. Rev.*, November, 1790, 241-44; *European Mag.*, November, 1790; and Drake, *Essays*, p. 142.

of intellect." He carried the book with him thereafter wherever he went;

> and when I, at about twenty years old, lost it in a box that fell overboard in the Bay of Funday in North America, the loss gave me greater pain than I have ever felt at losing thousands of pounds.[1]

4

Gulliver's Travels

In the fourth book of Gulliver's Travels we find the most intense expression of Swiftian misanthropy. Its satire, unlike that of the first three voyages, is almost universal. It attacks no single vice and satirizes general classes rather than specific persons; but as a sweeping indictment of all mankind, it spares no portion of humanity--least of all the eminently human literary critic. It should not then be matter for wonder that the eminently human literary critic, his thin skin violently bruised, has seldom failed to recoil from the merciless portrait of himself which Swift has painted. With a few important exceptions, our interest in tracing the reputation of Swift's masterpiece through the Romantic and Victorian periods will lie, I think, less in the critiques themselves than in the philosophies behind them. Men, as we shall see, tend to enjoy the first two voyages, to be bored by the third, and to turn again and again in anguish to the fourth, fascinated by its very repulsiveness. The reasons for their horror differ in interesting fashion one from another; but within each successive age the reactions of individuals, though varying, are likely to remain consonant with the unique standards of the period.

Morality played a major role in late eighteenth-century life and literature. Since man is created in the image of God, the misanthrope must of necessity be looked upon as immoral and irreligious; and so our early critics instantly recognized in the baleful latter portion of Gulliver the mark of Satan. Repelled and shocked, they rose to defend their deflated self-esteem by avoiding the main issue of Swift's purpose in creating his Houyhnhnms and Yahoos and concentrating upon obvious inconsistencies within those characterizations. Says James Harris:

> MISANTHROPY is so dangerous a thing, and goes so far in sapping the very foundations of MORALITY and RELIGION, that I esteem the last part of Swift's Gulliver...to be a worse Book to peruse, than those which we

[1]See *The Progress of a Plough-Boy to a Seat in Parliament*, ed. Reitzel, London, 1933. This passage comes from the *Political Register*, XXXVI, 19 February, 1820; 23-4.

> forbid, as the most flagitious and obscene.
>
> One absurdity in this Author (a wretched Philosopher, tho' a great Wit) is well worth remarking--in order to render the Nature of MAN odious, and the Nature of BEASTS amiable, he is compelled to give HUMAN Characters to his BEASTS, and BEASTLY Characters to his MEN--so that we are to admire THE BEASTS, not for being Beasts, but amiable MEN; and to detest THE MEN, not for being MEN, but detestable BEASTS.
>
> Whoever has been reading this unnatural Filth, let him turn for a moment to a Spectator of ADDISON, and observe the PHILANTHROPY of that Classical Writer; I may add the superior Purity of his Diction and his Wit.[1]

Had Swift intended to render the nature of beasts "amiable"? If so, Harris may be thought not unjust in his criticism of the absurdities in the fourth voyage. But even in this case, the mere substitution of the words "good" and "evil" for "human" and "beastly," respectively, might have neatly answered the major objection of the critic.

Beattie, equally obsessed by the irreligion and filth of the piece, approaches it, however, from a less assailable point of view. He had already mentioned the faults of the work in his Essay on Poetry and Music (Edinburgh, 1778), where he censured it as a malevolent fiction of rational brutes and irrational men; and he had been shocked by the idea of representing horses as "patterns of moral virtue," as "masters of reason," and yet completely lacking in religion. (Part I, p. 43) Horrified that a Christian Divine could trample on the nature assumed by Christ, he returned to the problem in his moral and critical Dissertations of 1783. Parts of Gulliver he praised highly: its style was a model of graceful simplicity; the fable itself and the characterization of Gulliver as a sea-faring man were supported with wonderful propriety and verisimilitude. And as far as the satire was leveled at pride and folly, "so far the author deserves our warmest approbation, and his satire will be allowed to be perfectly just, as well as exquisitely severe." (514-15) But this could not be said for the fourth voyage, for it made human nature itself the object of its contempt:

> But when a writer endeavours to make us dislike and despise, every one his neighbour, and be dissatisfied with that Providence, who has made us what we are, and whose dispensations toward the human race are so peculiarly, and so divinely beneficent; such a writer, in so doing,

[1] *Philosophical Inquiries*, London, 1781, III, 537-38.

> proves himself the enemy, not of man only, but of goodness itself; and his work can never be allowed to be innocent, till impiety, malevolence, and misery, cease to be evils. (515-16)[1]

Both Harris and Beattie then have found inconsistencies in the portraits of Yahoos and Houyhnhnms, and both have disapproved of Gulliver's tendency to scoff at divine Providence by debasing human nature. Beattie has gone further by pointing out the unhealthiness of the Swiftian attitude, if the fourth voyage be taken, as he and his contemporaries took it, to have a serious didactic purpose. Actually, neither Harris nor Beattie has succeeded in achieving more than a half-convincing rationalization of an irrational emotion aroused by the book; it remained for an anonymous reviewer to give authentic, because unambitious, expression to that emotion. In a short criticism of an obscure work modeled on Gulliver, the writer commends the new book. It surveys humanity with a less jaundiced eye than Gulliver and is therefore less disgusting, because it does not attempt to root up fellow-feeling or "to contradict what appears in shining characters throughout the universe," the wisdom and goodness of God. And he goes on to say, with almost Victorian clarity:

> It is not decent thus to expose wantonly the nakedness of our parent; nay, the disgust the representation inspires, silently destroys its force.[2]

Proud of their piety and taste, the critics are, no matter how they express their disgust, in agreement about the fundamental indecency of the work--all but two or three. The redoubtable Sheridan accepts the challenge with gusto:

> ...the whole apologue of the Houyhnhnms and Yahoos, far from being intended as a debasement of human nature, if rightly understood, is evidently designed to show in what the true dignity and perfection of man's nature consists, and to point out the way by which it may be attained. (op. cit., p. 479)

Thus Swift exhibits two portraits--one of "unmixed vice," the other of "unadulterated virtue"--in order to excite in us a hatred of the one and a love of the other. But by no stretch of the imagination can the wholly evil

[1]Beattie does not absolutely accuse Swift of impiety, but imputes his faults to a passion for ridicule. For example, he finds the poem on the *Last Judgment* especially shocking as a bit of irreligious wit.

[2]*Analytic Review*, May, 1789, 77-8. A review of *Mammuth*....by the Man in the Moon.

Yahoo be identified with man; it is a creature of Swift's fancy, resembling man in nothing but the make of its body "and the vicious propensities of its nature." (p. 480) How, Sheridan asks, can the Yahoos be considered human beings, when they are devoid of all the "characteristical" marks of human beings: speech, reason, and the power to walk on two legs? By giving the brute Yahoo vaguely human form, however, the Dean has brought his lesson home to man.

> But it may be asked, to what end has such an odious animal been produced to view? The answer is obvious: The design of the author, in the whole of this apologue, is, to place before the eyes of man a picture of the two different parts of his frame, detached from each other, in order that he may the better estimate the true value of each, and see the necessity there is that the one should have an absolute command over the other. In your merely animal capacity, says he to man, without reason to guide you, and actuated only by a blind instinct, I will show you that you would be degraded below the beasts of the field....
>
> On the other hand, I will show another picture of an animal endowed with a rational soul, and acting uniformly up to the dictates of right reason....What is the natural inference to be drawn from these two different representations? (483-84)

In conclusion, says Sheridan, "no mortal ever had a worse opinion of human nature" from Swift's portrait of the Yahoos, "nor a better of the brute creation, from that of the Houyhnhnms." (p. 486) And with delectable solemnity he caps the climax and routs all squeamish fools by citing the Hottentots and other savages as indisputably human, yet even more detestable than the Yahoos!

There are certainly absurdities in Sheridan's defense of _Gulliver_. He has mistakenly tried to refute the palpable humanness of Swift's Yahoos; and the eighteenth-century spirit of moralization, which was incapable of appreciating art simply as the expression of one man's personality, compelled him to counter didacticism with didacticism. But he did succeed in pointing out what other critics refused to see--the fact that, with all his misanthropy, Swift distinguishes carefully between virtue and vice and fulminates only at the latter. Sheridan could hardly be expected to realize the distinction between extended satire, which, though it includes elements of didacticism, is primarily indignant rather than educational, and moral allegory like _The Pilgrim's Progress_. That he did understand the basic _goodness_ of the flaming voyage to the Houyhnhnms reflects creditably upon his critical powers.[1]

Monck Berkeley answers the charge of misanthropy by interpreting the story of the Yahoos in much the same manner as Sheridan. "It only," he says, "paints mankind in that state to which habits of vice must necessarily sink them"; and Swift, being by profession a teacher of morals, can hardly be blamed for painting the deformity of vice "in colours the most glaring, and in situations the most disgusting." (loc. cit., p. xxiv) But Sheridan and Berkeley stand virtually alone, tilting their frail lances against a resolutely packed opposition. "What trifling is this!" exclaims one reviewer of the Literary Relics:

> The simple question is, whether Man, such as he is, is superior, in the scale of existance, (sic) to the other animals, by which he is surrounded. If he is, there is neither wisdom nor truth in representing him as their inferior.[2]

And there indeed the matter rests. Man, being superior to horses, finds neither wit nor truth in Houyhnhnm-land; and, though he will admit, as Drake does in 1805, the value of Swift's fertile imagination, his insight into the follies and vices of humanity, and his acute observations, he will go no further. The principal aim of Gulliver, says Drake, appears to have been to mortify human pride.

> ...the satire, however, has been carried too far, and degenerates into a libel on the species.[3] The fourth part, especially, notwithstanding all that has been said in its defence by Sheridan and Berkeley, apparently exhibits such a malignant wish to degrade and brutalize the human race, that with every reader of feeling and benevolence it can occasion nothing but a mingled sensation of abhorrence and disgust. (loc. cit., p. 148)

More gentle than most, Drake concludes by suggesting that Swift might not consciously have intended drawing so degrading a picture, but might have been betrayed into it by that gloomy discontent which afterwards became insanity.

---

[1]See also Henry Weber, *Popular Romances*, Edinburgh, 1812, xxv-xxviii. Weber agrees with the more conventional view, and accuses Sheridan of having wrongly concealed the faults of the work because of his friendship toward Swift.

[2]*Month. Rev.*, November, 1790, p. 242.

[3]To the best of my knowledge, this is the earliest use of this phrase.

From 1781 to 1814, I have discovered only a few remarks on Gulliver which lie outside the main line of attack; and for one of these--the only one of real significance--we must once again turn to Dr. Johnson. Amazingly enough, Johnson has very little to say about the book in his essay on Swift. But he does not neglect it entirely. In two characteristic sentences, which seem on first glance like bald statements of fact, he damns it more forcefully than others have done in pages. When Gulliver was first published:

> Criticism was for a while lost in wonder: no rules of judgement were applied to a book written in open defiance of truth and regularity. But when distinctions came to be made the part which gave least pleasure was that which describes the Flying Island, and that which gave most disgust must be the history of the Houyhnhnms. (p. 38)

And thus, without even bothering to soil his hands, the Doctor washes them of the whole matter. But Boswell records another interesting arraignment of the Travels:

> I wondered to hear him say of Gulliver's Travels, "When once you have thought of big men and little men, it is very easy to do all the rest."... Johnson at last, of his own accord, allowed very great merit to the inventory of articles found in the pocket of the Man Mountain, particularly the description of his watch, which it was conjectured was his GOD, as he consulted it upon all occasions. (II, 319)

I have found no other writer in all the history of Swift criticism with the impudence to echo that hasty judgment as to the simplicity of doing "all the rest." On the contrary, the impartial critic of the European Magazine (November, 1790) considers the original fiction of big men and little men a most simple and obvious device. "The genius of Swift," he says, "is rather to be acknowledged in supporting, than in producing them." (p. 331) It hardly matters, however, which of these contrary opinions comes nearer truth. They are equally one-sided; and equally sterile.

William Godwin alludes to the skilful and simple style of the book as an excellent example of "the degree of cultivation at which the English language had at that time arrived" and calls Swift the man "of the most powerful mind of the time in which he lived" (loc. cit., p. p. 446); but, since he is writing on English style, he has nothing more to add beyond a few observations on incorrect constructions in the work.

Between Johnson and Scott, then, Gulliver's Travels found only two men eager to defend it. Its religious and moral sentiments were decried; its fictional and technical virtues were questioned; even its grammar was partially condemned--not merely by Godwin, but by Sheridan himself in his edition of the Works! Yet it was read by young and old, and it continues to be read. In later sections of this study we shall see how it endured through the nineteenth-century, in spite of, and partly, perhaps, because of, much adverse criticism.

5

The Poetry

> IN the Poetical Works of Dr. Swift there is not much upon which the critick can exercise his powers. They are often humorous, almost always light, and have the qualities which recommend such compositions, easiness and gaiety. They are, for the most part, what their author intended. The diction is correct, the numbers are smooth, and the rhymes exact....
>
> . To divide this Collection into classes, and shew how some pieces are gross, and some are trifling, would be to tell the reader what he knows already, and to find faults of which the author could not be ignorant, who certainly wrote often not to his judgement, but his humour.

So Dr. Johnson in his Life of Swift. (65-6) With the faintest of praise he damns, and with the most cursory examination he dismisses, a body of verse which in bulk alone exceeds that of many an accepted English poet, and in merit is at least worthy of some slight study.

But we are not astonished at finding Johnson icily caustic. Let us search elsewhere: "His poetry in the main, with all its beauties, is prostituted to the most trifling subjects."[1] This will not do; the writer obviously dislikes Swift. Joseph Warton, on the other hand, in discussing Pope's Country Parson, speaks of Swift as the Hogarth of poetry, a painter of objects as they really exist, with no heightening circumstances, and mentions some of his poems incidentally as specimens of his excellency in "this way of writing." (loc. cit., p. 51) But Warton's is but a casual reference. The Dean as poet interests him only in passing.

We turn hopefully to Sheridan, but in vain. He speaks of the early Pindarics as "strained and crowded" in sentiments, "irregular and harsh" in numbers--the mistaken efforts of a "genius misapplied" (op. cit., p. 14); but, beyond this perfectly valid criticism of a few worthless poems, he pays no attention to Swift's verse.

[1] *Gent. Mag.*, October, 1782, p. 470.

He devotes much space, to be sure, to a discussion of "that beautiful poem called Cadenus and Vanessa" (p. 302), that history of an overwhelming love, warm-spirited and refined.[1] But he discusses it as biography, not poetry, and concentrates upon a defense of the lines which had so pained Orrery. Assuming that the crux of the matter lies in a correct interpretation of the word "conscious," which is too often used in a bad sense, he proceeds to explain away its criminal overtones in a long, ethical-philosophical passage and concludes, what he believes already sufficiently proved, that the love of Cadenus for Vanessa must have been "of the purest and most virtuous kind." (p. 322)

Interesting though it may be, this is not literary criticism. For the first significant judgment of Swift's poetry we must go once more to the essayist in the European Magazine of November, 1790. And here the spirit of an age which was to deny Pope and to woo the infinite with furious passion originally asserts itself. The Dean's verses, says the writer, are easy and natural, but in reality are to be regarded in the same light with his other compositions.

> They are nothing more than prose in rhyme. Imagination, metaphor, and sublimity constitute no part of their merit. Sir Isaac Newton was within a trifle as great a poet as Dr. Swift. (p. 332)[2]

Even today, I suppose, one would hesitate to ascribe "sublimity" to the poetry. Yet, like the voyage to the Houyhnhnms, it is still read; and Nathan Drake, though, with Hayley, he condemned Swift to perdition, saw more clearly than most of his contemporaries the enduring qualities of Swift's verse. Not romantic fervor, for the poems are largely humorous and familiar, but a richness of wit and a perfection of technique gives them beauty and permanence. In the accuracy of his rhymes the Dean has excelled all other bards;

> and so complete a master is he of similar terminations, that scarcely a single word appears to have been introduced for the sake of consentaneous sound, but strikes the reader as the very one which he should have chosen in plain prose as best adapted to express his meaning....
>
> With these technical beauties he has, in his best pieces, combined the most

[1]Compare *Month. Rev.*, November, 1790, which comments upon the name "Vanessa": "Another whimsical name! Surely, from these cold conceits, we might suspect that the good Dean, in all his amours, was rather in play, than in earnest." (p. 244)

[2]See also, for another expression of the idea that Swift's verse is poetry only in so far as it is "distinguished by the accident of measure," Mackintosh, *Memoirs*, December 29, 1811.

> poignant wit and humour, and a rich display of character; and these, so far from suffering from the necessary restrictions of metre and rhyme, are, in fact, rendered more graceful and impressive by their adoption. (loc. cit., 150-51)

Drake cannot, of course, approve--there have been few who could--of the revolting scatology so characteristic of some of the verse, but he assures the reader that there are several poems "which are not only free from anything which ought to revolt a correct taste, but exhibit much elegance, urbanity, and well-turned compliment." (ibid.)

Interest in the poetry, if only for the sake of calling it prose, increased during the nineteenth-century; but, besides the few scattered allusions already noted in the years before Scott, I have found only one other worth recording.[1] Barrett ascribed to Swift and published several bits of verse in his Essay of 1808.[2] The Critical Review (October, 1809) commented upon these in an ungracious manner perfectly expressing the attitude of the age:

> Many, we had nearly said, most, of the poems which are published in every former edition of the works of Swift, are heavy and flat to an extreme. It is hardly then to be expected, that pieces newly discovered at this time of day, should be above the state of the worst of those raked together by the industry of former collectors. (155-56)

---

[1]The story of Dryden's cutting remark to Swift about the Pindarics is first told by Joseph Warton, *loc. cit.*, p. 250.

[2]He also included extracts from the *Remarks* on Burnet's *History*. Selections from these were first printed in *European Mag.*, January, 1795, to February, 1796.

III

Swift the Writer

We have seen how prevalent conceptions of Swift the man took shape during the late eighteenth and early nineteenth centuries. We have followed criticism of individual phases of his art through the years and have discovered to some extent the part played by biographical prejudice in the theatre of literary criticism. To complete our picture we must learn what in general men thought of Swift the writer. After they had surveyed his life and judged him as a personality, after they had glanced judicially at his various works, what was their final verdict of his genius? What did they think of his choice of subject matter, the manner in which he handled it, and the style in which he expressed it?

It might be well to state at the outset that not even his worst enemy denies Swift a goodly measure of talent. But this is an age which urges the distinction between earth-rooted talent and heaven-born genius, rolling its eye in a fine frenzy. Rare indeed are the critics who grant the Dean more than a portion of the latter element. One commentator acclaims his "native genius," his inexhaustible fancy, his "lively and comprehensive" conceptions, his quick penetration, and above all his facile, clear, correct style.[1] Another considers him to have been blessed above all his contemporaries with "the powers of a creative genius" and admires him intensely for the naked strength of his style, "familiar, without vulgarity or meanness; and beautiful, without affectation or ornament."[2] But for the most part admiration for Swift is tempered with a careful intermixture of fault-finding.

His style taken alone comes in for high praise, however. Sheridan conceives of him as having carried propriety and purity of diction "to a greater degree of perfection than any English writer whatsoever." (op. cit., p. 27)[3] And Blair's Lectures on Rhetoric cites his language, in spite of its frequent inaccuracies and in spite of the fact that it is less elegant than Addison's, as a model of purity and propriety, distinguished for its freedom from embellishment and its masterful treatment of every subject, whether serious or ludicrous. Much the

---

[1] *Month. Rev.*, November, 1779.

[2] This is quoted from the notes of the Reverend J. Granger by Mark Noble in his continuation of Granger's *Biographical History of England*, London, 1806, II, 166.

[3] Sheridan, incidentally, seems to idolize Temple, and attributes Swift's masterly style to "a frequent revisal of that great man's works." (p. 27)

same sentiments have been repeated time and again since, and we should gain little by listing any more.[1] The idea of "proper words in proper places" becomes a shibboleth in the history of Swift criticism; and the student eventually grows to welcome even the slightest defection from the common opinion.

From technique we proceed to problems of a deeper nature--from the mechanics of expression to the thoughts expressed. For this Dr. Johnson's essay provides a perfect bridge. Swift's style, says Johnson, suited his thoughts, for his thoughts were as prosaic as his style. They were neither subtle nor sparkling, neither elevated nor variegated, neither learned nor profound.

> He pays no court to the passions; he excites neither surprise nor admiration; he always understands himself, and his reader always understands him: the peruser of Swift wants little previous knowledge;... he is neither required to mount elevations nor to explore profundities; his passage is always on a level, along solid ground, without asperities, without obstruction. (p. 52)

Though he grants the Dean a large share of originality and praises him for his "easy and safe" mode of writing, Johnson, as we should expect, stops far this side idolatry: Swift's style may instruct, but it does not persuade; it may satisfy the requirements of mere didacticism, but it never soars to higher truths.

It is perhaps not without significance that Johnson, whom some have considered so earthbound, should thus anticipate so-called Romantic criticism. This new search for the super-earthly, the wild and sublime, is, however, already apparent in two or three essays which appeared soon after the Lives of the Poets. In an article called "Some Outlines of the Character of Dr. Swift" in the European Magazine of September, 1790, the writer notes that, though all are agreed upon Swift's extraordinary talents, none has yet specified exactly what those talents were, nor wherein Swift differed from, or excelled, other wits. The analysis which follows hardly answers the questions thus posed, but it does exemplify a tendency. Dr. Swift, according to the author, has been improperly called a great genius. He had neither large comprehension nor clear discernment. As a poet, "he was little more than an excellent crambo player, if we except the good sense he abounds with." (p. 185) And his talents were "left-handed" ones; that is, they tended toward the wicked rather than the sublime. In satire and wit he never approached Dryden, who, had he studied the foibles of mankind as Swift did, would have been as great a

[1]See, for example, *European Mag.*, November, 1790; Chalmers, *British Essayists, loc. cit.;* and Mackintosh, *Memoirs*, December 29, 1811.

master of ridicule. The critic muddles his discussion somewhat by bringing in the name of Pope, and the following passage ends, for that reason, in an anticlimactic and almost ludicrous fashion, but it is worth quoting:

> Whether his prose be better than Dryden's, I shall not say; more chaste, as critics term it, less adulterated with foreign words, and correct, it certainly is; but I have more pleasure in reading Dryden, where I rove thro' a wilderness of fruits and flowers, than in pacing through a garden laid out by line; and trimmed by art, as is Pope's artificial prose. (p. 184)

That longing for the wild and fanciful as opposed to the calm and limited is expressed again by the impartial critic of the European Magazine (November, 1790), whom I have so frequently cited. He characterizes Swift's age as one deficient in many qualities, first of which is originality. And though the Dean transcended his age in some ways, he too often shows himself typical of it. His style is nervous and manly; but we have gained in purity, in strength, in melody, in grace, since he wrote. By rigidly abjuring the flowers of rhetoric and the flow of eloquence, he attained to precision--but not to greatness; for above all he lacked fancy!

> ...he does not lose himself in fields of his own creation. The mind that is not turned either to the sublime or the pathetic, cannot certainly rank in the first class of writers of imagination. (p. 331)

The dry, irresistible march of his humor can never be too highly praised; but the essence of genius resides not in humor or vigor or clarity, but in the fancy. Thus is the author of Gulliver's Travels, the creator of Bickerstaff and Drapier, put in his place. Thus does the brave new world of romance dismiss the great satirist of whom, coupling him with Arbuthnot, Cowper had said:

> That constellation set, the world in vain
> Must hope to look upon their like again.[1]

The indelicacies of his work turn many writers against the Dean. Chalmers, finding few Tatlers which can be assigned to his pen, describes him as ill-qualified "for this species of composition." (loc. cit., p. 54) His wit was so licentious that, no matter how sacred the subject, nothing was safe from his malignant ridicule. No salutary spirit of correction marks his satire; and his invective is inspired not by virtuous indignation but by sheer ill temper. And, according to Dr. Barrett, the one sure way to recognize a production of Swift's is to search for indecent imagery and nauseous

[1] *Table Talk*, 1782, ll. 660-61.

ideas. In this strange propensity for filth he is almost singular among English writers, "and it forms the strong outline that distinguishes him from almost every other writer."[1]

"The dirty language, and the noisome jest," said Byron a few years later,

> Which pleased in Swift of yore, we now detest;
> Proscribed not only in the world polite,
> But even too nasty for a city Knight![2]

Later in the same poem he cries, "Peace to Swift's faults! his wit hath made them pass;" but Byron, as we know, felt a kinship with the age of Pope. In the "nice" years of the nineteenth-century, wit was not enough to satisfy those who aspired to "taste." Men would occasionally arise to champion Swift's cause, but the grand defamation of his character and work had only just begun when Byron wrote those lines.

---

[1]*Essay*, p. 29. See also Drake, *loc. cit.*, p. 171; and *Crit. Rev.*, October, 1809, p. 154.

[2]*Hints from Horace*, 1811.

PART TWO
(1814-1841)

I

Swift the Man

Walter Scott, who had already brought out a successful edition of Dryden, turned his hand to Swift in 1814. The popularity of the "magician of the North" gave him access to much hitherto unpublished material, and such men as the Reverend Edward Bèrwick and Theophilus Swift aided him in compiling a Life and Works which was completely to supersede the editions of Nichols. Despite its innumerable errors botn of omission and inclusion,[1] the fruit of Scott's labor is eminently deserving of respect; and for many years, even after others had attempted the same task, it remained the major edition of Swift. The biography which forms its first volume did more, I think, to arouse a new and lively interest in the Dean than any other single work of the time.

Yet that biography, facile and readable as it is, authoritative as it may sound, stems, as M. Pons shows, from the tradition of romantic scholarship inaugurated by Berkeley in the eighteenth-century.[2] Scott's vivid portrait of Swift has a historical color not unlike that of his novels; but it is derived from any and all sources, no matter how suspect; and though the biographer attempts to stress the more sympathetic side of Swift's nature, his love for the anecdotal and dramatic involves him in countless inconsistencies and absurdities. The work remains a brilliant synthesis of prior biographies, which fails lamentably in that it makes no distinction between such authorities as Delany, on the one hand, and Wilson or Theophilus Swift, on the other. In its attempt at final amalgamation, it places contradictory stories side by side; the author takes his choice, but the reader is left with an impression of both. Thus the Memoirs must in large part be held responsible for the development of a nineteenth-century picture of the Dean as a living paradox. In it can, in fact, be found the germs of most of the conflicting opinions of later critics. Scott pays, for example, equal attention to the Dean's charity and benevolence, and to his parsimony and misanthropy. He praises highly Swift's zeal in assisting his political enemies, but he admits that at times, especially in his scurrilous quarrel with Steele, he overstepped the bounds of decency. Sincerely devout, he was prone to a peculiar sort of scoffing levity; a lover of liberty, he yet

[1] See *Blackwood's*, December, 1825, 724ff., for a commendatory review, which yet censures Scott for printing too much trash obviously not Swift's.

[2] See Pons' discussion of Scott, *op. cit.*, 62-70.

joined the Tory party; and, hating Ireland, he none the less fought for it all his life.

In his attitude toward the Stella-Vanessa question Scott's remissness reaches its nadir. So much impressed is he by the romantic melancholy of the story that he embellishes it with naive bits of legend; and he seems to incorporate material for its value not as fact but as pathos. Thus we are given scenes with appropriate dialogue, and the background is filled in with the careful attention to detail of a Robertson or Pinero. Swift emerges as a vain, proud, sexually impotent man, admirable in his writings, pathetic in his life.[1]

It is no wonder that from 1814 on men thought they knew the Dean of St. Patrick's as well as they knew Isaac of York or Jeanie Deans. But Swift was not a character in fiction. The facts of a novel are selected to create a definite impression; the facts of Swift's life, however, as Scott narrated them, could be interpreted in various ways. A monster lay dormant between the sympathetic lines of Scott's biography--and Francis Jeffrey, clad in the spotless armor of prudish Whiggism, was the first to pounce upon him.

Despite his notorious attacks upon his contemporaries, Jeffrey was of opinion that "the writers who adorned the beginning of the last century have been eclipsed by those of our own time." The reputation of the Augustan age was dead, and the editor of the Edinburgh Review danced delightedly on its grave. In a long review of Scott (September, 1816) he found an opportunity, then, for annihilating the most typical Augustan of all. He insisted, first, that Scott had been far too favorable to the personal character of the Dean,[2] "whom we think, it would really be injurious to the cause of morality to allow to pass, either as a very dignified or a very amiable person." (p. 10) And he proceeded to the most scorching condemnation of Swift that had yet been written. Insolent, coarse, selfish, brutal, destitute of tenderness and fidelity, unprincipled, patronizing toward his dependents, servile toward his betters, Swift's first great crime lay in his betrayal of the Whigs. He turned Tory only for his own advantage and only when it became both safe and profitable to abuse his former friends; and after the Queen's death he "retired in a state of despicable despondency and bitterness to his living, where he continued, to the end of his life, to libel liberty and mankind with unrelenting and pitiable rancour." (p. 11) He is called a "pious neophyte" who thoroughly despised sincerity, and a "low-bred underling" with the ridiculous airs of a parvenu, a vain beast who at last joined the

[1]Two persistent Swift anecdotes were first given currency by Scott: Archbishop King's mysterious statement to Delany after the marriage that Swift was the unhappiest man on earth (p. 239); and the story of the treasured lock of "only a woman's hair." (p. 241)

[2]Lockhart, *Life of Scott*, 2nd edition, Edinburgh, 1839, IV, 164-65, attempts to refute this charge.

Irish cause out of personal pique. His Irish politics arose from one principle:

> a desire to insult and embarrass the government by which he was neglected, and with which he despaired of being reconciled.... His object was not to do good to Ireland, but to vex and annoy the English ministry. (p. 22)

And so completely did Jeffrey abhor the whole story of Swift's political career that he found him worthy of not the slightest claim to lenity, but only of "contempt and infamy." (p. 24)

This is far different in tone from even the more vigorous denunciations of the previous age. The moralizing tendency of earlier critics has been colored by an element of actual personal spite, and Swift is not even allowed the mitigating virtue of good intentions to brighten the picture of his bad manners. Jeffrey's influence was tremendous and his powers of vitriolic expression unparalleled. Without questioning the sweep of Scott's popularity, we must admit that his gently vague lucubrations on the merits and failings of the Dean are likely to be forgotten as soon as read, while Jeffrey's poisonous dart wounds deeply and permanently. Casual readers of both men retain one impression--a clear image of demoniacal vice. Thus it is that incidental remarks on Swift to be found in writings after 1816 reflect not the calm, unsure impartiality of Scott, but the incisive, vehement loathing of Jeffrey. Hitherto, casual commentators had been as likely as not to balance the bad with the good; but hereafter we shall find little indulgence or mercy among them. Upon all but the most independent thinkers, Jeffrey has left his indelible mark.

He has done more. He has cleared a path for the sentimentalists in his account of Swift's love affairs. He has shown Thackeray the way to a female audience's heart; and, in his passionate account of the injustices done to Stella, Vanessa, and Varina,[1] has so far overgone all prior anti-Swiftians as to have succeeded virtually single-handed in engendering the most virulent Swift criticism of the chivalrous nineteenth century. For, more and more, in spite of Jeffrey's preoccupation with Swift's political treachery, hatred of the Dean was to center on his treatment of women. To Jeffrey's followers this was to become the most interesting, as well

[1]Jeffrey was, I believe, the first critic actually to include Jane Waring as the third "victim" of Swift's brutality.

as the most disreputable, part of Swift's history.[1] Here is an example of his attitude toward the subject:

> Vanessa was now dead. The grave had heaped its tranquillizing mould on her agitated heart, and given her tormentor assurance, that he should no more suffer from her reproaches on earth; and yet, though with her the last pretext was extinguished for refusing to acknowledge the wife he had so infamously abused, we find him, with this dreadful example before his eyes, persisting to withhold from his remaining victim, that late and imperfect justice to which her claim was so apparent, and from the denial of which she was sinking before his eyes in sickness and sorrow to the grave. It is utterly impossible to suggest any excuses or palliation for such cold-blooded barbarity. Even though we were to believe with Mr. Scott, that he had ceased to be a man, this would afford no apology for his acting like a beast. (p. 41)

Unhesitatingly he pronounces Swift the "murderer" of Stella and sees as the most shocking crime of all his apparent lack of self-condemnation. For the gloom of his latter days resulted, not, as it should have, from remorse, but from "the rancour of disappointed ambition, and the bitterness of proud misanthropy." (p. 42)

The dark impression created by Jeffrey's essay could not capture all minds alike; as we shall see, there were some who brazenly defied the edict of the Edinburgh Review. But Jeffrey's was the line of least resistance--especially for the rising crop of pro-female critics. One of the first of these was herself a woman, Anna Jameson, whose own love had been notedly unsuccessful, and who in 1829 wrote her Memoirs of the Loves of the Poets. She devotes a long chapter of this book to Stella and Vanessa, with a pitying little paragraph too for Varina, and expatiates at length on their sweet natures as opposed to the Dean's beastliness. Stella, for example, gave herself every day new claims to his love and compassion by her virtue and gentle devotion;"--and all availed not!" (Chapter XXXIV, p. 434)[2] Vanessa, dazzled by his fame and conversation, proffered her hand and fortune and received nothing in return but protestations of everlasting friendship. So, by his inhumanity he brought both women to untimely graves.

[1]See, besides the critiques discussed below, Aiken, *Select Works of the British Poets*, London, 1820, p. 389; Landor, *Imaginary Conversations* (Johnson and Horne), *Works*, London, 1876, IV, 222-23; *New Monthly Mag.*, July, 1826, p. 140; *Dublin U. Mag.*, September, 1838, 269ff. These are all sentimental strictures of Swift's relations with Stella and Vanessa.

[2]My quotations are from the Boston edition, 1857.

I can hardly hope thus summarily to convey Mrs. Jameson's powers of narrative and well-bred invective to the reader. She and her contemporaries, having given up the eighteenth-century search for factual truth, know every emotion of the long-dead human heart; they see only too clearly what must have happened, and they tell what they see with no respect for mere unadorned fact. What, says Mrs. Jameson, must have been Swift's feelings after Vanessa's tragic death--"_if_ he felt at all"?

> ...what agonies of remorse, grief, shame, and horror, must have wrung his bosom! he had, in effect, murdered the woman who loved him, as absolutely as if he had plunged a poniard into her heart...(p. 450)

Thus two "innocent, warm-hearted and accomplished" women perished as sacrifices "to the demoniac pride of the man they had loved and trusted." Their memories will never die, but, "good God! what an immortality! won by what martyrdom of the heart!" (p. 453) The grossly odious author of their misfortunes continued to live. But:

> Look at him in his last years, when the cold earth was heaped over those who would have cheered and soothed his dark and stormy spirit; without a friend--deprived of the mighty powers he had abused--alternately a drivelling idiot and a furious maniac, and sinking from both into a helpless, hopeless, prostrate lethargy of body and mind!--Draw,--draw the curtain, in reverence to the human ruin, lest our woman's heart be tempted to unwomanly exultation! (p. 454)

Mrs. Jameson's sketch represents the nineteenth-century attitude in its logical extreme. But Swift as the tormentor of chaste femininity is not the whole man. Swift the politician and Swift the man of society must also be tortured into congruence with the rest in order to prepare the way for Thackeray's three-dimensional ogre. This preparation was the combined work of Stanhope and Macaulay among others.

In 1836 Philip Stanhope (later Lord Mahon) published the first volume of his _History of England From the Peace of Utrecht to the Peace of Aix-La Chapelle_, which dealt in large part with the years of the Harleian ministry. The work became instantly famous, and Stanhope's characterization of Swift common knowledge. That characterization is simply Jeffrey's once removed. The Dean "had a thorough knowledge of all the baser parts of human nature --for they were his own." On an allegation of personal neglect he turned from the Whigs, "having evidently no better reason for deserting his cause than that he thought it in danger." (I, 69) Gross and selfish, he never scrupled "at allowing his underlings to suffer in his place, nor thought of relief to them by exposure of himself." (I, 95) This was Swift--a man without heart, a veritable wild animal. Nothing was needed to complete the disgusting picture but to deprive him of even the superficial social graces of a human being; and to this end Thomas Peregrine Courtenay bent his pen in his Memoirs of the life of Sir William Temple (London, 1836). Courtenay tirelessly comments on Swift's offensive habits, his mode of eating, his propensity for swearing, his utter disregard for chivalrous convention. Here indeed we find an early statement of a false impression popularized by Macaulay: that Swift's disagreeable manners, extremely unpolished at that time of his first coming to Temple, resulted in his not being admitted to a seat at the table of his patron. (II, 132)

The various comments upon the Dean by Macaulay himself are too well known to require much discussion. This greatest of English unscientific historians, so completely the slave of his violent party prejudices, naturally took all the worst things that had been said of Swift, mixed them with care, and transformed them magically into his unforgettable portrait of a dark and fierce spirit: "the apostate politician, the ribald priest, the perjured lover,--a heart burning with hatred against the whole human race,--a mind richly stored with images from the dung-hill and the lazar-house."[1] His remarks on the Dean appear in several places and range over a period from 1833 to 1855, but no change in attitude occurs from first to last. The characterizations create a single impression, and I shall treat them together as a unified whole.

First of all, Macaulay makes no attempt to belittle Swift's genius. He stands awed at the Dean's power "to shake great kingdoms, to stir the laughter and the rage of millions";[2] he attributes to Swift "some of the choicest gifts that have ever been bestowed on any of the children of men";[3] but here his appreciation stops. With unconcealed glee he introduces his readers whenever possible to the unpleasant picture of the coarse, haughty, and irascible Swift at the home of Temple--a "disagreeable, young Irishman, who had narrowly escaped plucking at Dublin,"[4] dining at the second table, being invited to play at cards with his patron only "when better company was not to be had," foolishly flirting with a black-eyed waiting maid,[5] addressing Temple with the language of a lackey, "or rather of a beggar"; a tiger, in short, caged and starved. "The humble menial was at heart the haughtiest,

[1]In a review of Stanhope's *History of the War of the Succession in Spain*, *Edinburgh Rev.*, January, 1833, p. 538.

[2]In a review of Courtenay's *Memoirs* of the life of Temple, *Edinburgh Rev.*, October, 1838, p. 178.

[3]In *The History of England*, 1855, Chapter 19. I quote from the Whitehall edition of the *Works*., New York, 1898, VIII, 179.

[4]*Edinburgh Rev.*, October, 1838, p. 178.

[5]Esther Johnson was, as Macaulay should have known, only a child at this time!

the most aspiring, the most vindictive, the most despotic of men."[1] And, of course, Macaulay no less than Jeffrey despises Swift for "ratting" from the Whigs. The incontrovertible fact of his continued friendship with Addison Macaulay finds an inexplicable mystery:

> It is not strange that Addison, who calumniated and insulted nobody, should not have calumniated or insulted Swift. But it is remarkable that Swift, to whom neither genius nor virtue was sacred, and who generally seemed to find, like most other renegades, a peculiar pleasure in attacking old friends, should have shown so much respect and tenderness to Addison.[2]

Impressionistic criticism of this type flourished throughout the period from 1814 to 1882, reaching its greatest heights of vituperation in the middle decades of the century. Before 1841, however, the monster-idea of Swift had already become the accepted one. No vice was too dreadful to be associated with him. None of his apparent virtues escaped a vicious interpretation. According to George Cunningham, in his Lives of Eminent and Illustrious Englishmen (Glasgow, 1838), we "cannot allow Swift credit for sincerity even in his high-churchism. That too was but a part of his cool, selfish, unprincipled, calculating system." (V, 194) And even W. C. Taylor, who in 1840 edited the best edition of Gulliver's Travels of the period, an edition copiously illustrated and annotated and courageously unexpurgated, unwaveringly added his voice to the opprobrious chorus. He calls Swift, in his Biographical Notice, one who became "politically powerful, and morally powerless; dreaded by all, loved by few, respected by none." (p. ii) In his intense dislike for the Dean he regards him as an utter criminal, believes the story of the rape at Kilroot,[3] misquotes Johnson's Vanity of Human Wishes,[4] and compares Swift as a lover with "eastern guardians of the Harem"--sometimes spiritualizing his passion for "three lovely and amiable women," and sometimes passing into the opposite extreme and wallowing "in the filth of the most disgusting obscenity." (p. iii)

This then was the popular impression of the great Dean as the century approached its half-way mark. A few there were, however, who refused to concur. And among them was William Hazlitt. "Oh," he cried, "when shall we

---

[1]*History of England, loc. cit.*, p. 180.

[2]In a review of Lucy Aikin's *Life and Writings of Addison, Edinburgh Rev.*, July, 1843, p. 246.

[3]In his thirst for anecdotes he also accepts the other account of Swift's departure from Kilroot, so that we see the Dean raping a woman *and* benevolently giving up his prebend to a poor clergyman!

[4]"And Swift expired, a changeling and a show." Johnson had written, "a driv'ler and a show."

have such another Rector of Laracor!"[1] And his admiration for Swift the writer caused him to scoff at strictures on Swift the man--especially at those of Jeffrey. "I do not," he said, "carry my political resentments so far back: I can at this time of day forgive Swift for having been a Tory." (loc. cit., p. 111) To Hazlitt the works were the man; his quick intellect grasped that fact and asked no more. He remains an anomaly in his age, or indeed any age.

Others preferred to fight Jeffrey on his own ground. In 1819 appeared an anonymous pamphlet in defense of Swift,[2] which accused the Edinburgh Review of partiality, argued that its critic should have read before he reviewed, and quoted many contemporary and complimentary allusions to Swift as proof of the esteem in which he was held by men of his own time. The Dean was a great Irish patriot, willing to encounter any risk for the sake of his country. Was this courage simply the outgrowth of an embittered nature, asked the writer? And had not Scott's publication of the correspondence between him and Vanessa sufficiently dispelled all possible conviction of the harmfulness of their connection? Indeed, Swift, like all men, was guilty of crimes, but crimes, after all, such as "a good-natured man might commit, and a good-natured man repent of." (p. 49) In detached views he was often mistaken; but surely "liberal men should have taken into consideration these detached views, and compared them with his entire conduct, and singular disposition and humour, before they had pronounced so decisively as they have done on his character." (p. 37)

The gently admonitory tone of this soothes the mind of a modern student of nineteenth-century Swift criticism; but a soft answer was hardly sufficient to turn men from the inspired wrath of Jeffrey's essay. A reviewer of the pamphlet in the Edinburgh Monthly Review (July, 1820) finds it a feeble performance, incapable of removing the powerful impression already created.[3] The worst charge against Swift, says the reviewer, is that of political apostasy; and he proceeds to prove it false by acquitting Swift of having had strenuous Whig sympathies in his youth. Less gently than the pamphlet it reviews, this article offers a clear statement of the fallacies underlying Jeffrey's biographical methods: he has handled Swift roughly, making no allowances for the natural infirmities of man, and, in order to make out a strong case, his essay is guilty of random assertion and absolute disregard of fact.

---

[1]*Lectures on the English Poets*, 1818. I quote from the *Works*, London, 1902, V, 104ff.

[2]*A Defence of Dr. Jonathan Swift, Dean of St. Patrick's, Dublin...*, London, 1819. Attributed to Edward Berwick.

[3]For a more appreciative review of the pamphlet see *Gent. Mag.*, February, 1819, 156-57.

> It is chargeable moreover, as we think, with sundry peculiarities which materially vitiate it as a biographical composition; a convenient forgetfulness and confusion in regard to dates; an exaggeration of every unfavourable circumstance, and a total omission of every thing of a contrary tendency; a suppression of all mention of any redeeming virtue, and, we believe, there was much in the character of Swift. (p. 4)

That there were redeeming virtues, that Swift often did wrong but seldom with criminal intent--these were the contentions of his less militant champions. In such manner did the Reverend John Mitford timidly defend him in the biographical preface to his edition of the poetry (London, 1833). In such manner even did the usually original-minded Carlyle add his word to the discussion:

> In his conduct, there is much that is sad and tragic, highly blameable; but I cannot credit all that is said of his cruel unfeeling dissipation. There are many circumstances to show that by nature he was one of the truest of men, of great pity for his fellow-men....a man of much affection, but too impatient of others' infirmities.... He was well called by Johnson a driveller and a show, a stern lesson to ambitious people.[1]

But the light of true scholarship, already faintly visible, begins to burn more brightly at this period. With William Monck Mason, great, though too little appreciated, historian of St. Patrick's cathedral, careful research leads to the strongest defense of Swift to be found in the first part of the nineteenth century. Mason's methods are truly those of a scholar. A healthy scepticism compels him to accept nothing until he has proved it to his own satisfaction; and thus, for example, he becomes the first important biographer of Swift actively to disbelieve the traditional story of the marriage to Stella and the death of Vanessa. His book[2] is hard to read. On every page a few lines of text are complemented by gargantuan notes in which, since they contain the most essential material, the unfortunate reader finds himself submerged. But it cannot be over-valued as a thorough antidote to the impressionistic school of criticism whose dicta it was Mason's intention to disprove. Palpably in sympathy with the Dean, the author none the less considers and discards many well-beloved legends with calm impartiality. He searches for truth, even if truth must redound to the discredit of his hero;

[1] *Lectures on the History of English Literature*, 1838. First printed, New York, 1892, ed. J. R. Greene, 177-79.

[2] *The History and Antiquities of the Collegiate and Cathedral Church of St. Patrick...*, Dublin, 1820. Swift is discussed in pp. 225-444.

and he searches for it, not, like his predecessors, in gossip and hearsay, but in a careful weighing of factual material. That the conclusions drawn are generally favorable to Swift need not lessen their value.

It is not my object to discuss the decisions which Mason makes concerning the facts of Swift's life. It is sufficient in order to understand his literary criticism that we see the picture of Swift as he paints it, after having refuted the Dean's detractors by means of a hitherto unknown scholarship. One by one he denies validity to the categorical statements of Orrery, Delany, Scott, Jeffrey, and the rest; and Swift emerges as a lover of undisguised truth, a hater of flattery, a true friend, a liberal benefactor, and a noble patriot. Entirely innocent of political dereliction, he remained all his life a High-Church Tory and a Whig statesman; but "Whig" and "Tory" are merely names, and interchangeable ones at that. And his exalted friendship with Stella, so misunderstood by his critics, never became anything more than friendship. Partly because of a cold temper, and partly because of forebodings about his madness and a laudable desire not to transmit it to posterity, he abjured sexual love. The complete absence of self-reproach in later life, instead of being shocking, as Jeffrey finds it, simply disproves the charge of unnatural cruelty.

Mason's work should have influenced common-sense opinion of the time, but it seems to have passed virtually unnoticed. Instead of superseding the essays of Scott and Jeffrey, it supplemented them in the minds even of those who took the trouble to read it. The Gentleman's Magazine (March, 1822), for example, acclaims it as an excellent vindication of the Dean, unhesitatingly calls the old marriage story a giant libel, and lauds Swift's patriotic and charitable nature; but the reviewer's disapproval of the "cruel aspersions" of other biographers is vitiated in the end by his willingness to accept their general impression. Mason's work has gone for naught; Swift still remains to this writer a fiery comet of idiosyncratic genius, who reveled in the "mammoth bulk of his mind, and the eighty-horse power of a blow from his monstrous paw," and who acted "upon the principles of a pirate." (p. 248) And the writer anticipates one of Thackeray's most famous remarks when he says that Swift "was not a man with whom, in our opinion, it would have been desirable to live, or be intimate." (ibid.)

For the most part, then, Mason's labors took but shallow root in the barren soil of his time. The British world was hardly prepared for vigorous, realistic scholarship. Yet scientific research was gaining ground in other fields; and science, in a somewhat romanticized form at first, was to contribute much to a new understanding of Swift. It was in 1835 that his skull and that of Stella were disinterred and examined by phrenologists. Articles on the subject appeared in the Scotch

Phrenological Journal; and, though the transaction was considered indecent by many,[1] it aroused in the public a new interest in Swift and his malady and cleared a path for the excellent later work of Sir William Wilde and others. In 1835, however, fashionable phrenology found in Swift's skull signs of large "amativeness" and small "wit"! Embryonic scholarship, indeed, this is, but at its present stage we are glad to turn from it into more profitable channels.[2]

The last, and perhaps the most revealing, essay with which we shall deal here appeared in four instalments in the Dublin University Magazine for 1840. The portrait of Swift was one of a series known as a Gallery of Illustrious Irishmen, and we should therefore expect it to be unadulterated panegyric. But the writer, meritoriously enough, proposed to answer former attacks not with encomium but with impartial common-sense to exhibit Swift as he was, "neither above nor below the standard of humanity, neither all good nor all evil, but, like other men, a mixture of conflicting ingredients." (131-32) The article is less interesting, however, for its enviable aims than for the manner in which it carries them out. Scott's two-way portrait, as I have shown, could provide material for the vicious indictments of Jeffrey and Macaulay; it could, if necessary, furnish enough information for a characterization of Swift as an angel of light --though there were few enough of these; but it could also involve the mind of the reader in a contemplation of paradox. And this third effect was to grow increasingly stronger, until, years later, it was to become the normal attitude toward Swift. In the Dublin sketch of 1840, then, we find this tendency resulting from a laudable attempt at impartiality. The writer speaks of the Dean's external harshness, his real benevolence; his ambition, his disinterestedness; his parsimony, his liberality; his levity, his piety; and to these contradictions in Swift's nature he ascribes the one-sidedness of most biographies.

The essayist is no scholar. He accepts all the old stories and interprets them--and this is always the danger of the "paradox" theory in studying Swift--according to the side of the Dean's character which he believes to have been uppermost at the time of the occurrence. Thus he makes no effort to palliate Swift's conduct toward Stella and Vanessa; this was the cruel, unfeeling Swift. The benevolent, soft-hearted Swift is to be found in the man who gave his life to Ireland. Licentious and violent in English politics, he was not a man to be trifled with:

---

[1]See, for instance, *London Medical Gazette*, October 24, 1835, 115-19. The writer says that Swift, ever the scourge of blockheads, is now scourging pseudo-scientists; and he reduces the rather amazing conclusions of the phrenologists to the absurd.

[2]See Teerink, pp. 388-89, for a more extended list of the phrenological articles.

> There was an energy in his wrath, a blasting scorn in his sarcasm, a searching fiery scrutiny in his satire; and withal, he had a presence noble at all times, but in the excitement of aroused indignation, actually awful; a presence before which, we venture to say, an Edinburgh Reviewer would have turned pale, even behind his mask. (p. 341)

Yet, when the writer turns to Ireland, he paints a far different picture. Gone are the violence and the ferocity:

> Swift loved and pitied his country--he mourned in her tears, he groaned in her oppression. He saw that to be her patriot was to be a martyr, but he saw that she needed a patriot, and he gave himself to her. (p. 549)

We conclude this section of our study with an incidental remark of the Irish essayist: "Of all historic characters that ever lived, Swift most stood in need of a Boswell." (p. 656) The modern student raises his voice in hearty approbation.[1]

[1]Besides the articles discussed here, I must mention Francis Mahony's humorous "Dean Swift's Madness," a nonsense essay with no bearing upon our present study, except as it shows a persistent interest in Swift even as the subject of utter foolishness, *Fraser's*, July, 1834.

II

The Works

Scott's edition of 1814, containing all the prose and poetry of Swift--and much that was not Swift's--immediately became the standard. Revised and reprinted in 1824, it was not to be replaced for many decades. In 1833-34 appeared Mitford's Aldine Edition of the Poetical Works and in 1840 Taylor's Gulliver. These were not the only publications of Swift's works during our present period;[1] but Scott and Mitford were the established authorities for the prose and poetry throughout the greater part of the century; and Taylor's Gulliver, though it never received the popularity it deserved, is of critical value, especially since it is one of the few unabridged editions of the work--even for adult consumption--to be published in its age.[2] The years from 1814 to 1840, then, inimical though they may have been to Swift, seem to have treated his writings, from this point of view, with respect. The question arises: could literary critics, obsessed with an idea of the monstrosity of the man, admire his art?

1

Personal Papers and Political Writings

To an extent the Dean was his own Boswell. Few works of so personal a nature as the Journal to Stella have ever been given the public; it has always had a wide appeal for critics of Swift, not merely for its interesting accounts of social and political intercourse in the early eighteenth century, but for its qualities of tenderness and self-revelation, for its alternate display of great-hearted generosity and queer little petulances. The "little language" especially, so unlike the usual biting simplicity of Swift's style, has perplexed and delighted countless commentators. In the years following Scott's biography, when men still believed the latter part of the Journal to be less affectionate toward Stella, virtually everyone accepted the fact as proof of Swift's love for Miss Vanhomrigh. It is often discussed from this aspect,[3] with the only dissenting voice that of Mason, who, in his History of St. Patrick, speaks of seeing no sign of waning love for Stella in the gradual disuse of affectionate gibberish; "for it would have been

[1] For other collections of and selections from Swift's works, see Teerink, pp. 132-35.

[2] See Teerink, pp. 193-97. I have not been able to ascertain when the first expurgated edition of *Gulliver* was published.

[3] See, for instance, Taylor's edition of *Gulliver*, p. xxii; and Mrs. Jameson's *Loves of the Poets*, p. 443.

quite preposterous to continue it, without ceasing, during a correspondence of three years." (p. 315, note v) Mason, however, stands alone in this contention; and I shall not, therefore, attempt to record any other allusions to the "little language."

Of the Journal itself more is written than during the preceding period. Scott calls it a minute and authentic record, a "wonderful medley" of grave reflections, important facts, trivial occurrences, and intimate tendernesses, which, though it wants system and gravity, is intensely interesting. (op. cit., p. 122) Jeffrey admires it--almost against his will--not for its literary value, but as a minute view of an extraordinary political crisis and of "the private manners and public taste and morality of the times." On the whole, he admits, it exhibits a more favorable picture of Swift's mind than can be gathered from the rest of his writings; and, surprisingly enough, he calls it "the most interesting of all his productions." (loc. cit., p. 49) Berwick, in his anonymous Defence of 1819, calls the attention of the Edinburgh Reviewers to examples of tenderness displayed in it by the man whom they accused of being destitute of the finer passions. And Monck Mason extols its verisimilitude. To those grave critics who disparage it Mason replies:

> Such dull cavillers had better refrain altogether from the perusal of this author's works; the reader of true taste will feel gratified at being introduced to intimate, familiar, acquaintance with this great genius, for no correspondence that has ever yet been published represents actual living conversation so expressively as those letters; verisimilitude was a quality peculiar to the works of Swift. (op. cit., 256-57)

Others, however, were struck not so much by the lifelike quality of Swift's correspondence as by its occasional indelicacies. In 1822 William Wilberforce looked into the Dean's letters and recorded the shocking experience in his diary: "...what a thoroughly irreligious mind--no trace of Sunday to be found in his journals...."[1] George Wingrove Cooke, the biographer of Bolingbroke, almost unique in his contemptuous attitude toward the women in Swift's life, invariably speaks of the "reverend deceiver" himself with equal contempt. Of the Journal he says, "...his overweening vanity impelled him to retail to a foolish woman every minute acknowledgment of his usefulness" accorded to him by Oxford and Bolingbroke.[2] And the grossness of many of his allusions, "even when writing to a young, an unmarried, and a virtuous woman," destroys any other value the work may

[1] *The Life of William Wilberforce*, London, 1838, V, 132.

[2] *Memoirs of Lord Bolingbroke*, London, 1836, I, 188.

possess for Lord Mahon.[1]

All critics agree, however, that Swift's letters give an excellent picture of his time. They also, unfortunately, give a picture of the man who wrote them--so frank a picture of human failings that what to the more sympathetic reader might seem like normal traits of occasional fretfulness and vanity can readily be used to bear out the arguments of Swift's enemies. Thus the militant Whigs were likely to judge the political pamphlets with the little petulances of the Journal as a touchstone. No one pretended to deny them merit as Philippics and beautifully reasoned pieces of disputation; but many questioned their sincerity and censured their brutality. Even Scott, for example, who, in discussing the Proposal for the Universal Use of Irish Manufactures, commends the Dean for the risks he was willing to incur for the sake of a country which he hated and which hated him, nevertheless disapproves of the Drapier's Letters as over-bitter, wrong-headed, and vulgar.

Swift, to Jeffrey's mind, never acted on any principle of dignity or fairness. In the Journal we see him alternately eulogizing or abusing various men according as they gratified or thwarted his personal vanity; thus in his political works he disregards all laws of "polished hostility," and writes magnificent invective out of pique, not "from the fulness of the mind, or the desire of instructing mankind--but on the spur of the occasion." (loc. cit., p. 44) His party writings have therefore long since lost all interest, "except as memorials of the manner in which politics and personalities were then conducted." (p. 8) Of only one formidable talent was he actually possessed, according to the contemptuous Edinburgh Reviewer:

> He was, without exception, the greatest and most efficient libeller that ever exercised the trade; and possessed, in an eminent degree, all the qualifications which it requires:--a clear head--a cold heart--a vindictive temper--no admiration of noble qualities--no sympathy with suffering--not much conscience--not much consistency--a ready wit--a sarcastic humour--a thorough knowledge of the baser parts of human nature--and a complete familiarity with everything that is low, homely, and familiar in language....Almost all his works are libels; generally upon individuals, sometimes upon sects and parties, sometimes upon human nature. (p. 45)

I have already posed the question: could men who neither respected nor admired Swift respect and admire his art? In the lines just quoted Jeffrey answers for

[1] *History of England From the Peace of Utrecht...*, I, 70.

his generation. Grudgingly they respected, unwillingly they admired; they could not sincerely deny the force of his argumentative prose. And so, with their notions of the man-monster, unable to restrain their applause of the monster's art, they applauded it as an excellent specimen of superior monstrosity. In his Lives of Eminent Englishmen, for example, Cunningham finds the Dean's Irish politics, like his other politics, to have resulted from an ambition not to aid his countrymen, "but to harass and perplex a ministry whom he hated, and from whom he had nothing to expect." (p. 196) Of the Proposal for using Irish manufactures and the Drapier's Letters he says that they achieve perfection only in their "dogged misrepresentation and invective." (p. 196) And Stanhope, who admits that he loses his contempt for the man in his admiration of the author, who even doubts the authenticity of The Four Last Years of the Queen because of its inferiority to Swift's other works,[1] cannot record his delight in the pungent satire, simple style, and easy deductions of the Drapier's Letters without prefacing his remarks with the statement that, after all, they were written simply as an opportunity for Swift, pining in obscurity, to display his powers.[2]

Only two important works of the period break from the prevalent conception of the pamphlets as having been composed out of a desire for personal aggrandizement, or out of political pique. These are Mason's History of St. Patrick and the article in the Dublin University Magazine of 1840. The latter essay speaks of the English tracts as having again and again saved the government from ruin. Dazzling and powerful as they were, however, his "wondrous efforts in the political battle of England have left no mark behind them;" (p. 540) but in Ireland it is not so--every Irish lover of liberty breathes the breath of Swift. And all this he accomplished by appealing to the reason, and not the passions, of his people. Mason devotes several paragraphs in his gigantic notes to a discussion of all the political tracts, commending each in turn for this same virtue. Swift's ability to assemble strong facts and to present them logically and forcefully cannot be too highly praised; and Mason finds Johnson's slighting judgment of the Conduct of the Allies merely amusing, coming, as it does, from one whose own political works fail simply because they attempt to substitute imaginative qualities and fanciful language for the unimpassioned accuracy of Swift.

---

[1]See his *History of England Comprising the Reign of Queen Anne until the Peace of Utrecht*, London, 1870, p. 445.

[2]*History of England From the Peace...*, II, 100.

2

Bagatelles and Miscellaneous Works

The early nineteenth century was in its way no less moralistic than the late eighteenth. Yet one of the great differences between the two periods lay in their attitudes toward Swift as a teacher. We saw in the first part of our study how his lighter works were condemned because they seemed frivolous and casual. One hears that cry less often after 1814; and the reason is, I think, not hard to find. Swift was no longer expected to teach. A moral reprobate, compounded of evil, may provide us with food for thought from the pages of his own life; his vices may serve, as Swift's served Jeffrey, for horrible examples to the rising generation; but his literary achievements can teach the pure-souled no lessons, except by contrary inference. Thus we see a salutary effect arising out of false and harsh conceptions of the Dean as a man. No longer under constant obligation to moralize, he can in part be appreciated simply for his keen wit. While admiration of the more ambitious works is tempered more than ever by a revulsion against the man behind them, the frolicsome _jeux d'esprit_ begin to come into their own.

Scott, to be sure, qualifies his enthusiasm for the lesser works, but he censures only gently and in passing:

> We may often think the immediate mode of exercising his talents trifling, and sometimes coarse and offensive; but his Anglo-latin verses, his riddles, his indelicate descriptions, and his violent political satires, are in their various departments as excellent as the subjects admitted, and only leave us room occasionally to regret that so much talent was not uniformly employed upon nobler topics. (_op. cit._, p. 489)

Yet, despite his occasional regrets, he accuses Orrery of lacking a sense of humor in sneering at the _Directions to Servants_; and he expresses great admiration for the _Polite Conversations_--a series of dialogues which Coleridge, not an unqualified admirer of the Dean, called "the most stupendous work of human memory, and of unceasingly active attention to what passes around us, upon record."[1] Even Jeffrey, as Monck Mason gleefully notes, liked these two works. Simply as pleasant, witty reading, with nothing to jar the prudent intellect, they found a ready audience; for the age, as one critic tells us, thought itself in one way especially suited to enjoy Swift: it was prone to read for amusement alone and valued laughter

[1] *Lectures on Shakespeare and Milton*, 1812. I quote from the Bohn edition, London, 1914, p. 86.

above other qualities in its literature.[1] I have found only one writer who feels compelled to defend the bagatelles as moral works. The anonymous Defender of 1819--who was after all the Reverend Edward Berwick--found in them "a moral tendency...to lessen the vanity and promote the good humour of mankind." (p. 52)[2]

All agree in the unrivaled excellence of Swift's humor and irony, as we shall see later in our discussion of Swift the writer. His humor, according to Jeffrey, consists in expressing shocking statements in a calm way, as though they were commonplaces, and then gravely and ingeniously maintaining them. This is especially true of the Modest Proposal and the Argument against Abolishing Christianity, both of which our critics generally agree in praising as inimitable specimens of irony and refined raillery.[3] As always, however, references to these pamphlets and to the more straightforwardly serious ones, like The Sentiments of a Church of England Man and the Proposal for Correcting the English Tongue, are scattered and infrequent, Mason alone providing an appreciative line or two for each of the Dean's better-known works.[4]

3

The Battle of the Books and A Tale of a Tub

We turn to the masterpieces, and a brilliant light floods the stage of critical opinion. Swift's greatest works are not merely superb outpourings of wit and humor; they cannot possibly--not even Gulliver, for an adult--be read and enjoyed *in vacuo*. The man Swift makes himself and his ideas heard through them. In the Partridge Papers, in the satirical letters, in the Meditation upon a Broom-stick, even in A Modest Proposal, his purpose, though not indeed lost to the average reader, can be forgotten in a contemplation of sheer magnificence of wit and expression. The deafest of ears, on the other hand, *must* listen to the ideas which immediately underlie the Tale and Gulliver, chiefly perhaps because those ideas sweep widely across the plains of human experience. Men react similarly when confronted with the prospect of quack astrologers, of bloated and platitudinous moralists, or of starving children; but in their attitudes

[1]See the *Scots Magazine*, November, 1814, p. 848. This observation occurs in a review of Scott's edition.

[2]Hazlitt, *Lectures*, p. 112, ascribes Swift's occasional disposition to trifling to a need for relaxation from "excessive earnestness of mind."

[3]See, for example, Scott, *op. cit.*, 363-64; Mason, *Hist. St. Pat.*, p. 248 note z, p. 375, and p. 376 note 1; and Taylor's *Gulliver*, p. xvi.

[4]He does not like the *Proposal*, but apologizes for its lack of erudition as the result of philological ignorance of the time. The *Dublin U. Mag.* of 1840 echoes eighteenth-century opinion of its negligent style.

toward life and humanity in general they are much more at variance with each other. Thus the critic of one of Swift's lesser pamphlets may overlook its purpose when that purpose is neither great in scope nor remarkable for its originality. With the masterpieces, he faces a different problem.

We should expect those who dislike Swift to disapprove of A Tale of a Tub, and so it is during the years from 1814 to 1840. Accordingly, the tide of critical opinion carries the work to a new low--and with it the Battle of the Books. The Battle indeed suffers most; it becomes the object not of literary discussion but of another battle. Scott opens the lists by declaring its source to have been a "spirited poem" by one Coutray, called Histoire Poétique de la Guerre nouvellement déclarée entre les anciens et les modernes, which strongly resembles Swift's work in both plan and management. (op. cit., p. 45) Mason, after inspecting the "poem," retaliates by describing it as a spiritless piece of prose in twelve books, bearing not the slightest resemblance to the Battle; and he thus re-establishes Swift's claim to complete originality. (op. cit., p. 239, note d) For the next twenty years critics pay little attention to the book except to speak of its source and thereby either to accuse Swift of, or defend him from, the charge of plagiarism. One commentator, following Scott--Mason's scholarship goes for naught, as usual--says that the Battle is borrowed from Coutray's poem, but that its humor and satire are sustained in a manner peculiar to Swift; that is, "the wildest offsprings of an all-licensed fancy" are given an air of probability.[1] Henry Hallam, in his Introduction to the Literature of Europe (London, 1839), calls the Battle "such an improvement of the similar combat in the Lutrin, that we can hardly own it is an imitation." (IV, 559) But the most significant remark of the age is that of W. C. Taylor:

> The Battle of the Books, is said by Dr. Johnson, to be an imitation of the French Combat des Livres: there is no use in discussing the question of originality, for both the French and English works have been long since consigned to unhonoured oblivion. (op. cit., p. xvi)[2]

"The Tale of a Tub," said Hazlitt in his Lectures, "is one of the most masterly compositions in the language, whether for thought, wit, or style."

> It is so capital and undeniable a proof of the author's talents, that Dr. Johnson, who did not like Swift, would not allow that he wrote it. It is hard that the same

[1]James Henry Monk, *Life of Bentley*, London, 1830, p. 88.

[2]The name of the author of the French book in question was not Coutray but de Callières. This was first discovered by Craik!

> performance should stand in the way of a man's promotion to a bishopric, as wanting gravity, and at the same time be denied to be his, as having too much wit. (p. 110)

Yet Hazlitt's own contemporaries were already denying both gravity and wit to the Tale. Scott, more appreciative than many, sadly admits that Swift's wit, luxurious as it may be, too often has led him, even if unconsciously, to ridicule sacred subjects. (op. cit., 85-6) The sympathetic Edinburgh Monthly Review (July, 1820) uses the work chiefly as proof that the Dean was fundamentally opposed to the low church party and that, therefore, he did not assume this opposition simply as a pretext for his defection from the Whigs; but the reviewer incidentally calls the Tale a "dangerous experiment" and is unwilling to comment "either the object of the work, or the means by which it is attempted to be attained." (11-12) A shocked horror at the prospect of a beneficed clergyman inditing a sarcastic allegory on the principal sects of Christianity pervades the thought of the period.[1] Even Mason defends the book not for literary merit, of which he speaks only incidentally, but because it is quite free "from the schismatic principles which Mr. Scott so ingeniously insinuates," for it exalts not any one party of the English reformed church, but the church itself. (op. cit., p. 237, note c)

It has been found unprincipled and dangerously facetious. But that is not all. Two critics remark upon its actual dulness and minimize its wit. Jeffrey says:

> It is by far too long and elaborate for a piece of pleasantry;--the humour sinks, in many places, into mere buffoonery and nonsense;--and there is a real and extreme tediousness arising from the too successful mimicry of tediousness and pedantry. All these defects are apparent enough even in the main story, in which the incidents are without the shadow of verisimilitude of interest, and by far too thinly scattered; but they become unsufferable in the interludes or digressions, the greater part of which are to us utterly illegible, and seem to consist almost entirely of cold and forced conceits, and exaggerated representations of long exploded whims and absurdities. (loc. cit., p. 46)

This is unexpectedly obtuse criticism even from Jeffrey, who, in spite of his hatred of the Dean, cannot forbear according some admiration to his vigorous powers of satire. Yet what he had said little men must needs repeat;

[1]See, for instance, Dr. Aiken, *Select Works of the British Poets*, London, 1820, p. 389; Stanhope, *Hist. From the Peace...*, I, 95; Monk, *Bentley*, p. 71; and Taylor, *op. cit.*, p. xv.

and we find George Cunningham, whose observations are seldom original, echoing him twenty years later in his Lives of Eminent Englishmen: the Tale of a Tub, which appealed to the sceptical Voltaire as well-calculated to lower the claims of religion, is after all merely "an elaborate, but tedious, whimsical, and inconsiderate production." (p. 193)

Comment of a different sort brightens the last years of the period under discussion. Hallam, in his enormous history of European literature during the fifteenth, sixteenth, and seventeenth centuries, mentions the Tale as a work sufficient to redeem England's name in the annals of fiction. He calls it Swift's masterpiece, to which Rabelais has nothing superior, "nor any thing so condensed, so pointed, so full of real meaning, of biting satire, of felicitous analogy." (IV, 559) Coming, as they do, from the pen of an ardent Whig, those words help to renew our faith in the future of disinterested literary criticism. And the loyal Dublin University Magazine (1840) praises its deep learning and its "minute and wonderful completeness of allegory, which no ingenuity either before or since has ever equalled, along with an energy of thought, a quickness and brilliancy of wit, a keenness and justness of satire, a purity of language, and an almost vivid distinctness of expression, which in one grand and matchless combination, exhibit all the peculiar excellencies of the genius and the style of Swift." (p. 139)

4

Gulliver's Travels

From Johnson to Scott, as we have seen, discussion of Gulliver was concentrated upon the fourth voyage as a specimen of misanthropy, either salutary or vicious in effect according to the bent of the commentator. This discussion continues after Scott, but it is less emphasized as fresh critical by-words begin to appear. At this point, however, it might be well to make a brief survey of the field as it stands in regard to the perplexing problem of Gulliver and the Yahoos--or, at any rate, of the moral effect of Gulliver's Travels as a whole.

We shall begin with Scott, whose judgments of the book advance far beyond those of his predecessors in many respects, but whose reaction to the fourth voyage differs little. An editor of Swift, he says, must always consider it with pain; only an indignation terrible beyond words could engender such a diatribe against human nature. Granting a moral use to the picture of the Yahoos, "even a moral purpose will not justify the nakedness with which Swift has sketched this horrible outline of mankind degraded to a bestial state." (op. cit., p. 338) And Scott agrees with Delany and Beattie in scoring the improbable fiction of a nation of horses "performing an hundred purposes of rational and social life, for which their external structure altogether unfits them." (p. 339)[1]

Jeffrey, on the other hand, finds himself quite unmoved by the tremendous power of the voyage to the Houyhnhnms, which, though it forces most readers to react violently in one way or another, seems to produce in him an impression not so much of disgust as, again, of dulness. "The picture is...bald and tame in the highest degree." (loc. cit., p. 48) So heretical is this statement that I can find no other critic who dares to repeat it; and I think it may be attributed to sheer perversity rather than to any firm conviction.

It is interesting to observe that, after Scott, critics no longer seek arbitrarily to brand the portrait of the Yahoos as false. They may find it repulsive, even libelous in places; but they are less firmly convinced of the majesty of mankind than were their immediate forbears, and they tend to admit in part the truth of Swift's indictment of humanity, though they refuse to swallow the bitter pill without making a wry face. This new timidity may have resulted from the doubts already assailing the nineteenth-century mind, or it may have come about through the pervasive influence of such frank spirits as William Hazlitt. In 1818 Hazlitt lectured at the Surrey Institution on the English Poets; and what he said about Swift's misanthropy is worth quoting in full. His answer to the objections to Gulliver has, I believe, never been surpassed for clarity and force:

> He has taken a new view of human nature, such as a being of a higher sphere might take of it; he has torn the scales from off his moral vision; he has tried an experiment upon human life, and sifted its pretentions from the alloy of circumstances; he has measured it with a rule, has weighed it in a balance, and found it, for the most part, wanting and worthless--in substance and in shew. Nothing solid, nothing valuable is left in his system but virtue and wisdom. What a libel is this upon mankind! What a convincing proof of misanthropy! What presumption and what malice prepense, to shew men what they are, and to teach them what they ought to be!... I cannot see the harm, the misanthropy, the immoral and degrading tendency of this. The moral lesson is as fine as the intellectual exhibition is amusing. It is an attempt to tear off the mask of imposture from the world; and nothing but imposture has a right to complain of it. It is, indeed, the way with our quacks in morality to

[1] Scott repeats most of what he says in the *Life* in a slightly different form in his introduction to *Gulliver, Works,* XII, 3ff.

> preach up the dignity of human nature, to pamper pride and hypocrisy with the idle mockeries of the virtues they pretend to, and which they have not: but it was not Swift's way to cant morality, or any thing else; nor did his genius prompt him to write unmeaning panegyrics on mankind! (loc. cit., p. 111)[1]

Mason, naturally, vehemently defends certain aspects of the voyage. He refutes, for example, Beattie's argument that a Christian divine ought not to have tried to trample upon humanity by showing that if the argument has any force it must apply equally to every species of satire--a manifestly untenable proposition. But even he finds that, despite its laudable intentions, the fourth voyage is unpleasant to contemplate; and Swift's picture of the Houyhnhnms is a cold, insipid one, utterly devoid of lights and shades.[2] In the same way, other commentators loathe while they admire, admire while they loathe. Mitford, in his biographical introduction to the poetical works, calls attention to the rich vein of ridicule in Gulliver, while decrying the nauseating brutality of the book--"a work so wide in its temper and feeling from the spirit of Christianity." (p. lxxxii) The Dublin University Magazine of 1840, finally, accepts the portrait of the filthy Yahoo as melancholy and disgusting evidence of mental disease in the author; and yet:

> ...however indignant we may feel at the insult of the implied identity, it is, nevertheless, true, hide it as we may, that the portrait would not have been a libel had it not been like.... Exaggerated and intense as was the contempt of human nature which Swift expresses in this revolting satire, it did not spring from what is usually termed misanthropy. (p. 635)

Gulliver's Travels, for the rest, receives its warranted approbation from the critics. In many respects it comes into its own during this period. Scott says much of its charm and its verisimilitude. In the contrast between its simple style and unimaginative protagonist, and the marvels which it relates, he sees the work of a master. Lilliput and Brobdingnag are especially worthy of praise; with superb artistic effect Gulliver is made to lose his own ideas of comparative size and to adopt those of the pigmies or giants who surround him, thus heightening the naturalness of the whole effect. And Scott remarks at length upon the infinite art "with which human actions are divided between these two opposite races of ideal beings, so as to enhance the keenness of the

[1]Much the same thing is said by William Roscoe in his *Life of Pope, Works of Alexander Pope, Esq.,* London, 1824, I, 288-89.

[2]Peculiarly enough, Mason is here using the exact words of Orrery, *op. cit.*, p. 189.

satire"; (op. cit., p. 342) thus ridiculing political intrigue by transferring it to a court of tiny creatures and rendering monstrous the lighter follies and female levities by attributing them to a race of giants. Here indeed is a masterly art which virtually defies analysis. But it is to an admiring contemplation of verisimilitude that Scott constantly returns. The Dean's creation of living characters--Gulliver, Mary the cook-maid, Bickerstaff, the modest proposer--"all persons as distinct from each other as they are from the Dean of St. Patrick's" (p. 496)--has seldom been excelled. Though like Defoe in his enumeration of minute incidents, in this respect he is infinitely less limited than the author of Robinson Crusoe. And he remains unique in his amazing trick of neglecting to relate in detail circumstances of seeming importance, while dwelling upon the inconsequential; thus Gulliver communicates vaguely information which he could have acquired only from hearsay, and expatiates at length upon his own most trivial experiences.

> In short, the narrator is the centre and main-spring of the story, which neither exhibits a degree of extended information, such as circumstances could not permit him to acquire, nor omits those minute incidents, which the same circumstances rendered of importance to him, because immediately affecting his own person. (p. 497)

Scott, then, has succumbed completely to the charm of Gulliver, with the sole exception of the fourth voyage. And his idea, that the fable, after the first improbability, never once loses its air of truth, is carried through the years by other critics.[1]

The comparison with Defoe becomes a common one, though two men refuse to share Scott's preference for Swift. John Dunlop, for instance, considers Robinson Crusoe the most instructive work of fiction ever written; but from Gulliver he rises "not as from the work of De Foe, exulting in our nature, but giddy, and selfish, and discontented, and, from some parts, I may almost say brutified."[2] And Coleridge found in Defoe a satisfaction for the soul only partly to be gained from reading Swift. "Compare," he says, "the contemptuous Swift with the contemned De Foe, and how superior will the latter be found!"[3] In general, however, comparisons made by the

[1]See, besides those hereafter mentioned, Aiken, *Select Works*, p. 390. Mitford alone in this period finds food for cavil. He thinks the Brobdingnagians *too* gigantic for the imagination to cope with and believes that giants of a *"moderate size"* would have been better! (*op. cit., p. lxxxi*)

[2]*History of Fiction*, Edinburgh, 1814. I quote from the second edition, 1816, III, 491.

[3]*Literary Remains*, New York, 1860, IV, 312. These words date from 1830.

critics redound to Swift's credit.[1]

The severest anti-Swiftian of the age makes no effort to detract from the reputation of Gulliver. Jeffrey calls it the Dean's greatest work--a masterpiece of fictitious travel literature, done with such spirit, originality, and success as never before.[2] Its air of truth and simplicity palliates its extravagances and enhances the effect of its satire. But Jeffrey seldom indulges in pure encomium; and he concludes that, though without its satire the book would have appeared preposterous, it pleases chiefly by the novelty and vivacity of its story. The least satisfactory parts are those in which satire predominates over narrative; for the "greater part of the wisdom and satire" appear to him to be commonplace and unimpressive, "if presented without these accompaniments." (loc. cit., p. 48) Hazlitt commends the verisimilitude of the book, as usual, with a happier turn of phrase than most of his contemporaries. He begins by scoffing at Dr. Johnson's denial of its merits. Whether, he says, the excellence of Gulliver lies in its conception or its execution matters little; the fact remains that its power is somewhere--a power, indeed, "that has moved the world." Nor is that power, he continues, thrusting briskly at Johnson's florid English style, "that of big words and vaunting common-places." Swift has accomplished something which only an acute mind could enable a man to perform; in order to strip empty pride of the glamor in which external circumstance has clothed it, he has disillusioned the prejudiced imagination "by reducing every thing to the abstract predicament of size."

> He enlarges or diminishes the scale, as he wishes to show the insignificance or the grossness of our overweening self-love. That he has done this with mathematical precision, with complete presence of mind and perfect keeping, in a manner that comes equally home to the understanding of the man and of the child, does not take away from the merit of the work or the genius of the author. (loc. cit., p. 110)

Mason, too, speaks of the appeal of Gulliver to all ages and ranks of society. And as examples of Swift's admirable finesse in the application of conceptions of size, he cites the delectable solemnity with which the unimaginative English sailor talks of the immense Lilliputian trees, the tops of which he could barely reach

---

[1]See, for example, Mason, *Hist. St. Pat.*, p. 355; and Mitford, *op. cit.*, p. civ. Most of Mitford's criticism is, of course, of little importance. It derives almost entirely from Johnson and Scott, even to the point of unacknowledged plagiarism.

[2]See also Stanhope, *Hist. From the Peace...*, II, 343, for a most appreciative discussion from the pen of one of Swift's least sympathetic critics.

with his clenched fist, or the impression he gives of censuring his own rashness when he prosaically recounts his fatal leap over the bit of Brobdingnagian cow-dung, instead of attempting to describe its prodigious size. Thus, says Mason, "instead of trespassing upon the credulity of the reader, he appears scarcely to take credit for all he might be allowed, and clothes with an air of probability the most improbable fictions." (op. cit., p. 358, note 1) This strikes even the modern reader as good criticism; and Mason makes another observation of equal value--an observation to which no later critic has paid due respect. Much as he dislikes the fourth voyage, Mason is not entirely in agreement with strictures based on its improbability. After all, he says, it is quite likely that it was not Swift's intention to follow the scheme of the preceding books in this portion:

> ...can we reasonably deny to Swift the same privileges which have been allowed to all fablers, from Aesop, down to his contemporary, Gay: that of conveying a useful moral under the mask of an improbable fiction? (p. 360, note n)

Obviously, this does not furnish an adequate explanation of the fourth book from every point of view. It does not remove the greatest stumbling block to complete appreciation of Gulliver's Travels--the fact that the latter portion of the work is so different in tone and treatment from the first two books as to detract from the artistic unity of the whole; but it remains a plausible defense of the fourth voyage as a separate entity, and as such its value is incontrovertible.

From the outset, the voyage to Laputa has neither pleased nor greatly interested commentators. Its failure to make the most of its opportunities, its overdrawn satire, its lack of a centralizing theme, its tendency to ridicule phases of science of which the Dean had but slight knowledge--all these come in for their share of criticism from most of the early nineteenth-century writers;[1] and there has, in fact, been little change in critical opinion from 1726 to the present day.[2]

---

[1]See, for instance, Scott, *op. cit.*, 333-35, also vol. XII, 9-10; Jeffrey, *loc. cit.*, p. 48; and Mitford, *op. cit.*, lxxx-lxxxi. Mason, *op. cit.*, p. 358, does not attempt to defend it beyond explaining that it satirizes spurious and chimerical studies, and not true science. See also Henry Lord Brougham, *A Discourse of Natural Theology*, 1835, note to Section V, for an unsympathetic discussion of the Struldbrugs as just one more indication of the Dean's unnatural misanthropy.

[2]For a late restatement of the conventional objections to *Laputa*, see Quintana, *op. cit.*, 315-19.

Interest in Gulliver's Travels culminates with the publication in 1840 of W. C. Taylor's edition. In his biographical introduction Taylor explains the general meaning of the satire, and in his notes he points out the more minute allusions. He also offers a brief essay on the development of satirical fiction. Thus, though his critical judgments are seldom stimulating, his work is of value from the scholarly point of view. The primary object of the book was, he thinks, simply to caricature the exaggerations of travelers' tales; the satire on human nature developed as the work grew; and Gulliver, originally conceived of by his creator as a philosopher, was changed to a blunt sailor because of the popularity of Robinson Crusoe. In general, Taylor does not try to enlarge or destroy accepted criticism; his sentiments are, in great part, at one with those of Scott. Only in the Essay on Satirical Fiction does he strike a new note: Swift's works, he says, were written according to the fashions of his time, but they transcended those fashions. They mark the transition from religious to political allegory; in the Tale of a Tub politics are subsidiary to religious discussion, and obscure allusions make the allegory difficult to follow, the story sometimes being sacrificed to the controversy and then again regaining its ascendancy. Gulliver, however, in which religion becomes a secondary consideration, is free of this defect. It and Reynard the Fox "are probably the only works of satirical fiction which afford us much pleasure, taken merely as stories." (p. lix) But though the story tends to assume primary importance, the discovery of the secondary purpose "opens a new source of pleasure, by affording scope for the exercise of our own ingenuity, and directing our attention to that of the author." (ibid.) And Swift, like Bunyan, has succeeded in sustaining a long allegory without falling into inconsistencies--has succeeded chiefly by choosing a simple character as his hero; "the sturdy sailor and the humble Christian remain the same in all their adventures; known once, they are known for ever." (p. lx)

5

The Poetry

Mrs. Jameson's Loves of the Poets introduced its chapter on Stella and Vanessa with the following words:

> It is difficult to consider Swift as a poet. So many unamiable, disagreeable, unpoetical ideas are connected with his name, that, great as he was in fame and intellectual vigor, he seems as misplaced in the temple of the muses as one of his own yahoos. (p. 431)

To most nineteenth-century minds, the ideal of poetry was of something rainbow-tinted, a mystical emanation from Heaven to which nothing could be more foreign than the hard brilliance of Swift's verse. Yet the critics pay far more attention to his poetry than we should expect from Mrs. Jameson's words. Matthew Arnold was later to call Dryden and Pope classics of English prose, without actually denying them the merit of a certain facility in numbers. If this judgment applies to the two greatest poets of Swift's age, it certainly applies to him; and we find it expressed at length by many critics.[1]

Only Hazlitt displays real enthusiasm for the Dean's verse. He dislikes the many "lack-a-daisical, slip-shod, tedious, trifling, foolish, fantastical" pieces which Swift wrote simply to oblige others; but, otherwise, he maintains that had Swift never composed anything else his name would justly have gone down to posterity as one of the most sensible of poets, belonging "in the first rank of agreeable moralists in verse."

> There is not only a dry humour, an exquisite tone of irony, in these productions of his pen; but there is a touching, unpretending pathos, mixed up with the most whimsical and eccentric strokes of pleasantry and satire. (loc. cit., p. 109)

Scott considers the Dean pre-eminent in the species of poetry which he cultivated; but it is not the highest species. His wit, lambent or blasting as the subject requires, lends a resounding forcefulness to his lines, and his powers of versification are superb. He wears rhyme--"a handcuff to an inferior poet"--as a "bracelet"; thus his lines fall "as easily into the best grammatical arrangement,...as if he had been writing in prose."

---

[1]See, besides those here discussed, Cunningham, *Lives of Englishman*, p. 199: "His verses are nothing more than rhymed prose."

(_op. cit._, p. 490) But he fails utterly to attain to the sublime or the pathetic. It is due to the accidental intensity of his invective that the lines often seem to border on grandeur, and never to sublimity either of conception or expression. For the most part, his failure lies in his lack of imagination. Thus _Cadenus and Vanessa_, his best non-satirical poem, though graceful, has neither depth of tenderness nor emotional power; of all his poems, the _Rhapsody on Poetry_ most nearly approaches sustained flight. Naturally, also, the refined tastes of Swift's great Scotch editor compel him to regard the more indecent verse with disgust. Yet he shows a certain indulgence toward it, since filth abounded in the writings "even of the most esteemed poets of that period." (p. 385) And he goes so far as to defend the Pindarics, "the only kind of writing which he seriously attempted without attaining excellence," on the ground that they are not, generally speaking, "worse than the pindarics of Donne and Cowley, which...gained these authors unbounded applause." (p. 34)

Jeffrey, on the other hand, found it as difficult as Mrs. Jameson to persuade himself that the unamiable Swift was a poet. "The merit of correct rhymes and easy diction, we shall not deny him," (_loc. cit._, p. 49) but the diction remains that of prose, and only an occasional mention of the Muses or some other person of heathen mythology gives a slightly poetic coloring to the lines. The Edinburgh Reviewer calls _Cadenus and Vanessa_ complete proof of the Dean's incapacity for poetic feeling. Written at the height of his powers, in a moment of true emotion, it is yet as cold and flat as the ice of Thule; and "we take it for granted nobody reads it now-a-days." (p. 50) Only the _Rhapsody_ and the _Legion Club_ contain any more glow of poetical animation than a series of lines "out of Coke upon Littleton"; but in the former it is lost in the midst of "the usual small wares of cant phrases and snappish misanthropy," (p. 51) and in the latter it takes the shape of coarse invective, with no approach to a dignified high-mindedness.

Jeffrey's articulate contempt is hardly adequately countered by the diffident statement of Berwick in his _Defence_ that the poetry has many excellencies, that its indecencies were desperate remedies required for desperate diseases, and that its happy blending of rhyme and reason makes it, if not poetry, "something as good." (_op. cit._, p. 60) This, though, however weak it may seem, remains the strongest defense of Swift the poet to be found during the next score of years. We might, of course, look hopefully for something better in Mitford's introduction to his 1833 edition of the poems; but his discussion of the poetry is entirely quoted from Scott--without the additional encumbrance of quotation marks.

Even the Dean's most persistent apologist, Mason, says comparatively little about the poetic value of the verse. He concentrates upon an aspect which has given him pain--the scatology and over-vehement invective--and defends it, not unlike Berwick though more at length, by ascribing it to Swift's office of "censor" and his own habitual cleanliness which compelled him to correct offensive errors by the most forcible means possible, even at the expense of his reputation.

> It is true these pieces do no longer serve to any purpose but to fill the mind of the reader with disgust; we behold them now like nauseous drugs, without any regard to their sanative qualities, although to them we are perhaps indebted, in a great measure, for the present soundness of our constitution. (op. cit., 381-82)

Swift, in other words, submitted voluntarily to a sort of literary martyrdom, "having renounced some portion of his posthumous fame for the benefit of the community." (p. 382) And Mason, though he disapproves of Jeffrey's strictures on the Legion Club and sees poetic fire and almost sublimity in the poem, yet calls attention to its viciousness and labels it the "most censurable" of all the Dean's works. (p. 397)

I opened this section with a quotation from Mrs. Jameson, and it might not be amiss to close it in the same way; for in many respects her point of view brings us back to one of the major questions underlying the problem of nineteenth-century Swift criticism--the degree to which hatred of the man was capable of influencing judgment of his works. And Anna Jameson expresses even better than Jeffrey the lengths to which antagonism toward the Dean could carry the critic of his art. She is only incidentally a literary critic in her essay on Stella and Vanessa; she touches solely upon the poetry and even that in passing; but her attitude in general is clear and significant: Swift's verse, utterly worthless as such, derives interest alone from the beauty of the character of the women to whom he addressed it. Cadenus and Vanessa, his most admired poem, with its insipid, tawdry fable, its inconclusive conclusion, and its unchivalrous hints at secret sin, "would have given but an ignominious celebrity to poor Vanessa, if truth and time, and her own sweet nature, had not redeemed her." (loc. cit., 431-32) In that same poem Swift showed his utter want of taste by bitterly satirizing women in general. And what right, cries Mrs. Jameson, had he to accuse us--he who was playing the Abelard in his forty-fifth year, and who was "one of the ugliest men in existence"? (p. 443) Assuredly, the perusal of Cadenus and Vanessa "never conveyed one emotion to the reader's heart, except of indignation against the writer; not a spark of poetry, fancy, or pathos, breathes throughout." (p. 442)

Thus we see one critic at least who, with a woman's merciless logic, identified her contempt for Swift with her scorn of his work!

III

Swift the Writer

The masculine mind, not entirely a slave to consistency, unflaggingly records its admiration of Swift the writer. From 1814 to 1840 tribute is accorded almost without exception to his rare genius and to his phenomenal, if often misused, powers of creation and expression. Scott describes his work as distinguished by three peculiar characteristics: extreme originality,[1] indifference to literary fame, and complete success in every style of composition attempted, with the exception of history and the unimportant fugitive odes. He executed his works solely as a carpenter forms implements of his trade, not for their value as art but in order to accomplish a purpose. Yet, though he owes the extent of his popularity and permanence as an English classic to his great prose masterpieces, even his trifles are perfect as far as they go. Nor can there be too much praise for his literary economy. He never introduces a word, an episode, or an allusion for its own sake, but always for the "express purpose of strengthening and supporting the whole." (op. cit., p. 498)

Two ideas predominate in the thought of the period after Scott: that of Swift's power and influence in spite of the occasional nature of his writings and his evident indifference to literary fame,[2] and that of his amazing mastery of the art of verisimilitude.[3] The minor motifs--his coarseness, his wit, the vehemence of his invective, his originality, and the simple effectiveness of his style--are woven incidentally into the major theme by most of the critics.

Thus, according to the Scots Magazine (November, 1814), Swift's works, though composed chiefly for some immediate purpose, have survived because of a nervous and unique turn of thought and a magnificent wit, not excelled even by that of Butler. Their grand excellence lies in irony, "the most difficult, and, as we rather think, the most exquisite species." (p. 848) With all this, except the sweeping glorification of irony, even Jeffrey must agree. Of all the "ingenious" Augustans, he

---

[1]But see Landor, *Imaginary Conversations, loc. cit.:* He was not really original, says Horne to Johnson; he frequently copied from rare books.

[2]Besides those hereafter discussed in this connection see *Gent. Mag.*, March, 1822, p. 251: the highest token of Swift's genius was that he rendered literature "the power of a magician"; and *Dublin U. Mag.*, 1840, p. 635: he was wholly devoid of "the sordidness of a trading writer."

[3]I have discussed this more at length above in the section on *Gulliver*.

says, Swift was indisputably the most original. He possessed a vigor denied to his contemporaries and "a sort of heartiness of abuse and contempt of mankind, which produces a greater sympathy and animation in the reader than the more elaborate sarcasms that have since come into fashion." (loc. cit., p. 9) It is no small proof of the vivacity of his genius that his careless and hasty productions have been thought worthy of preservation by posterity. With amazing perspicuity he lends an air of truth to the least plausible of propositions:

> To deliver absurd notions or incredible tales in the most authentic, honest and direct terms, that have been used for the communication of truth and reason, and to luxuriate in all the variations of that grave, plain and perspicuous phraseology, which dull men use to express their homely opinions, seems to be the great art of this extraordinary humourist, and that which gives their character and their edge to his sly strokes of satire, his keen sarcasms and bitter personalities. (p. 46)

From the pen of Jeffrey we may accept all this as the highest praise. Even though he qualifies it in innumerable ways--the homely richness of Swift's style lacks grace (p. 56), and is tame compared with the "sonorous diction" of Johnson and Junius (p. 8); his intelligence is that of practical good sense without profound judgment or fancy (p. 8); and his greatest talent lies in the dextrous manipulation of a copious and degrading vocabulary of abuse (p. 45)--in spite of such inevitable strictures, his grudging respect inevitably breaks through the clouds of defamation.

Mason echoes Scott's praise, with appropriate encomiums of his own on the consummate irony, the verisimilitude, and the variety and scope of the Dean's writings.[1] He also calls attention to the stylistic variations at Swift's command:

> Throughout his works he has given very different specimens both of sentiments and expression. His first production, the Tale of a Tub, exhibits a vehemence and rapidity of mind, a copiousness of images, and a vivacity of diction, such as he never afterwards exerted. In his later prose works there is an equable flow of easy language; purity and simplicity is their predominant character: his few metaphors seem to be received rather of necessity than of choice. (op. cit., 431-32)

---

[1]See *Hist. St. Pat.*, 429ff.

In general our critics are no less appreciative of the Dean's style than were their eighteenth-century predecessors. Even Stanhope, as great an enemy of Swift the man as we find during the period, unreservedly commends his plain and homely language and admits himself to be lost in admiration for the Dean's literary achievements.[1] I find, in fact, only one reference to his style which swerves from the beaten path; in an article called "Prodigality of Words," he is accused, with many others, of scattering around him as he proceeds a multitude of idle and unnecessary words, "the uselessness of which a superficial reader is often hindered from perceiving by the force or beauty of their arrangement."[2] But the express purpose of this essay is to point out the almost universal fault of excess verbiage in the great English masters of prose, and so the argument carries little weight when applied to Swift apart from the context. The Dublin University Magazine (1840) revives the old theory as to the grammatical incorrectness of the Drapier's writings, which abound in "painful" inaccuracies and "syntaxical blunders." But the critic proceeds in more conventional fashion: setting aside mistakes of a purely grammatical kind, all must agree that "no where is to be found a more perfect, pure, and nervous sample of genuine English." Plainness of thought and expression, effortless and seemingly honest argument--these stamp Swift's style with the mark of greatness:

> Each stage in the inductive progress is so gradual, and, as it were, so natural, that the reader is unconscious while he follows it step by step, until he arrives at his journey's end, that he has been led leagues beyond his calculation, and in a course perhaps diametrically opposed to that which he would have followed had he not taken Swift for his companion. (p. 658)[3]

A constant source of displeasure to commentators is the Dean's indelicacy. But I have already referred to many of their remarks in previous sections, and I need add little. No one in the age of Jeffrey and Macaulay pretends to enjoy the nauseating portions of Swift's

[1] *Hist. Eng. From the Peace...*, I, 70. See also Berwick, *Defence*, p. 47: Swift taught the world "what is the best style to influence a Nation"; *London Medical Gazette*, October 24, 1835: Swift, the most subtle reasoner that ever wrote a political pamphlet, used the vernacular as a tool; and Cunningham, *Lives of Englishmen*, p. 199: Swift clearly and precisely pours forth an inexhaustible vocabulary of abuse "with all the fertility and exuberance of true genius." In *Blackwood's*, December, 1825, we find an entire article, pp. 719ff., proving that Swift could and did use metaphors.

[2] *Blackwood's*, May, 1826, p. 583. The article is initialed "D".

[3] Compare Dr. Aiken, *Select Works*, p. 390. He scoffs at Swift's prose style as having *only* the merit "of expressing the author's meaning with perfect precision"!

work--not even Mason; certain passages remain pretty strong meat even for us moderns. The Gentleman's Magazine of March, 1822, is most vehement in insisting that no excuse can possibly be offered for Swift's offense in this respect; and the charming Mr. Mitford leaves off copying Scott long enough to pen a delectable note on the subject. I quote it in full, without comment:

> Perhaps the most offensive and indelicate passage in all Swift's Works, is an Examination of Certain Abuses in the City of Dublin, p. 271, ed. Nichols. (op. cit., p. xcix, note 5)

Swift's superb wit, granted him by all his critics from the very beginning, comes in for fresh treatment after 1814. The three greatest wits of modern times, according to Hazlitt, were Swift, Rabelais, and Voltaire;[1] but Swift differed from the others in that there was no element of sportiveness in his wit. His was the wit of sense--a serious wit, a saturnine wit, a practical wit. This it was that drove him mad:

> There is nothing more likely to drive a man mad, than the being unable to get rid of the idea of the distinction between right and wrong, and an obstinate, constitutional preference of the true to the agreeable. (loc. cit., p. 111)

The ludicrous in him arose from his keen sense of impropriety, his hatred of absurdity, his caustic separation of truth from falsehood, of folly from wisdom; "and it is the force, the precision, and the honest abruptness with which the separation is made, that excites our surprise, our admiration, and laughter." His seemingly playful irony resulted from inward bitterness of thought. Thus he escaped into the regions of fancy and invented his Lilliputians and Yahoos: "they only made him laugh, while men and women made him angry." Rabelais luxuriated in delightful nonsense, but, "except for the sparkling effervescence of his gall, Swift's brain was as 'dry as the remainder biscuit after a voyage.'" (p. 112)

It is perhaps in this astute statement from the always brilliant Hazlitt that Coleridge found his inspiration for the famous characterization of Swift as "anima Rabelaisii habitans in sicco,--the soul of Rabelais dwelling in a dry place."[2] At any rate, the dead earnestness at the root of the Dean's humor is remarked upon by two other renowned writers. Carlyle speaks of his sarcasm as carried to an epic pitch, of his irony as

[1]To Henry Crabb Robinson this was an ingenious but "not very intelligible parallel"; and he censures Hazlitt for eulogizing "the modern infidel." *Diary of Henry Crabb Robinson,* ed. T. Sadler, London, 1869. February 17, 1818.

[2]*Table Talk,* June 15, 1830.

great and fearful.[1] And Macaulay, contrasting him with Addison and Voltaire, calls his mirth the "mirth of Mephistophiles,"[2] of a man of sour aspect, who moves others to laughter without joining in it himself. Thus Macaulay, though he respects Swift's abilities, finds Addison's humor more inimitably delicious.[3]

The significant fact about Macaulay, however, is that he does respect Swift's abilities. And that, as it applies to all the men who helped shape the monstrous portrait of Swift the man, remains the significant fact of Swift criticism in the period between 1814 and 1840. Only one unswerving apologist arose for Swift the man during those years--Monck Mason; but, however they might carp and cavil at his individual works, his most insistent antagonists bowed in humble, if surly, submission to the power of his genius--

> a genius equally suited to politics and to letters;--a genius destined to shake great kingdoms, to stir the laughter and the rage of millions, and to leave to posterity memorials which can perish only with the English language.[4]

---

[1] *Lectures*, 177-79.

[2] *Edinburgh Rev.*, July, 1843, p. 231.

[3] But see Stanhope, *Hist. Eng. Comprising...*, p. 548: Addison's grace was no match for Swift's "withering irony."

[4] *Edinburgh Rev.*, October, 1838, p. 178. (Macaulay)

PART THREE
(1841-1865)

I

Swift the Man

Scott's edition was necessarily expensive and therefore virtually inaccessible to men of limited means. This fact, and the fact also that it abounded in errors, appeared to Thomas Roscoe to warrant the publication of a new edition. In 1841 Roscoe brought out the Works in two volumes--in a cheap format which should appeal to Swiftians who could not afford the magnificent edition of Scott. The new editor's high-minded design of correcting his predecessor's errors led him simply to revert to the work of Sheridan and Nichols, but in his biographical introduction he displayed a certain amount of originality. Roscoe's attitude toward the story of Swift's life is that of an over-exuberant sentimentalist, with hot Tory prejudices[1] and a faint predisposition toward the scholarly method wherever it does not interfere with sentimental preconceptions. Thus he follows Monck Mason as his final authority for most factual matters, but relegates his doubts about the marriage with Stella to a note and tells the old stories of Stella and Vanessa with evident relish for each detail.

The portrait of the Dean belongs to the paradox genre. Swift's vices are softened and his virtues heightened, but he remains a brooding figure of mystery, acting upon the most exalted principles at one moment and tearing holes in his hostesses' table-cloths at the next. At one time happy, celebrated, and "making it his delight to honour and promote his friends, of whatever party they might be," his "day of life grew dark almost before its noon." (p. ix) Between the morning and the evening, however,--the poetic imagery is Roscoe's own--Swift shone forth as the brightest of suns: a "truly great man," with "wondrous powers," a "pertinacious love of truth and integrity" (p. xi), great wisdom and a mighty heart, which, though they could have regenerated the world, "were arrested at the source, and, like a wound bleeding inwardly, gave no sign of the pain and suffering to the eye." (p. xii) Morally beyond reproach, he exerted a real influence over the Tory ministry without resorting to flattery and without losing his charity and forbearance.

Swift's conduct as a lover, finally, though not open to complete extenuation, was not unforgivable. Of a naturally cold temper, his remarkable personality none

[1]He misses no opportunity to cast opprobrium upon the Whigs, and even blames the famous "forged" letter, in favor of Mrs. Barber, on Walpole. *The Works of Jonathan Swift*, London, 1841, I, lxxix.

the less fascinated all who met him; and women constantly fell in love with him. He himself never made the first advances nor replied in the usual love-terms, never assumed the character, "much less the usual assiduities," of a lover. (p. xlvii) He married Miss Johnson in "a moment of grief, anguish, and remorse,...in the vain hope of snatching that once beloved object from an untimely grave" (p. lviii); and his conduct is deserving of strong denunciation solely in the case of his final cruelty toward Vanessa. For this the only explanation can be that "he was labouring under a species of distraction, arising from a combination of causes, and in some part from that morbid sensibility and irritation of temper which, far from bearing the evils of life with becoming humility and patience, forming no part of his character, hurried him into gloom, misanthropy, and despair, and terminated in confirmed insanity." (p. lix)

Roscoe is not alone in his attempt to couch his effusions in lush language. Others, too, make an art of avoiding the mot juste in favor of eloquence; and their emotions become as rhetorical as their style. Sometimes they weave their airy dreams about the character of the Dean himself; sometimes they sentimentalize the story of the loves and deaths of Stella, Vanessa, and Swift; more often they waste few tears upon the man, but shed them rapturously over the fate of the ladies. The emotion of pity in some form, at any rate, manages to creep into the pages of most of the early Victorian essays--pity for the sad-eyed primeval monster or the monster's victims; it hardly mattered which. Sentimental effusions about Swift himself often made much of his sickness. To one writer, for example, he seemed a living enigma, soluble by only one hypothesis: "From the beginning to the end of his days Jonathan Swift was more or less MAD."[1] A mass of contradictions, he combined within his nature contending forces of the angelic and the diabolic; his virtues became vices, his vices "were not without the savour of virtue"; he was cruel, he was proud, he was vehement, he was merciless, he was tender and generous and brilliant--but he was never free of insanity! The ruling trait of his character was "morbid eccentricity, much less of which has saved many a murderer in our days from the gallows."[2]

In 1853 Thackeray published his lectures on The English Humourists of the Eighteenth Century, which unmasked Harlequin and showed him to have, for all his

[1]Samuel Phillips, "Essay on Dean Swift," London *Times*, October 3, 1850, p. 3. The essay was inspired by the appearance of Lady Duff Gordon's fictional romance, *Stella and Vanessa.*

[2]For similar opinions see *Chambers's Cyclopaedia of English Literature,* 1844: "Kisses and curses were alternately on his lips." (I quote from the revised edition, London and Edinburgh, 1876, I, 487); *Hogg's Instructor,* July, 1853. In an otherwise colorless review of Thackeray the writer accuses him of having too lightly taken into account the dash of insanity that tinged Swift's life; and *The Critic,* July 15, 1853, a similar review of Thackeray.

laughter, a breaking heart. The most notorious of the famous series is that on Swift, thinking of whom was to Thackeray like thinking of "an empire falling."[1] And with his study of the very gloomy, very beastlike Dean we reach the high point of the movement toward emotionalizing and debasing Swift's character. The essay is so well-known, however, that I need not quote from it at length. Everyone knows the picture of the Dean as Thackeray has painted him: the bullying coward; the lonely eagle; the bitter, raging, servile slave; the religious hypocrite; the harsh-mannered ruffian.[2] With not the slightest regard for fact, the great Victorian novelist creates a work indisputably artistic--lavish, richly colored, amazingly eloquent--but specious beyond the wildest flights of fancy of his predecessors.

He must have held his audiences spell-bound. The lecture casts its spell even over the modern reader, and the impression it creates is not easily dissipated. Thackeray's charm illuminates its every line; the most bold-faced mis-statements become attractive through the delightfulness of the medium in which they are expressed. When the author says that he would have preferred a potato and a kind word from Goldsmith to a guinea and a dinner from the Dean, who insulted a man as he served him and made women cry (p. 438), when he calls Swift a lifelong hypocrite before the Heaven which he adored, when he speaks of him "alone and gnashing in the darkness" (p. 455), suffering as he deserved to suffer, the cautious reader must keep his emotions firmly under control, or he may find himself, like his ancestors, becoming prey to the insinuating ingenuousness of it all. It is only in his almost nauseating account of the Stella-Vanessa episodes that Thackeray completely loses his grip upon the modern reader. To him Stella, whom he prefers to Vanessa, is "one of the saints of English story" (p. 448); the "pure star in that dark and tempestuous life of Swift's" (p. 449) is his love for her; and the lecturer writes a "sweet epitaph" over her grave:

> Gentle lady, so lovely, so loving, so unhappy! you have had countless champions; millions of manly hearts mourning for you. From generation to generation we take up the fond tradition of your beauty, we watch and follow your tragedy, your bright morning love and purity, your constancy, your grief, your sweet martyrdom. (p. 448)

He sheds a tear too, not merely for Miss Vanhomrigh, but also (in a note) for Varina. In fact, he says, "the book of Swift's life opens at places kept by these blighted flowers!" (ibid.) And when Stella died and Swift had nothing but a lock of her hair, then followed memory and

[1] *Works*, New York, 1899, VII, 455.

[2] For a fictional portrayal of all these characteristics see *Henry Esmond*, *Works*, VII, 339-44.

remorse "for the guilty lonely wretch, shuddering over the grave of his victim." (p. 454)[1]

I am sure, said a later essayist, that "if Jonathan Swift had entered the room while the Lecture upon him was going forward, he would have eaten William Makepeace Goliath, white waistcoat and all."[2] But Jonathan Swift was unfortunately dead, and Thackeray was suffered to spread the gospel of his monstrosity unharmed. His lecture probably sank more deeply into the consciousness of Victorian England than any other single work on Swift; its influence over non-scholarly opinion even of today can hardly be over-estimated. And we find reviewers of 1853 commending it highly as a life-like presentation of the Dean, that brain-blasted genius who spent his life in raging against marriage and against children--"those tiny blossoms of humanity who make life an everlasting May."[3]

It would perhaps be too much to say that the sentimental, color-lavishing school was ever carried to extremes beyond those of Thackeray.[4] But in some respects he had simply approached the gates through which a flood of vituperation not his own was already pouring. Admittedly he admired the Dean; admittedly he felt a kind of self-satisfied pity for the great fallen genius of a fellow-satirist. Others were less kind. Of the definitely anti-Swiftian essays of the time I find only two which follow Thackeray in sorrowing rather than exulting at the fall of an empire. The first of these is David Masson's review of The English Humourists in the British Quarterly Review (October, 1854).

Swift, according to Masson, was a bundle of paradoxes, religious and irreligious, insulting and kindly, parsimonious and charitable. Gifted beyond all his

[1]Thackeray believes, of course, in all the traditional stories concerning both Stella and Vanessa, including that of the former's illegitimacy.

[2]Sir Arthur Quiller-Couch, *Adventures in Criticism*, London, 1896, p. 95.

[3]The quotation is from *The Critic*, July 15, 1853. See also *Hogg's Instructor*, July, 1853; and Thomas Irwin's *Versicles*, Dublin, 1856, which includes a long poem, *Swift*, doubtless inspired by Thackeray's essay, a passage from which precedes the verses. The poem is not, however, vituperatively anti-Swift. The Dean is rather well-called "Too mighty for the mean of earth--Too critic clear for happiness." Charlotte Bronte, in a letter to Mrs. Gaskell, May, 1853, speaks of Thackeray's eloquence and force, though she admits that she does not always agree with his opinions.

[4]Except, perhaps, by Taine in his *Histoire de la Littérature Anglaise*, Paris, 1864, IV, Ch. 5. This, the most romanticized study of Swift that I have yet encountered, was published in Edinburgh in 1871, done into English by Van Laun, and was widely read. Since Taine's theories and methods are well-known, and since the essay does not, after all, fall within the geographical limits set for this study, I do no more than mention it here. It should, however, be read by those who think Thackeray's smug myopia shocking!

contemporaries but racked by mysterious passions and ambitions, he was a great, melancholy genius, with some dark secret in his life diffusing a black poison throughout his whole existence; an "unruly, rebellious, gloomy, revengeful, unforgiving spirit, loyal to no authority, and gnashing under every restraint" (p. 556), in closer communion with the devil than with God, slinking through life as though "with a murder on his mind." (p. 558) Yet, totally free of cant, he hated hypocrisy with a fine strength.

> Indeed, it might be given as a summary definition of Swift's character, that he had cleared his mind of cant, without having succeeded in filling the void with song. (p. 560)

Masson gives up the Stella-Vanessa problem as an insoluble mystery, consonant with the rest of Swift's inscrutable career, but he makes one interesting statement in this connection which is not, perhaps, without foundation. From the evidence afforded by the story of Swift's relations with women, and from a study of certain doctrinal passages in the works, he thinks one thing plain:

> Those who in the present day, both in this country and in America, maintain the intellectual equality of the two sexes, and the right of women to as full and varied an education, and as free a social use of their powers, as is allowed to men, may claim Swift as a pioneer in their cause....
>
> This fact that Swift had a <u>theory</u> on the subject of the proper mode of treating and educating women, which theory was in antagonism to the ideas of his time, explains much both in his conduct as a man and in his habits as a writer. (p. 550)

The mystery behind the man appeals with equal force to John Francis Waller, an Irishman who brought out a new edition of <u>Gulliver's Travels</u> in 1864. Like Masson a lover of paradox, he is more akin to Thackeray in his insistent expressions of compassion; nor is he far removed from Jeffrey in his constant tendency to point a moral. In his biographical introduction to <u>Gulliver</u> we frequently find such interpretations of fact as the following, which grows out of the story of Swift's public apology to the Dean on bended knee during his school days:

> Truly we can understand how this degradation lacerated his proud heart, and was one of the many reasons which made him through life observe his birthday in sorrow and mourning. (p. viii)

But Waller's sympathy generally borders on scorn. Despite his desire to portray Swift as an Irish patriot, he finds it impossible to acquit him of the charge of political infidelity in England; though he hesitates to believe in the alleged marriage to Stella, there is no hesitation in the manner in which he brands the Dean with deliberate baseness in his treatment of her and Vanessa; and, not unlike Thackeray, he turns with a feeling of terror, after telling of Stella's death, "to look in, upon that wintry night, at that bereaved and miserable man, as he sits down in his room in the midnight stillness, in the presence of his mighty sorrow, to meditate upon and write of her with a calm despair that is more pathetic than violent, passionate grief." (p. xxxii)[1]

But the plaintive note of the essays just discussed is lacking in many others of the period. The vindictiveness of Jeffrey and Macaulay is echoed and reinforced by writers from 1840 to 1865, some of whom express their contempt for Swift with unprecedented vitriol. William Howitt, a militant Whig, thinks Scott too tolerant. He follows Macaulay in speaking of Swift's designs upon Stella as having commenced during his first residence at Moor Park; and he believes the Dean to have been a destroyer of women, playing with them "as a cat does with mice."[2] Cold-blooded, brusque, blunt, selfish, solely responsible for the criminal peace of Utrecht, he sacrificed everyone for the promotion of his comfort or his ambition; but justice triumphed in the end, for he never got a mitre. Katharine Thomson in her Literature of Society (London, 1862) speaks of his "few good and many bad qualities," (II, 160) and considers that, "heart he had none." (II, 181) His heartlessness, his selfishness, his insincerity--these are so much the common talk of our critics that we should gain little by following each one individually.[3] It might be well, however, to summarize briefly the sentiments of two of the more influential writers of the age, Thomas De Quincey and George Gilfillan.

---

[1]This word-picture is illustrated by a drawing of Swift at his desk, head in arms, the sheet-clad spirit of Stella hovering over him!

[2]*Homes and Haunts of the Most Eminent British Poets*, London, 1847, I, 189.

[3]For conventional unsympathetic criticism see Thomas B. Shaw, *Outlines of English Literature*, 1848, Ch. XIII; *Dublin Review*, March, 1849: in an article on the Duke of Marlborough Swift is called "the most intrepid liar whom political controversy...ever brought forth" (p. 125); Frederick Lawrence, "Private Life and Personal Character of Dean Swift," *Sharpe's London Journal*, XI, 303-10 (1850). This, a review of Wilde's *Closing Years*, traces Swift's life "with little pleasure" and takes from Wilde the idea of Swift's becoming a toper in old age; W. F. Collier, A *History of English Literature*, London, 1862: the author wishes Swift had accepted King William's offer of a troop instead of writing poisonous books; and Thomas MacKnight, *The Life of Henry St. John, Viscount Bolingbroke*, London, 1863, *passim*, but especially pp. 154-55. Leigh Hunt's *The Town*, London, 1858, contains chatty remarks which display his palpable disapproval of the man Swift.

We find De Quincey's remarks on Swift in Tait's Magazine for September, 1847, in a review of Schlosser's Literary History of the Eighteenth Century.[1] It is a scorching review; but, while the German Schlosser comes in for the greater part of the vituperation, many others are excoriated in typical De Quincey fashion--from the literary men of the eighteenth century themselves to their "commonplace" readers of the nineteenth. In his discussion of Swift De Quincey's chief interest lies in the works, but he casts an occasional wry glance at the Dean's "scowling face," and speaks in passing of his "villainies for the sake of popularity, and still more for the sake of wielding this popularity vindictively." (p. 12) And he restrains his constant ridicule of Schlosser only once, to agree with the German's opinion of Swift's philosophy of life as characteristic of savagery:

> This is undeniable. The meanness of Swift's nature, and his rigid incapacity for dealing with the grandeurs of the human spirit...is absolutely appalling. His own yahoo is not a more abominable one-sided degradation of humanity than is he himself under this aspect. (p. 14)

For a short time George Gilfillan exerted a telling influence over British critical opinion; and his judgments of Swift, coming as they did during the period of his great power, are of importance in the history of the Dean's nineteenth-century reputation. In three different essays Gilfillan returns to the subject, charmed by its repulsiveness. And each time he returns, he returns with a new vocabulary of abuse. Swift, he says in a laudatory discussion of Jeffrey's attack upon the Dean, was "strong, naked,coarse, savage, and mud-loving, as one of the huge primeval creatures of chaos."[2] Later in the same book, an amazing critique of Thackeray's English Humourists commends Thackeray for having composed, if not so elaborate a sketch as Jeffrey's, a more humane one. However, though Thackeray rightly pities Swift, he has allowed his gentle nature to carry him too far. He has, for example, called him a pious spirit--called that black libeler who reveled in "downright beastliness," who ruined the happiness of three females, who "mocked and gibbered" at the profoundest mysteries of Christianity, a pious spirit!

> We are not the least charitable of critics; and we feel deep and solemn sorrow over the mountain of ghastly ruin which Swift at last became: but we dare not apply to him epithets which would fit a Jack Wilkes, a

[1]My quotations are from the *Collected Writings*, Edinburgh, 1890, vol. XI.

[2]*A Third Gallery of Portraits*, 1854. I quote from the New York Sheldon and Company edition, n. d., p. 194.

> Mirabeau, or a Tom Paine, as well as the miserable Dean of St. Patrick's. (p. 223)

Thackeray, indeed, wrongly conceived of Swift as a great humorist. He was strong but without moral grandeur: like the "fearful hybrids described in the Revelation, his power was in his tail," (p. 219) and he dealt out scorpion-like pain with it. His bitterness brought him at last, "as if on demon wings," to deny his Maker; and in this respect, as a "moral monster," he must be classed with that "Yankee-Yahoo," Edgar Poe:

> Neither of them could believe that a race which had produced them had any link relating it to the Divine. They saw all things and beings in the vast black shadow cast by themselves. (p. 220)

And in an essay called "Satire and Satirists," in the Scottish Review (January, 1856), Gilfillan makes an even more apt comparison:

> (As) Nero wished that all Rome had one neck that he might destroy it at a blow, so Swift dared, to rear himself so to speak, on the back of his own personal disappointment, and to hurl out scorn at man and suspicion at his Maker. It was not, it must be noticed, enmity at the evil which is in man, which excited his hatred and contempt, it was man himself.... His was the very madness of Manicheanism. That heresy untruly held that the devil was one of two aboriginal creative powers, but Swift believed him to be the only God.[1]

Harsh vindictiveness could not possibly go beyond all this. Short of accusing the Dean of having been the devil incarnate, Gilfillan has brought us to the ultimate goal of romantic criticism; and Swift has become a kind of brute Faust condemned to eternal critical torture as the result of his pact with Mephisto. But, though the middle of the nineteenth century thus saw the reputation of Swift as a personality at its nadir, it also witnessed the beginnings of a strong movement in the opposite direction. For modern methods of scholarship were at last rising to the fore; and with them came a new orientation toward Swift, an attempt to see him as a human being, clearly, impartially, without sentimentality.

The year 1849 is a doubly memorable one in the history of Swift criticism. First of all, the inaugural issue of Notes and Queries, a magazine for students of literature, appeared; and that excellent periodical naturally became during the following decades a storehouse of

[1]I quote from the reprint in *A Gallery of Literary Portraits*, London, 1909, 236-37.

fragmentary information about Swiftian problems as well as others.

Eighteenth and early nineteenth-century magazines had acted as a repository for anecdotes and legends about the Dean; but more and more a desire had arisen in the minds of scholars and critics for less questionable material--unpublished letters, for example, and other miscellaneous bits not in themselves of transcendent importance and yet grist for the judicious student's mill. Notes and Queries strikingly filled this need and by so doing gave a great impetus to scholarship in general.[1]

To Swiftian scholarship in particular W. R. Wilde's The Closing Years of Dean Swift's Life, published in Dublin in 1849, furnished a greater impulse than probably any other single force. Wilde's work is not of great critical value, though it does print some of the Dean's "hitherto unnoticed" writings. But its careful scholarship and cautious discussion of some of the more important biographical problems mark it as of signal worth in an age when caution and care mattered little to most men. In the course of his work, the author discusses Swift's insanity and the physiological cause of his malady, refutes Sheridan's assumption of the Dean's cruelty to Stella by a perusal of her will, and pricks the bubble of phrenology.[2] In some respects Wilde's work leaves something to be desired; sheer weight of testimony inclines him to a belief in the marriage, and, with no real authority, he accuses Swift of a fondness for liquor in later life. (p. 39) But in general he adheres admirably to the scientific method; and of all British personalities Swift's was perhaps most in need of scientific study.[3]

Wilde was not alone in his quest for a different kind of truth from that sought by the early biographers or fashioned by the romantic critics. Some of his contemporaries, with a healthy caution as their guide, were also trying to see Swift as he might actually have been.

---

[1]A volume of the magazine chosen at random even during its early years will yield two or three references to Swift. See, for example, the numbers for January to June, 1857, where we find unemotionally discussed the question of the illegitimacy of Swift and Stella, the meaning of the name *Gulliver*, some questions as to the publication of Swift's works, and a portrait of the Dean. See also, as examples of the same tendency in other periodicals both before and after 1849: *Gent. Mag.*, January, 1826, February, 1855, March, 1855, July, 1855; *New Monthly Mag.*, January, 1842; and *Dublin U. Mag.*, September, 1838.

[2]See also *British Quarterly Review*, November, 1846, for a discussion of phrenology by Dr. Skae, in which he exposes its fallacies in the case of Swift and Stella.

[3]See the *Dublin U. Mag.*, March, 1849, for an approving review of Wilde and his methods; and *Chambers's Edinburgh Journal*, November 6, 1847, for an equally appreciative review of the work as it originally appeared in the *Dublin Quarterly Journal of Medical Science* for 1847.

One of them, in reviewing The Closing Years,[1] concentrates upon deflating old romantic notions about the Dean, from the tale of the benevolent resignation of Kilroot to the marriage story. The writer, a disciple of the neglected Monck Mason, considers most of the early biographies as rubbish compiled by a group of "old women," whose gossip was foolishly perpetuated by Scott. The business of future biographers, he says with prophetic insight, will be to blot out "some of the pleasant stories told without anything of sufficient authority." (loc. cit., p. 185) Charges of political dishonesty and irreverence have, he says, their roots in unauthenticated anecdotes; and though the fierceness of many of Swift's deeds was "symptomatic of mental disease" (p. 194) of which he was always in some degree the prey, nothing in his conduct or habits as we see them can lead us to believe in his innate viciousness. His sometimes intolerable manners resulted, apart from the germs of insanity residing in his nature, from a "galling sense of social inferiority." (p. 189) And, from a perusal of the letters, the reviewer comes to the conclusion--false perhaps, yet indicative of a carefully impartial study of existent material--that Swift's real love affair was with Vanessa and not Stella, in spite of a determination on the part of commentators "to make a romance out of this Swift and Stella story."

> The world will not allow people to be happy in their own way; and Swift and his female friends had to pass through the same ordeal that in an after generation tortured Cowper and Mrs. Unwin. The people of the place did not understand it--Swift was to marry her--then he had married her--then he would marry her but for some mystery connected with their birth, which precluded the possibility of marriage--then the fact of marriage had taken place, but on the very day of the marriage came a mysterious revelation, whispered in the ear by Archbishop King, believed by Dr. Delany and some other old women, and now preached on the housetop by Dr. Wilde. (p. 186)

In its way, obviously, this is as arbitrary as the statements of Jeffrey or Thackeray, but it is an arbitrary scepticism; and from scepticism grows matter-of-fact scholarship. At all events, those of the time who went to Swift's own works to find out about the man came away with a more sympathetic view of his personality than that of their contemporaries. We find John Eagles, in an article called "Thackeray's Lectures--Swift" in Blackwood's (October, 1853), scourging Thackeray for his whimsy, his lack of a "fair, honest, truth-searching and truth-declaring spirit," and his misuse of consummate ability in painting a monster instead of a man. Swift was, Eagles

[1]"Swift and his Biographers," *North Brit. Rev.*, August, 1849.

avers, a human being; biographers have been too fond of dwelling upon the contradictions in his character, but he was neither cruel, unfaithful, nor avaricious, and his coarseness was the coarseness of his age. The great enigma of his life lies in his amours. "These apart, no man would ever have ventured to assert the life-long madness of Swift" (p. 497); but gossip and curiosity, instead of solving their mystery, have merely succeeded in deepening it. Not knowing the truth, we have, therefore, no right to judge.[1] And the reviewer insists, finally, upon Swift's intrinsic goodness:

> Nature gave him a biting power, and it was her instinct that made him use it; and what if he exaggerated? It is the poet's license. What did Juvenal? and what did he more than Juvenal? Oh, this at once bold and squeamish age!--bold to do bad things, and to cry out against having them told or punished, but delighting in dressing up an imaginary monster and ticketing it with the name of Jonathan Swift, dead a century and a half ago!!... and if we think him too much inclined to view mankind ill, we should reflect that he lived in such times as we have been describing, and had ill-treatment enough from mankind to render his best struggles for contentment at times hard, and that he preserved his friendships to the last. (511-12)

That Swift transcended his age and that the men of Queen Anne's day were incapable of appreciating his greatness is also the thesis of another excellent apologist. James Hannay[2] has in some ways, I think, very nearly captured the essence of the Dean. He admits the strangeness of Swift's personal story, the morbid bitterness of his attitude toward the world, the unfathomable mystery underlying so many of his actions. And, admitting all this, Hannay makes it his business to try to learn its explanation, to learn it by treating Swift not as an every-day fellow, but as an exceptional man in exceptional surroundings. "It is," he says, with reference to Jeffrey's essay, "natural to us to love and believe in great men; and if they look bad and ugly, we wish to see the fact explained, not crowed over and exulted in." (loc. cit., p. 133) Thus, though Thackeray's picture is lifelike, it is also unappreciative, and Hannay proposes to give a notion of the Dean's person "more consonant with the admiration which (whether we love him or not) we must have for his genius." (133-34)

---

[1]Eagles tends to believe in the story of the kindred illegitimacy of Swift and Stella. In summarizing the ways of accounting for Swift's treatment of her, he finds this perhaps the best. But he makes no categorical statements.

[2]*Satire and Satirists*, London, 1854, Lecture IV. I quote from the New York edition, 1855.

First of all it must be understood, says the writer, that Swift deserved more than he got from the world. Was he a "highwayman," was he necessarily self-centered, simply because, with his gigantic intellect, he rightfully expected power and position consonant with his abilities? Why should he not have been embittered at being exiled in Dublin, decently enough placed, perhaps, for an ordinary parson, but certainly not for the first man of the age? In Ireland he was like "the giant under Aetna."

> But before I grumble at his misanthropy, I must have more respect than I have at present for the men whom he hated.
>
> I like Swift for this,--he was a great, genuine, brawny, outspoken man. He moves about, in the court-world of Anne's time, the most genuine man in it, at all events; the man whose talk, action, writing, loves and hates, are most of a piece, and most coherent and natural. (p. 139)

No matter what his faults, he stands out above his contemporaries "as a specimen of manhood and real honesty, and generosity, and nobility of tendencies."

> And I beg your attention to this, that but for his openness, and his general daring way, we should never have had a chance of hearing these stories of occasional rudenesses, and the like, which, taken in a lump out of his long struggle in a chequered and embarrassed life, look so formidable. (p. 144)

That he was a misanthrope of sorts cannot be gainsaid, but all his misery is traceable to the fact "that in an age of hollowness and falsity he found his great genius not duly employed in the world." (ibid.)

Swift, Hannay continues, had more heart than many a smoother person; his offences were not against the heart, but rather against society--

> against a body existing with certain codes of mutual flattery and compromise, concealments, and polite hypocrisies, and servilities, and cowardices.
>
> Poor Swift! He was bent on acting greatly and bravely; he had a right to expect that room should be made for him in the palaces of the world. No wonder that destructive literature--that Satire--was his forte! (p. 147)

He also concedes to the Dean--what is so often forgotten even today--a large measure of sheer robust humor; he speaks with evident appreciation of his "manly enjoyment of the ludicrous and the low" and of his relish for "mere buffoonery, and even practical jokes." (p. 150) And though he arbitrarily states the fact of the marriage to Stella,[1] and though he somewhat gratuitously calls Vanessa "a vain dilettante kind of a woman," (p. 149) who fell in love with Swift's reputation, yet he is temperate in his judgments even here. Swift's biography, he insists, is still in too obscure and uncertain a state to allow us to judge of the Dean's conduct.

> Much depends upon mere suppositions; and when he is attacked, the worst of what is supposed is generally taken for granted. I remark this, to show how cautious we should be in condemning him wholesale.... (p. 148)

And thus we find in the midst of what we have generally thought to be the period of most unrelieved gloom in the history of Swift criticism brilliant rays of light heralding the new sun. The modest work of Hannay, to the best of my knowledge utterly overlooked by later critics, is more than a ray of light. For originality of approach and vitality of thought it merits a more detailed discussion than I have been able to accord it here. Its superiority over the work of more famous men becomes doubly striking when we turn to an essay which, though well conceived and sympathetically executed, returns to all the old platitudes and answers all the conventional objections to Swift's personality in conventional fashion. In his youth W. E. Lecky published a study of Swift[2] which later, in an enlarged and modified form, became the biographical introduction to the Temple Scott edition of the Works.[3] It says nothing new. The youthful author makes much of the Dean's coarseness, palliated, however, by its lack of lascivious or voluptuous qualities; he calls him, platitudinously, "a hypocrite reversed" (p. 25); and he defends him from the charge of religious scepticism by blaming the period in which he lived, "when Christianity seemed to have perished" and society was "corrupted to the very core" (p. 27);[4] he accepts the traditional stories of the marriage to Stella and the love affair with Vanessa with only casual reservations and censures Swift for his cruelty; and, finally, he sums up his characterization of the man in a sentence which might well have been written by Scott:

> To represent him as a perfect character, either morally or intellectually, would be

[1]He later reversed this opinion. See below, Part Four.

[2]In *Leaders of Public Opinion in Ireland*, London, 1861. Published anonymously.

[3]Between 1861 and 1897, when the revised version was printed, Swift scholarship made advances necessitating changes in factual material as well as critical judgments. Thus, for example, in the 1861 essay Lecky speaks of *A Tale of a Tub* as having been written when Swift was only nineteen.

[4]This passage is omitted in the 1897 version.

> of course absurd; but his faults were redeemed by devoted friendship and noble generosity, and his weaknesses by a colossal and versatile intellect. (p. 59)

Lecky's judgments of Swift the writer are equally unstimulating.[1] Yet he was chosen to contribute the introduction to what became the standard edition of the Works. One hesitates, however, to wonder why. The field of Swift criticism is already over-crowded with mysteries.

---

[1]See below, Part Four, for another sample of Lecky as a critic of Swift.

II

The Works

The period between 1840 and 1882 saw no important new editions of the Works. That of Roscoe in 1841 and the selection made by D. Laing Purves in 1869 are perhaps the most valuable before 1897, when the first volume of the Temple Scott edition was published. It is only, indeed, in comparatively recent years that really estimable work has been accomplished in the printing of hitherto unpublished material and the careful re-editing of the whole of Swift's literary product. For the men of Thackeray's time Scott's edition sufficed.

1

Personal Papers and Political Writings

The reason why Scott's edition sufficed may be found perhaps in the fact that Swift was being less widely read toward the middle years of the century than ever before. We find a commentator in 1881 saying:

> There are perhaps few acknowledged English classics who are so seldom read in the present day as Swift. Of course everybody knows, or pretends to know and understand, 'Gulliver's Travels,' and the 'Tale of a Tub,' and there are people who have dipped into the 'Journal to Stella,' and the 'Battle of the Books;' but whether from the unfortunate vein of coarseness which runs through most of his writings, or on account of the dark sayings which abound in subtle satire, it is more common to hear opinions about Swift deliberately quoted from Thackeray's essay than to find judgment based upon independent study.[1]

If it was true that Swift was not being read in 1881, he must have been equally neglected by the preceding generation. After all, we today, with our admiration for the Dean, make no claim to a thorough reading of his works--though not, indeed, for the same reasons. I doubt, for example, whether many besides the special student delve very deeply into the political pamphlets. Dead issues, even when vigorously discussed, can hardly hold much interest for the general reader. He has, I think, a right to demand something more. Thus we shall find Swift's lesser writings receiving little attention during the period from 1840 to 1865. The critics concentrate upon

[1]Stanley Lane-Poole, *Fraser's*, September, 1881, p. 385.

his personality and his art in general; as a writer he interests them, but they waste little time in discussing pamphlets or miscellaneous works with which their audiences may have had but a passing acquaintance, if any.

For biographical reasons Roscoe quotes frequently from the Journal to Stella, which he calls an "interesting narrative," but in his usual fashion he avoids aesthetic discussion; he is at best a second-rate and unoriginal critic. The Journal appears "a strange but fascinating medley" to Chambers's Cyclopaedia (loc. cit., p. 575); and the North British Review (August, 1849) calls its style fraternal and indulgent, and finds in its utter lack of restraint one more proof of the fact that Swift never loved Stella romantically. Hannay, whose criticism in Satire and Satirists tends toward the general rather than the specific, sees in it evidence of the Dean's tenderness and his "vein of most cordial, homely fun." (loc. cit., p. 146) And Thackeray characteristically knows of "nothing more manly, more tender, more exquisitely touching, than some of these brief notes." (loc. cit., p. 449) Perhaps the most original comment is a vigorous denunciation of the Journal in Thomas MacKnight's biography of Bolingbroke. MacKnight finds it a strange picture--but not an elevating one:

> Neither the reverend doctor nor the young lady to whom this journal is really addressed rises in our estimation....Coarse jokes and coarse oaths, the plainest allusions and double meanings of the broadest kind, are all mingled together in this strange medley of wit, vanity, affection, and secret history. (128-29)

Remarks about the political works are scattered and infrequent. Roscoe mentions most of them with more enthusiasm than judgment. The picture he gives us is of Swift taking up "the controversial flail with the strength of a giant and the resolution of a martyr" against the vile Whigs (op. cit., p. xxx), or of Swift in Ireland founding his objections to Wood's patent not on prejudice but "upon strong principle." (p. lxiv) This is not, however, literary criticism. In the same way, whether Swift was or was not an apostate has but slight bearing upon the English tracts as literature. They are noticed as such by only two or three writers of the time. In an essay on political satire in England, The Quarterly Review (April, 1857) quotes from the Examiner paper in which the rewards of Marlborough are contrasted with those of Roman generals[1] and commends the satire here for the business-like way in which Swift carries on a baseless argument, adding gravity and minuteness to the humor and giving "a wonderful air of plausibility to the statements themselves." (p. 414) Waller speaks in his introduction to Gulliver of the skill with which Swift

[1] See *Works*, Temple Scott edition, IX, 96ff.

addressed the prejudices of the nation without offending its pride or insulting its sense in The Conduct of the Allies and the Remarks on the Barrier Treaty (p. xxi); and MacKnight casts aspersions upon the History of the Four Last Years of the Queen as partial, historically inaccurate, and inferior in force of argument to the Conduct of the Allies and in wit to the Examiner. (loc. cit., p. 177)

None of this is quite satisfying; the Irish pamphlets, though, receive a better treatment. This is not to say that they are universally admired, for they are not. Perhaps the best statement of approbation comes from George L. Craik, who traces the birth of patriotism in Ireland to Swift's efforts in the Wood affair.[1] Craik, while admitting that the Drapier's Letters are not economically sound, sees in them feelings and principles which go beyond material considerations and describes them as the most Demosthenic compositions since Demosthenes:

> It would perhaps be difficult to produce any modern writing in which the most remarkable qualities of the old Greek orator are so happily exemplified,--his force, his rapidity, his directness, his alertness and dexterity, his luminousness of statement and apparent homeliness or plainness, the naturalness and at the same time aptness of his figures, his wonderful logic (whether for fair reasoning or sophistry and misrepresentation), his ever-present life and power of interesting, his occasional fire and passion, his bursts of scorn, indignation, and withering invective, and the other resources of his supreme art. (p. 233)

Craik was an Irishman, and his was a fairly temperate Irish opinion.[2] The English are less certain of the greatness of the Drapier. A belligerent Whig calls Swift's conduct in the matter of Wood unjust and his pretences hollow. Wood's coinage was really very good, says Howitt in Homes and Haunts, and he and the people of Ireland suffered innocently because the Dean "wanted a cause of annoyance to Walpole, and against the government generally." (p. 207) De Quincey, flaying the old "erroneous" account of Wood's contract and the "imaginary" wrong it inflicted, considers this the most "scandalous" of

---

[1] *A Compendious History of English Literature*, 1861. My quotations are from the New York edition, 1875, vol. II.

[2] See also Lecky, *Leaders of Public Opinion*, p. 49; and Waller, *op. cit.*, p. xlii: Swift "saved," "improved," "adorned," and "exalted" Ireland.

all Swift's "villainies for the sake of popularity."[1] Thackeray too refuses to call the Irish pamphlets a sign of patriotism in the writer; the Letters are "masterpieces of dreadful humour and invective," (loc. cit., p. 442) logically enough reasoned, but fabulous as Lilliput, the outpourings of a soul not greatly grieved but rather roused to mad wrath through enmity and rage! And even the consciously unromantic North British Review (August, 1849) considers their "rabid fierceness" to be "symptomatic of mental disease." (p. 194) Another writer, finally, compares them unfavorably with Sydney Smith's Peter Plymley: Swift, "a detective in a dean's wig," a diseased and frightful caterer to the mob at the same time as he hated them, was immeasurably inferior to the buoyant, bounding Smith.

> Plymley's letters are true; the treatment may be incomplete...but the main principle is sound; the common sense of religious toleration is hardly susceptible of better explanation. Drapier's letters, on the contrary, are essentially absurd; they are a clever appeal to ridiculous prejudices.... No doubt there is a clever affectation of common sense in these, as in all of Swift's political writings, and the style has an air of business; yet, on the other hand, there are no passages which any one would now care to quote for their manner and their matter; and there are many in "Plymley" that will be constantly cited, so long as existing controversies are at all remembered.[2]

2

Bagatelles and Miscellaneous Works

This section must be a short one, for our critics have little time for Swift as a composer of pleasant trifles. That he has drawn perfect pictures of a coarse society in the Directions to Servants and Polite Conversations, and that his least remarkable tidbits are after all "toys constructed by a master's hand" are the sole remarks upon the subject from the pen of one writer;[3] and most are so taken up with their picture of a misshapen

[1] *loc. cit.*, p. 12. See, for an equally venomous attack, Lord Brougham, *Historical Sketches of Statesmen...*, London, 1845, Third Series, II, 209-11. Swift is called impudent, perfidious, unprincipled, ribald, *etc.*

[2] In "The First Edinburgh Reviewers," *National Rev.*, October, 1855, 280-81. But compare Abraham Hayward in the *Edinburgh Rev.*, July, 1855, p. 273: though the sour-tempered Swift was inferior to Smith as a moralist and a man, "an impartial posterity will probably prefer the Drapier's Letters to Peter Plymley's."

[3] Shaw, *Outlines of Eng. Lit.*, 234-35.

monster that they have neither time nor inclination to mention his lighter side.[1] Of the Modest Proposal, however, Thackeray provides the classic example of wilful misunderstanding. Chambers had already termed it, though an extraordinarily powerful and ingenious production, "rather too strong for modern taste" (loc. cit., p. 575)--at least an understandable judgment. But to Thackeray, it seems, the pamphlet was merely Swift's sarcastic method of showing "the unreasonableness of loving and having children" (loc. cit., (p. 443); it was one more example of his contemptible rage against mankind:

> Could Dick Steele, or Goldsmith, or Fielding, in his most reckless moment of satire, have written anything like the Dean's famous "Modest Proposal" for eating children?[2] Not one of these but melts at the thoughts of childhood, fondles and caresses it. Mr. Dean has no such softness, and enters the nursery with the tread and gaiety of an ogre. (p. 442)

For such incredibly vicious obtuseness the author of Vanity Fair deserved the punishment he received at the hands of a reviewer courageous enough to fight him with his own weapons. Ah, Mr. Thackeray, said John Eagles, in Blackwood's (October, 1853):

> ...you wind up your appeal so lovingly, so charmingly, so insinuatingly to your fair audience, upon the blessings of conjugal love and philoprogenitiveness, that you must be the dearest of lecturers, the pet of families, the destroyer of ogres; and, as to that monster Swift, the very children should cry out, as they do in the Children in the Wood, "Kill him again, Mr. Thackeray." And this you did, knowing all the while that the Modest Proposal was a patriotic and political satire--one of real kindness to the people....All this you knew very well; it was shabby and shameful of you by your mere eloquence to make this grave irony appear or be felt as a reality and a cruelty....Yes,--you knew the while these your words were awakening detestation of Swift, you were oratorising a very great sham--all nonsense--stuff--that would never pass current but through the stamp of lectureship. (p. 503)

[1]See, however, Roscoe, *op. cit.*, and Lecky, *loc. cit.*, who at least mention many of the lesser works, *passim*, and find them good. Katharine Thomson, *Lit. of Society*, II, 201-02, expatiates upon their indelicacy; Chambers's *Cyclopaedia*, p. 575, commends the minute observation of the *Directions for Servants;* and Hannay, *loc. cit.*, p. 147, speaks pleasantly of the "playful facetiae."

[2]Fielding not only could but did! See above, Introduction.

3

The Battle of the Books and A Tale of a Tub

It is impossible to deny the pungent wit of the Tale of a Tub; yet, as one nineteenth-century critic expresses it, "None but an inspired madman would have attempted to do honour to religion in a spirit which none but the infidel could heartily approve."[1] That the Tale justly gave offense to Queen Anne, that it rightly stood in the way of a bishopric for Swift, and that the sceptic Voltaire could recommend it as a satire against religion--for these reasons it is almost universally damned by the Dean's enemies in the middle eighteen-hundreds. Thackeray, for example, sees Swift as a man who, in entering the church, bound himself to "a life-long hypocrisy" (loc. cit., p. 441); the man who wrote that "wild book," who was a boon companion of Pope and Bolingbroke, must have known what he was doing. "The Queen, and the bishops, and the world, were right in mistrusting the religion of that man." (p. 439) And when, in old age, he exclaimed over his genius as expressed in his early work, he was, Thackeray believes, admiring not the genius but the consequences to which that genius brought him--

> a genius wonderfully bright, and dazzling, and strong,--to seize, to know, to see, to flash upon falsehood and scorch it into perdition, to penetrate into the hidden motives, and expose the black thoughts of men,--an awful, an evil spirit. (p. 441)

And De Quincey, less gentle, speaks with contemptuous amazement of Swift's astonishment at Anne's refusing to confer a bishopric upon one who had treated all the profoundest mysteries of Christianity not merely with scepticism or a casual sneer, "but with set pompous merriment and farcical buffoonery." The Dean was, indeed, says the mystic opium-eater, constitutionally incapable of religion, and in his astonishment at Anne's coolness "was in that state of constitutional irreligion--irreligion not from intellectual scepticism, but from a vulgar temperament--which imputes to everybody else its own plebeian feelings." (loc. cit., 14-15)[2]

One of Swift's most persistent calumniators, on the other hand, shows high enthusiasm for the Tale. In spite of its irreligion and its coarseness, Gilfillan finds it full of fire, rich imagery, and freshness of thought: "the wildest, wittiest, wealthiest book of its size in

---

[1]Samuel Phillips, in the *Times*, October 3, 1850.

[2]See also Chambers's *Cyclopaedia*, p. 574; Masson in the *Brit. Quart. Rev.*, October, 1854, p. 536; MacKnight, *loc. cit.*, 154-55; Waller, *op. cit.*, p. xviii; and Lecky, *loc. cit.*, 24-5, and *passim*.
Mrs. Thomson also finds the work dull--as dull "as if written in a dead language." (*loc. cit.*, p. 175)

British literature."[1] It is, he thinks, replete with such fertile, if not elegant, metaphor that it equals in this respect Shakespeare or Jeremy Taylor!

Other critics concentrate upon other aspects of the work. Roscoe calls it "an astonishing production, of which the fervid vehement style, sparkling wit, and vivacity of genius, seem to distinguish it above the happiest efforts of his own resistless pen." (op. cit., p. xx) And Hannay also considers it Swift's greatest literary effort. Both men attribute his failure to advance in the church not to the Tale, but to the Windsor Prophecy, in which he had satirized the Queen's backstairs favorite, the Duchess of Somerset; and Hannay grows really wrathful on this score. That eighteenth-century piety could not bear the notion of giving a bishopric to the author of the Tale is, he cries, odious cant! For Swift was, if anything, too good to be "an eighteenth-century bishop." (loc. cit., p. 143) And the North British Review (August, 1849), remarking incredulously upon the fact that "the Church was actually offended at being so saved from dangers that were far from imaginary," (p. 188) agrees in thinking it incomparably Swift's best work, a work of such absolute freedom and "fulness of power" as nothing that he afterwards produced. To Thomas Shaw it appeared a richly imaginative religious lampoon, whose events are recounted "in the broadest, boldest, most unreserved language of farcical extravagance" and whose digressions as well as its main theme "are absolute treasuries of droll allusion and ingenious adaptation of obscure and uncommon learning." (loc. cit., p. 228) But by far the strongest apology for the work comes from the pen of Eagles, who so intelligently reviewed Thackeray's lecture in the pages of Blackwood's (October, 1853):

> This Tale of a Tub has often been condemned and excused, and will be while literature lasts, and is received amongst persons of different temperaments. There are some so grave that wit is condemned by them before they know the subject upon which it is exercised. To many it is folly, because beyond their conception. We know no reason why the man of wit should not be religious; if there be, wit is a crime; yet it is a gift of nature, and so imperative upon the possessor that he can scarcely withhold it. (p. 508)

George Craik's Compendious History provides us with a long and sometimes interesting discussion of the Tale and the Battle. (II, 208-28) Swift, we are told, though neither a Cervantes nor a Rabelais, combined in his nature considerable portions of both; but these two

---

[1] *A Third Gallery of Portraits*, p. 222.

masterpieces could have been written only by him.

> The torrent of triumphant merriment is broader and more rushing than anything of the same kind in either. When we look indeed to the perfection and exactness of the allegory at all points, to the biting sharpness and at the same time the hilarity and comic animation of the satire, to its strong and unpausing yet easy and natural flow, to the incessant blaze of the wit and humor, and to the style so clear, so vivid and expressive, so idiomatic, so English, so true and appropriate in all its varieties, narrative, didactic, rhetorical, colloquial, as we know no work of its class in our own language that as a whole approaches the Tale of a Tub, so we doubt if there be another quite equal to it in any language. (209-10)

And Craik commends the satire for the fineness of its edge, its force and liveliness. In Swift's youth, he says, his genius had a "fervor, exuberance, and florid gayety" (p. 222) which it later partly lost; here and there in both the Tale and the Battle the expression rises to eloquence, and even to a poetic glow not to be found in any of his later writings. For the rest, Craik provides the reader with long excerpts, mostly from the story of the three brothers in the Tale of a Tub. He shows, unfortunately, little interest in the rich digressions and the deeply serious meaning which underlies the whole. And of the Battle he quotes only one long section--the episode of Bentley and Wotton, with no comment beyond the fact that it is "a very happy Homeric burlesque." (p. 224)

The Battle of the Books, in fact, receives slight notice from the critics of this age. Discussion about its source seems to come to an end with Roscoe, who echoes Monck Mason on the subject; he also says much about Swift's "learned chivalry" and his "refined" taste in writing the Battle--"like some young heroic chief to defend the form of his aged sire from the assaults of his relentless foes." (op. cit., xix-xx) Lecky mentions it as a work "unrivalled in its kind" (loc. cit., p. 12); but the one other extended comment of the period, coming curiously from the pen of a man who found the Tale of a Tub an absolute treasury of delight, is distinctly unappreciative: for some inexplicable reason, Thomas Shaw considered this--perhaps the least terrible of all Swift's satires--to be a fierce and brutal piece of drollery, full of coarseness and savagery, some of the incidents of which "are worthy of the hand which painted the Yahoos." (loc. cit., p. 228) It is impossible for the historian of Swift's reputation as a writer to fit criticism of this sort into any pattern of thought. We must assume that Shaw's obvious admiration for Dryden blinded him to the charms of the Dryden-baiting Battle.

4

Gulliver's Travels

Critics of the age were, as I have said, interested primarily in the personality of Swift. The task of sizing up the man--and the man's genius as expressed in his work in general--kept them so busy as to leave little room for an extended appreciation of single works; and so the years from 1840 to 1865 brought forth virtually nothing in the way of new criticism of Gulliver. It goes without saying that contemporaries of Dickens and Thackeray loved a good tale. Without exception they enjoyed the story of Lemuel Gulliver's voyages into strange realms; but almost as universally they hooted the moral of that story, thus creating a dichotomy between the narrative and its teachings, and commending the one and censuring the other on grounds already too well-trodden by critics of past generations.

Roscoe characteristically shirks his duty by quoting from the judgments of Sheridan, Johnson, Scott, and W. C. Taylor. He defends the voyage to the Houyhnhnms in his own person, however, against the traditional belief in its inferiority as a work of art by explaining the author's object as "not so much to depict mankind as to expose their corruption and degeneracy" (op. cit., p. p. lxxv);[1] yet he partially vitiates this courageous dictum by admitting that at the same time the "picture is overcharged, and the condemnation of too sweeping and unsparing a character." (ibid.) Others are less sympathetic. Chambers's Cyclopaedia, for instance, takes it for granted that all parties "seem now agreed in the opinion that the interest of the work diminishes as it proceeds," that Lilliput is delightful, that Brobdingnag abounds in excellent moral and political observations, that the voyage to Laputa is ingenious but tedious and absurd, and that the last part "is a gross libel on human nature, and disgusting from its physical indelicacy." (p. 575) Shaw, finding it an exquisitely rich adventure story, narrated with superb verisimilitude, especially in the first two sections where an identical satiric aim is attained by looking through opposite ends of a telescope,[2] stops short at the Brobdingnagian King's remark that human beings seem like little odious vermin. This, he cries, "is neither just nor useful," but defeats the very object of satire: to render "the species better, wiser, and more innocent." (loc. cit., p. 232) He finds the third voyage pointless and as coarse as, though far less genial than,

[1]See also Hannay, *loc. cit.*, p. 146.

[2]Compare Scott, *op. cit.*, p. 330. For other remarks on the verisimilitude, see Chambers's *Cyclopaedia*, p. 575; Sharpe's *London Journal*, XI, 309; and Katharine Thomson, *loc. cit.*, p. 200.

Rabelais; but he does admire the "Juvenalian" picture of the Struldbrugs. (p. 233) In the last section, however, he can find nothing at all to like; setting aside "the outrageous improbability of the leading idea," (p. 234) the portrait of the Yahoos exhibits hatred and contempt on every page and seems to have been dictated by unreasoning misanthropy. Its ferocity is excessive and absurd, and Swift lays himself open to the charge "either of having drawn not a portrait but a gross and odious caricature, or of having his eyes grievously blinded and perverted by prejudice." (p. 234)

Waller, in his edition of Gulliver, expresses delight in the realism and skill of the first two books, and even finds justification for the unsuccessful third voyage in that it strikes out against vicious pseudo-scientists--but draws the line conclusively when he approaches a discussion of the rest. The fourth voyage, he says, is more comprehensive, more malignant, and more unjustifiable than the others.

> To approve of this terrible libel on human nature is impossible; to extenuate it is difficult; and it is only the sense that an entire omission of this fourth voyage would be unwarrantable which induces us to present it, dealing with it, however, in such a manner as shall make it as suitable for general reading as any of the former ones. (p. 272, note)[1]

And he insists that such moral as may be drawn from it will no more justify the fable than will the practice of the ancients "in brutalising their slaves by making them drunk" as a warning to children! (p. 283, note)

But dangerous though they might think Gulliver's Travels, all men read it for its story with real pleasure; and some prided themselves on the fact that they were, so to speak, cheating Swift in neglecting his satire for his tale. The pathetic irony of a bitter indictment of mankind read by innocent childhood as a gay fairy tale amused them and inflated their self-esteem: they had conquered the monster and relegated him to the nursery. In 1842 Bulwer-Lytton writes, in a persistently rhythmic frame of mind:

> Lo! that grim Merriment of Hatred;--born
> Of him,--the Master-Mocker of Mankind,
> Beside the grin of whose malignant spleen
> Voltaire's gay sarcasm seems a smile serene,--
> Do we not place it in our children's hands,
> Leading young Hope through Lemuel's fabled lands?--

---

[1]See also Collier, *Hist. Eng. Lit:* Only "a bad man could have imagined its events, and none but impure minds can enjoy such revolting pictures." I quote from the revised edition, London, 1898, p. 286.

> God's and man's libel in that foul yahoo!--
> Well, and what mischief can the libel do?
> O impotence of Genius to belie
> Its glorious task--its mission from the sky!
> Swift wrote this book to wreak a ribald scorn
> On aught the Man should love or Priest should mourn--
> And lo! the book, from all its ends beguil'd,
> A harmless wonder to some happy child![1]

And David Masson, speaking of the inspired "ludicrous invention" of the story, remarks upon the fact that school-boys read it with delight, ignorant of its satire, and that even literary critics, though better informed, "break down in laughter from the sheer grotesqueness of some of the fancies."[2]

Thackeray, on the other hand, can never forget the meaning of this "dreadful allegory." Its surprising humor, its natural figures, its delectable "truth topsy-turvy, entirely logical and absurd" (loc. cit., p. 445)--all its manifold beauties fade into nothingness when confronted with its "horrible, shameful, unmanly, blasphemous" moral; "and giant and great as this Dean is, I say we should hoot him." (p. 446) In all seriousness Thackeray advises his audience not to read the last section of the book and speaks of it as Yahoo-language, the shameless shrieks and imprecations of a monster, "filthy in word, filthy in thought, furious, raging, obscene." (p. 446) And what is the meaning of this blasphemy against heaven? Thackeray's answer comes glibly: its meaning is "that man is utterly wicked, desperate, and imbecile, and his passions are so monstrous, and his boasted powers so mean, that he is and deserves to be the slave of brutes, and ignorance is better than his vaunted reason." (p. 447)

To such blind and empty pretence the critic of Blackwood's (October, 1853) applies his lash; he calls Thackeray's point of view "a morbid philanthropy, a maudlin philanthropy" (p. 510) and actually makes a plea for strong and vigorous--even coarse--satire! Hogarth, he says, depicted human vice in an even more realistic fashion than Swift, yet men call him a great moralist.

> Hoot him, Mr. Lecturer, hoot both or neither. No--the hoot of the lecturer was nothing but a little oratorical extravagance, for an already indignant audience, touched upon that tender modern virtue, general philanthrophy (sic). (510-11)

Even those, however, who hooted Swift most loudly, even Gilfillan and De Quincey, raised their voices in praise of the power which was Gulliver. Schlosser, in his

---

[1] From *The Souls of Books*, first printed in 1842 in the volume called *Eva and Other Poems*.

[2] *British Novelists and their Styles*, London, 1859, p. 94.

Germanic stupidity, thinks the book tedious and its style dull, said De Quincey; nothing could be further from the truth: it is one of the great books of all time, and its style is purposely touched with "an aerial tint of dulness" in order to give it "a comic air of downright Wapping and Rotherhithe verisimilitude." (loc. cit., p. 16) And Gilfillan, who makes much of Swift's magnificent poetic powers, writes with awe of the Dean's ability to create a poetic effect more fierce and terrible than Juvenal's, without the aid of rhythm or rhyme:

> ...think of his description of war and of statesmanship in the last parts of Gulliver's travels--descriptions in which, working with the barest and coldest words, he produces the effect of poetry, as though a hot furnace should be fuelled with snow.[1]

5

The Poetry

It is a curious fact that Gilfillan, arch-enemy of Swift the man, feels, more than any of his contemporaries, the poetic fire which animates Swift's verse. Indeed, he prefers Swift to Pope as a poet, partially for the romantic reason that the Dean seems to be the more natural genius, but even more because he sees a grandness, a power in Swift's meanest efforts never approached by the "tinklings" of the bard of Twickenham. Swift, he says, was, "if not truly great, immensely large; and even in his most careless verses you see a large black purpose--that, namely, of a wholesale libeller, who, as he said himself, loved many men but hated man--looming through; and some of his veriest trifles make you tremble."[2] This is, to be sure, admiration springing from terror rather than delight; but the fact remains that it is admiration, and it is admiration of poetry as such--a sense of a sublimity in Swift's verse grasped by few other commentators.

For the rest, this period yields no more stimulating criticism than we should expect. Roscoe offers nothing original; he echoes Scott in pronouncing the Pindarics not inferior to those of Donne and Cowley (op. cit., p. xvi); he calls Cadenus and Vanessa a beautiful poem, but discusses it only as a sincere exposition of the development of the Vanessa affair (xlviii-li); and he considers the poems in general a series of excellent occasional satires (lxxxii). Chambers's Cyclopaedia prints five of the poems (A Description of the Morning, the City Shower, Baucis and Philemon, On the Death of Dr. Swift, and The Grand Question Debated) and finds them all good. The truth and humor of the first two and the liveliness of the last appeal to the critic; and the sincerity,

---

[1] *Satire and Satirists, loc. cit.*, p. 238.

[2] *A Third Gallery...*, 221-22.

the touches of homely pathos, "which are felt like trickling tears," give an electrical effect to Swift's verses on his death--"the finest example of his peculiar poetical vein." (p. 488) But that peculiar poetical vein is limited. The perfection of the Dean's poetry is akin to that of the old Dutch school of painting. It is content with a faithful representation of the lower world, with no higher aspirations; it lacks, in other words, that overworked nineteenth-century attribute of sublimity. Even the Rhapsody on Poetry, Swift's most ambitious flight, "is pitched in a pretty low key." (ibid.)

With this judgment, dull as it may seem to the modern student, other writers loquaciously agree. Leigh Hunt, while calling Swift a powerful, a precise, a fastidious, and a truly original poet, who, though emulating Butler, yet developed a manner all his own, and who "had more music in him than he loved to let 'fiddlers' suppose," nevertheless compares his verse unfavorably with that of Pope or Butler. It is, he maintains, but "a kind of smart prose," utterly wanting in "pregnancy of expression."[1] Shaw, even less appreciative, finds in it none of the higher qualities of poetry: "not much harmony, no depth of feeling, no (or very rare) splendour of language." (loc. cit., p. 235) Like its author, it is dry, hard, and cold, though The Legion Club is "the most intense expression of hatred and contempt...that human pen perhaps has ever traced, or human heart conceived." (ibid.) And Waller, singling out the Rhapsody as an unsurpassable bit of bold and spirited satire, finds all the verse nervous and thoughtful, caustic and witty, but hopelessly lacking in the sublime and the pathetic--and therefore no better than rhymed prose. (op. cit., p. xliii) In the same way, George Craik regards the poems as admirable examples of that kind of poetry "which has scarcely any distinctively poetical quality or characteristic about it except the rhyme." (loc. cit., p. 238) Most of them belong to the humblest form of verse, and even those few which aspire to greater heights --Cadenus and Vanessa, the Rhapsody, and On the Death of Dr. Swift--are chiefly distinguished from the others by their greater length. Piquant wit and fancy Swift had; but true poetry demands grandeur of imagination and tender emotion.

[1]*Wit and Humour*, London, 1846, 309-10. Hunt, incidentally, censures the verses on Swift's death as the vulgar spleen of a loveless misanthrope. (p. 330) I have found no similar criticism anywhere else.

III

Swift the Writer

From our survey of the reputation of Swift's individual works in the period under consideration we are bound to conclude that they were being read less, or at least less thoroughly, than in former years. The age of Thackeray, peculiarly rich in invidious criticism of the man, seems to have displayed a remarkable apathy toward his writings. Traditional opinions have been echoed and re-echoed, with but slight effort to strike out into new paths of thought. In seeking to fashion a full-bodied portrait of the Dean, critics have, in short, had virtually no opportunity for a careful consideration of his works.

When we turn, however, to a study of Swift's art in general, we are confronted with an almost embarrassing wealth of material. Our critics, prone to indulge in broad generalizations about the man, carry on in their discussions of his art. They generalize with abandon, sweep into the discard all matters of fact not in accord with their respective theories, and, surprisingly enough, succeed at times--where they otherwise have failed--in scratching the surface of truth. For this very reason, perhaps, it is not easy to find many points of contact between the various critical approaches; and I propose, therefore, to discuss them as nearly as possible in chronological order, making no attempt to see consistent patterns of thought relating one critic to another, where such patterns obviously do not exist.

We can pass swiftly over the remarks of the persistently uninteresting Roscoe. His observations on the Dean's wit and on the vigor, simplicity, and conciseness of his style can hardly succeed in teasing the weary student into thought. Such ideas, though the very bread and meat of Swift criticism, tend at this stage of our study to exasperate rather than pique the glutted palate. It is to be expected that they will appear incidentally in most discussions of his art, but they are no longer of sufficient importance to merit our attention.[1] For the first bit of interesting criticism we turn from Roscoe to Chambers's Cyclopaedia; and here, in the midst of much conventional material on the purity of his style, his humor, his coarseness, and his ability to create realistic characters and situations, we find one rather amusing

---

[1]For equally conventional treatments see *Sharpe's London Journal*, XI, 309: Swift effected triumphs comparable to those achieved by Junius; Thackeray, *loc. cit.*, p. 432: Swift, possessing powers of eloquence, dared not use them, but, dreading ridicule, depended for effect upon elaborate simplicity; Collier, *loc. cit.*, p. 287: "He seems to have hated foreign words as he hated men"; and Waller, *op. cit.*, p. xlii.

assumption. The writer thinks Swift to have been deficient in purity of taste and loftiness of imagination, decries his willingness to find inspiration solely in the "palpable and familiar objects of life," and says, with evident disdain: "We can scarcely conceive him to have ever read the Faery Queen or Midsummer Night's Dream." (p. 576) In other words, the writer--no doubt typical of his age--felt vaguely cheated at finding in Swift nothing misty, nothing fairy-like, nothing delicate and aerial!

It is the Dean's coarseness, invariably at least mentioned by all commentators, which chiefly turns Leigh Hunt against his art. Hunt praises his qualities of wit and humor extravagantly; though he lacked the poetry of Aristophanes, the animal spirits of Rabelais, the delicacy of Addison, and the pathos of Sterne, he had no superior, ancient or modern, in wit, in "a sheer meeting of the extremes of difference and likeness."[1] But he was not a healthy man, and there was a morbidity in his excessive coarseness--a coarseness much more repulsive even than that of his own contemporaries. With Hunt's opinion another writer agrees: wit, says Howitt, in Homes and Haunts, need not be disgusting, and Swift's vulgarity cannot be charged to the temper of his age:

> Swift out-Herods the times and his cotemporaries....and his vilest parts are inextricably woven with the texture of his composition, as in Gulliver's Travels.... Youthful readers should at least be made aware that the wit that is praised is combined with obscenity or grossness that cannot be too emphatically condemned. (p. 208)

The foregoing evaluations, though interesting, are by no means revolutionary. During our century-long voyage on the sea of Swift criticism we have encountered many similar ones; but in Thomas De Quincey we meet our first great rebel of the present period. De Quincey, addressing the "commonplace" reader and calling him by inference a "blockhead," sets out militantly to prove the folly of current ideas about the excellence of the Dean's prose style. In this singular reaction against conventional shibboleths, the critic makes three points. First, Swift's sole merit as a stylist "is vernacularity, and nothing better or finer." This he exhibits, not in a graceful artlessness, but in "a coarse inartificiality." Secondly, he possesses this excellence in common with many other writers of his age:

> And what wonder should there be in this, when the main qualification for such a style was plain good sense, natural feeling, unpretendingness, some little scholarly practice in putting together the clockwork of sentences so as to avoid

[1] *Wit and Humour*, p. 308.

> mechanical awkwardness of construction, but above all the advantage of a _subject_ such in its nature as instinctively to reject ornament, lest it should draw off attention from itself? (_loc. cit_., p. 17)

And thirdly, he goes on, Swift would have broken down irrecoverably had he attempted to write upon grand, impassioned themes! Most "blockheads" regard Swift's style not as if relatively good, but as if absolutely so; but suppose he had been required to write a pendant for Sir Walter Raleigh's apostrophe to Death, or to passages in Sir Thomas Browne or Jeremy Taylor: "Are you aware what sort of ridiculous figure your poor bald Jonathan would have cut?" (p. 18)

This, then, is a fact of nineteenth-century criticism: Swift's powers are deprecated because he wrote _Gulliver's Travels_ and _A Tale of a Tub_ instead of _The Faerie Queene_ and _Hydriotaphia_. The same absurd theory is enlarged upon in Masson's essay in the _British Quarterly Review_ (October, 1854), where Swift is called a great genius, one who possessed in the highest degree what Goethe and Niebuhr call the "_demonic_ element"; yet one who does not rank with Spenser, Milton, Scott, Wordsworth, or even with Pope, Steele, Addison:

> The demonic element in a man...may, in one case, be the demonic of the etherial and the celestial; in another, the demonic of the Tartarean and infernal. There is a demonic of the supernatural--angels, and seraphs, and white-winged airy messengers swaying men's phantasies from above; and there is a demonic of the infra-natural--fiends, and shapes of horror tugging at men's thoughts from beneath. The demonic in Swift was of the latter kind.... One might say of Swift that he had far less of belief in a God, than of belief in a Devil. (p. 556)

As a simple humorist and a serious expositor, he remains a man of strong and sagacious English mind, plain-spoken and conspicuously free of cant, abjuring the profound and the trite alike. (p. 560) But, says Masson in another place, like his prototype Rabelais, Swift's more typical medium is always that of mad, obscene, ghastly, and infinitely sorrowful humor! His robust mind transcended in its awful scope the picayune problems of his day, even while it concerned itself with them; but more than his prosaic contemporaries he renounced sublimity and adopted a philosophy of the nether world, of universal despair. Thus, Masson concludes, although he will be remembered as long as our literature lasts, his works should be recommended only to the strong. To strong men he will be congenial, "for they can bear to look round and round reality on all sides, even on that which connects us with the Yahoos."[1]

Obviously, what disturbs Masson is the fact that Swift was a satirist who, instead of sweetly chastening, preferred to carry his satire to its reasonable extreme. It is the Dean's bitter tenacity, his insistent refusal to see anything through tinted glasses, that creates enmity in the souls of the more thin-skinned critics. Gilfillan, for example, ridicules those who praise his satirical powers. Swift was not a satirist, he cries, but a minor Satan, who surprised man naked and asleep, "looked at him with microscopic eyes," ignored his peculiar marks of "incipient godhood," and reported accordingly--not a satirist, but a heartless "monster of misanthropy."[2] Did the Dean, then, have no lighter side? Not, I fear, for the men whom we have been discussing. They generously accorded him his full measure of gloomy genius--and refused to look beyond.

But James Hannay proclaimed him without reservation the greatest of English satirists--not, perhaps, so polished as Pope, but more largely related to universal nature.

> He had more humor, for example, than Pope, who had it not in him to produce a downright side-shaking bit of rollicking fun. There is more laughter, altogether, about Swift's satire, as there was about the man.... Then he was a deep thinker; he has sayings about human nature which are as good as anybody's; and his satire goes very deep: it is not only bitter satire against individuals, it is philosophical satire, which goes to the root of things. He was a lord of all the weapons in this line,--invective, ridicule, humor; and includes in himself, like the Trojan horse, many different fighting-men. (loc. cit., p. 150)[3]

One feature of his art distinguishes him from many other satirists, according to Hannay: he was primarily a man of action, and his writings are eminently practical. He

[1] *British Novelists and their Styles*, 90-4.

[2] *Satire and Satirists*, p. 237. See also Walter Savage Landor, who extols Swift's humor but decries his gall, in a short poem of 1863: "Bitters and acids may excite, Yet satisfy not appetite." (*Works*, VIII, 343) Eagles, in *Blackwood's* (October, 1853), p. 512, defends his bitterness on the basis of the times and the treatment accorded him by mankind. Hannay, *loc. cit.*, p. 146, says much the same thing.

[3] See also the *Quarterly Rev.*, April, 1857, 410-11, for a similar, though less sympathetic, expression of a belief in Swift's powers. The writer classes him with Aristophanes and Rabelais and calls him more various than either: "He could hurl a rock like the Cyclops, or fling a pebble with the gayest warrior who ever came out to battle."

scattered them abroad fiercely and with consummate abandon. His imaginative works have the direct object of influencing opinion and affecting world institutions; he was for and of the world, and, unlike most men of letters, who are passive makers of "beautiful pictures," he never wrote merely for the sake of writing. (p. 134) This observation is perhaps open to serious question. One wonders whether Gulliver's Travels, whatever its ostensible purpose, or--better still--A Tale of a Tub came into being simply as a result of a need for action. But, though we may challenge Hannay's statement, we cannot challenge the fact that it is intelligent and stimulating. He stands out, I think, as the great forgotten prophet of modern Swift-sympathy.

That Swift never forgot himself, that he could not lose his own identity in the contemplation of beauty--this is perhaps what Hannay means in terming him a man of the world rather than a man of letters. He does not, however, imply that this necessarily detracts from the Dean's genius or art. George Craik, on the other hand, who expresses the idea more fully, finds in it the sole barrier to a place for Swift among the greatest immortals. Into everything that came from his pen he put a strong infusion of himself--not merely his intellect, but his passions and prejudices; and this is at one and the same time his strength and his weakness.

> The common herd of writers have no individuality at all; those of the very highest class can assume at will any other individuality as perfectly as their own,--they have no exclusiveness. Next under this highest class stand those whose individuality is at once their strength and their weakness;--their strength, inasmuch as it distinguishes them from and lifts them far above the multitude of writers of mere talent or expository skill; their weakness and bondage, in that it will not be thrown off, and that it withholds them from ever going out of themselves, and rising from the merely characteristic, striking, or picturesque, either to the dramatic or to the beautiful, of both of which equally the spirit is unegotistic and universal. To this class, which is not the highest but the next to it, Swift belongs. (loc. cit., p. 209)

And so, as we approach the last phase of our study, we see the rise of a new and brighter evaluation of Swift's art. Craik's search for universality and detachment in literature caused him to place Swift a little lower than the highest, but it did not compel him to deny all merit to the Dean. Nor did he recoil in fascinated horror, with trembling admiration admitting Swift's genius in the very act of denouncing it. Instead he coolly assessed it according to his lights; and, no matter what we think of his opinion, we must at least respect it. In his age the peak of anti-Swift hysteria was reached by such men as Thackeray and Gilfillan. But also in his age other critics arose who renounced hysteria and courted sanity, who tried to see Swift as a human being and to read his works accordingly. Their point of view, their efforts at understanding and sensible appreciation, may have had no perceptible effect upon general opinion of the time or even upon later scholars; but what they said was indicative of a great new trend toward level-headedness.

PART FOUR
(1865-1882)

I

Swift the Man

It is not to be expected that the harshly prejudiced or the sentimental attitude toward Swift should have completely given way to a more rational point of view in the space of a few years. Old impressions created by critics like Jeffrey and Thackeray lingered long after those men had ceased to be; Taine's History of English Literature, first given to the English-reading public in 1871, carried the work of debasing the Dean's reputation even further. The years from 1865 to 1882 are by no means totally free of adverse or ill-considered criticism. We find one writer, censuring the age of Anne as an irreligious one, saying of Swift that, when we think of him as a man, his sermons "seem to be a mockery."[1] Another quotes Orrery as an occasional authority, compares Swift to a lion in his lair, and creates a portrait in every respect consistent with the old monster-theory.[2] To Anthony Trollope, Thackeray's characterization was indubitably true: Swift was a man who, "from first to last, was miserable himself, who made others miserable, and who deserved misery."[3] Judgments like these are most likely to occur in works which do not deal specifically with the Dean, to whose story, therefore, the authors have been unable to devote the necessary amount of study.[4] But they also appear in more extended discussions; and we find D. Laing Purves prefacing his selection of the works of Swift with a biographical sketch in which nineteenth-century strains of sentimentality and ill-founded censure are inextricably woven together. Purves calls the Dean's life one which "points its own moral,"[5] repeats traditional anecdotes without questioning their authenticity, runs blithely through the list of Swiftian paradoxes, and altogether writes a thoroughly trite essay--in treatment, however, somewhat more gentle than those of many of his predecessors. Sentimentality, then, as well as bitter vituperation, is not yet dead, and even the monumental

[1]William Forsyth, *Novels and Novelists of the Eighteenth Century*, London, 1871, p. 22.

[2]*Englishwomen's Domestic Mag.*, January and February, 1874, 6-8 and 63-5.

[3]*Thackeray*, *English Men of Letters* series, 1879. I quote from the New York edition, p. 155.

[4]See, for example, F. W. Wyon, *The History of Great Britain During the Reign of Queen Anne*, London, 1876, II, 261; and J. H. Burton, *A History of the Reign of Queen Anne*, London, 1880, III, 267-84, but especially pages 274 and 279.

[5]*The Works of Jonathan Swift, D. D.*, Edinburgh, 1869, p. 1.

labors of Swift's late nineteenth-century biographers will not utterly kill it.[1]

A new, clearer thinking age has none the less begun. This is not to say that all men have learned fully to appreciate Jonathan Swift or even entirely to discredit long-credited legends about him. Much of the old antagonism persists; many of the old stories are repeated. But critics have learned to consider before judging and to base their judgments on firmer ground than personal bias. Whatever their failings, they have at least begun to make an attempt at impartiality; and though they may come to conclusions not wholly favorable to the Dean, they seem to make their decisions after, and not before, studying the facts of his life. Besides, if we can accept the word of James Hannay--and I have already shown him to be an acute and intelligent thinker--the Queen Anne writers were showing signs of regaining their lost popularity. In an essay called "Thackeray on Swift" in Temple Bar (October, 1867), Hannay applauds this fact as a relief from the mawkish turbulence of his own epoch and laments Thackeray's inability to understand the Dean. For the rest, he repeats the generous estimate of Swift's personality which he had already expressed in Satire and Satirists, speaks of him as "an eminently friendly man," (p. 323) and hopes that Thackeray and he have at last met "in the meads of asphodel and the amaranthine bowers." (p. 330)[2] It is a significant fact, also, that in this essay Hannay reverses his position in regard to the marriage question; now he believes that the marriage never took place and leans toward the theory of sexual impotence as an explanation of the mystery.

Hannay had answered Thackeray's question, "Would you have liked to be a friend of Swift's?", with a clear affirmative; and William Allingham, in an essay which Carlyle (in a letter to Allingham, November 1, 1867) called "the faithfullest and justest crayon sketch" ever, said much the same thing. Allingham, under the pseudonym of Patricius Walker, contributed a series of literary "Rambles" to Fraser's, in one of which, "Moor Park and Swift" (November, 1867), he tried to sift fact from fancy in the

[1]For a sentimental article couched in flowery language, see A. D. Vandam, *Amours of Great Men* ("A Bachelor from Conviction"), 1878, reprinted in *Tinsley's Magazine*, XXIV, 73ff., 1879: Swift imposed continence on himself as a result of his sad experience with Varina and his conviction that it was morally wrong to bring children into this worst of all possible worlds. See also "Dean Swift's Cathedral," *Belgravia*, April, 1867: the author muses upon Swift's "wild fitful soul" during a visit to St. Patrick's. Old-style vituperation can be found as late as 1880 in an article by J. Nichol in Ward's *English Poets*, III, 34-8; also in a review of Stephen's *Swift* (*Athenaeum*, September 30, 1882) which considers the Dean selfish, cruel, a religious sceptic, and in general depraved.

[2]See also James Hain Friswell, *Essays on English Writers*, London, 1869, 217-21. His estimate of Swift as a tender, noble, and misunderstood man is consciously influenced by Hannay.

biography of the Dean and came to the conclusion that Swift's rough exterior covered a fine good-nature, that he hated the stupidity of mankind, not men, that in all probability he never married Stella, that his "grand mistake in life was going into the church," (p. 652) and that, of all his set, he would have been the best and safest man to have as a friend. A writer in the North British Review (January, 1870), obviously repelled by Swift's personality, yet tries to give him his due as a man who meant well, whatever his faults. He was eternally kind, though self-centered; his joining the Tory party "was not the act of a man of stainless honour; but it was the most venial form of political apostasy." (p. 175) A sincere Irish patriot, he glowed with "a divine anger against oppression" (p. 181); but above all he had "a burning abhorrence of falsehood and wrong" (p. 185)--the noble feature which redeemed all his vices. Despite his imperfections he was a great man.

> Forget his coarseness, put aside the wretched egotisms of his private life, assume--what is surely true--that a man may be incapable of unselfish personal feeling, and yet upright, generous, and ardent in his general perceptions and sympathies; and then say if there be any man between Milton and Burke who is so essentially the Hebrew prophet inspired to detect and denounce wrong as Swift. (p. 188)

Critics like Jeffrey and Thackeray had made their greatest mistake in trying to judge Swift according to common standards. Later writers have realized that genius must not be so measured; and William Mackay clarified the issue in an essay entitled "The Mad Dean" in the New Monthly Magazine (September, 1870). Mankind, he said, must not be judged by a common standard: what has Joynt the butcher, who is the essence of mediocrity, in common with genius? Swift was after all a great and lonely spirit, a mighty intellect touched with madness. And the answer to all charges against him of cruelty, treachery, and dishonesty lies in the simple fact that he was loved by two women. Vanessa's vanity led justly to her downfall, but Stella never stopped loving the Dean; and only the cheap gallantry of the English has perpetrated and kept alive the cruel myth of her unhappiness. That Swift married her at all--and Mackay believes that he did--in that lax age redounds to his credit; for, whichever account of her parentage is true, she was of tainted--or at least low--birth. The story of Swift's ill-nature, says the writer, has been falsely engendered by the prejudiced statements of great and popular men; and it is matter for particular regret that these opinions are adopted by a host of smaller writers, "who take up the cry and prolong it feebly and clamorously in places where it receives unquestioning credence." (p. 346) As a case in point he mentions Collier's handbook,[1] now being read in hundreds of classrooms--a book whose chapter on Swift is a bit of "most nauseating Thackeray-and-water."

> When Thackeray speaks of Swift, it is one man speaking of another. But when from the highways and hedges of literature tiny hands are stretched forth to smite, and squeaky voices are raised to defame, it is Gulliver on the ground vast but inert, and held in the degrading meshes of the Lilliputians. (ibid.)

Gulliver was, however, already regaining his freedom when Mackay penned those words, for writers of all sorts had begun to reconsider long-established judgments. We find a reviewer of Stanhope's History of England incidentally defending Swift against Macaulay's charge of political apostasy;[2] we find J. A. Froude speaking of him as one who, "disdaining the tricks by which he might have flattered his way, even under Walpole and the House of Hanover, into the high places in the Church,...became, in the best and noblest sense, an Irish patriot"[3]--certainly a reversal of earlier criticism of the Dean as an embittered failure, who fought for Ireland out of mere pique; and even in a short story, a simple jeu d'esprit which deals in humorous fashion with the incident of an apparition believed by some "ould residenthers" to be the ghost of Swift, doomed to perambulate Ireland as a punishment for his treatment of Stella--even here we come across a passage which gratuitously offers an apology for Swift's eccentricity in the fact of his own knowledge of his impending madness.[4]

Everything else, though, fades into insignificance beside the memorable work of John Forster, who was to die soon after the publication of the first and only volume of his Life of Jonathan Swift (London, 1875). That book, though it carried Swift's story no further than the year 1711, was so solid a work that it gave a remarkable impetus to appreciative Swift criticism; it has, indeed, never lost its influence. From the biographical point of view it marks the beginning of the great era of nineteenth-century research--a short period when knowledge of the Dean was to progress by leaps and bounds, a period culminating in the publication in 1882 of two extended Lives of Swift and the first section of another.[5] Much

[1]See above, Part III.

[2]*Quarterly Rev.*, July, 1870, p. 25.

[3]*The English in Ireland in the Eighteenth Century*, London, 1872, I, 500.

[4]E. Owens Blackburne, "Dean Swift's Ghost," *Belgravia*, January, 1875. The passage mentioned occurs on page 399.

[5]That of J. Churton Collins, first published in book-form in 1893, appeared originally in two long articles in the *Quarterly:* April, 1882; and July, 1883.

has been accomplished since 1875. New editions of Swift's works have appeared; new material has been discovered; new and excellent biographies have been, and are being, written; but few scholars can be said to have contributed more to our understanding of the man than did John Forster in his pioneering work of 1875. When he wrote, only a score of years had passed since the days when Thackeray had regaled audiences with his story of a monster; yet, only a score of years after his death, scholarship in the field of Swift criticism was to attain to such proportions that a new edition of the Works could be undertaken, an edition which only now is beginning to be superseded. With Forster we see the first great result of the careful research and the meticulous sifting of fact which were beginning to characterize nineteenth-century scholarship, and to which most critics were already resorting, if somewhat diffidently.[1] His ardent love for everything Swiftian led him to search in every odd bypath for material which might cast some fresh light upon his subject. Unfortunately, such limitless erudition has its failings, and these are apparent in Forster's book: he attaches too great an importance to every little item which has come to his attention and discusses the inconsequential in as detailed a fashion as the really important. Thus, for instance, he devotes a long section to a description of the punning society of Laracor, and, having discovered some examples of "Castilian" dialogues, quotes from these with an interminable thoroughness.[2] In the same way, though he serves Swift scholarship well in clearing up the matter of the Dean's college life, his discussion of the subject wearies the reader by its length.[3] We should not, however, quibble, when we remember his restoration and deciphering of the "little language" in the Journal and his other sincere attempts to restore all the lost details of Swift's life.[4]

The volume, dealing, as it does, with the least important years of a long and fascinating career, can

---

[1]See, for example, A. W. Ward, "Swift's Love-Story in German Literature," *MacMillan's*, February, 1877. For carefully tracing the influence of the Swift-Stella story upon German poets in a manner not unworthy of a modern scholarly journal, the author apologizes, since many will regard this as mere idle pedantry; his sole excuse is that he finds the subject interesting! Of the other scholarly works of the period, perhaps the most significant can be found in C. W. Dilke's *Papers of a Critic*, London, 1875, I, 351ff; and in Dr. Bucknill's very scientific "Dean Swift's Disease," *Brain*, January, 1882. Both Elwin and Courthope, in their edition of Pope, of course, added much to our knowledge of the friendship of the two Augustan geniuses.

[2]See pages 204-11 and also note to p. 248. My references are to the New York edition, 1876.

[3]*ibid.*, 42-56. See also the lengthy discussion of the two versions of *Baucis and Philemon*, 171-89.

[4]Many of his discoveries, not utilized in his published volume, were deposited in the South Kensington Museum, where they have provided much material for later scholarship.

hardly be recommended to the casual student: in the mass of information accumulated therein the man Swift is virtually lost. His personality stands out less vividly than in many a slighter essay. Had Forster completed his work, Swift might have emerged as a living figure, but in this first volume even the outlines of his character are but barely sketched. We know little more after all our reading of it than that Forster is in enthusiastic sympathy with the Dean and that he believes him to have been sincerely religious, humane, and "naturally cheerful." (p. 212) Reserving extended discussion of the Stella-Vanessa problems for the never-to-be-written later volumes, the author hints at disbelief in the marriage, since he can find no sufficient evidence for it, and he scores any opinion that the relationship between Swift and Stella was unhappy:

> For what she was surrendering, then, she knew the equivalent; and this, almost wholly overlooked in other biographies, will be found in the present to fill a large place ....This young friendless girl, of mean birth and small fortune, chose to play no common part in the world; and it was not a sorrowful destiny, either for her life or her memory, to be the star to such a man as Swift, the Stella to even such an Astrophel. (153-54)

Forster himself apologizes in his Preface for his minute examination of detail; and his own expression of the necessity for such elaborate consideration of Swift's least importance years makes perfectly clear the purpose of his book--and its chief virtue:

> Few men who have been talked about so much are known so little. His writings and his life are connected so closely, that to judge of either fairly with an imperfect knowledge of the other is not possible; and only thus can be excused what Jeffrey hardily said, and many have too readily believed--that he was an apostate in politics, infidel or indifferent in religion, a defamer of humanity, the slanderer of statesmen who had served him, and destroyer of the women who loved him. Belief in this, or any part of it, may be pardonable where the life is known insufficiently, and the writings not at all; but to a competent acquaintance with either or both it is monstrous as well as incredible. (p. 3)

It was the biographer's object, then, to offer the reader all the available facts which should help him to a "competent acquaintance" with Swift. We cannot judge of his final performance by a fragment. Under his sympathetic, if somewhat lubberly, touch, the Dean would, I feel sure, eventually have come into full view.

Reviews of Forster's book were not unanimously laudatory. Each reviewer, while praising the biographer's scholarship, had his own little objection to offer. The Saturday Review (December 4, 1875) disagrees with Forster's defense of Swift's political change,[1] which can be explained only by the old theory of personal pique. The Quarterly (January, 1876) coldly refuses to give the Dean his due as a truly religious man and re-asserts his cruelty toward Stella and Vanessa. However, the reviewer continues, those who roundly denounce Swift the man and who yet enjoy his writings should never forget that had the man not been what he was the world would not have possessed the writer. And he concludes with the belief that Forster's work will, when completed, place Swift, "if not on so lofty a moral pedestal as seems designed for him by his biographer," at least in a more sympathetic position than ever before. (p. 80)[2] We find one reviewer indeed who goes far beyond these in dissenting from the very substance of Forster's work, and especially from his method. According to the Cornhill Magazine (February, 1876) he is a "judicious Dr. Dryasdust," (p. 172) who, by iconoclastic pedantry, may have succeeded in sweeping away many exaggerated prejudices, but has also destroyed much that was genuine; for legitimate conjecture is necessary in order to effect the portrait of a great man. Forster (constantly mis-spelled "Foster" by the writer) has wrongly tried to refute all old anecdotes, which must have had some basis in truth; he has deprived Swift of any excuse for his bitterness and has made him into a fine, amiable fellow. But we know that Swift was intensely bitter, we feel that there was something behind that bitterness, and we have a right to know what it was:

> How did a nature full of powerful and generous emotion become so strangely soured? Where did he learn the secret of that satire which resembles the stroke of a knout--cutting through skin and flesh by a single downright stroke, without preliminary flourishes or tentative blows? Where was the heart schooled which burnt so keenly against injustice, and could yet frame such hideous indictments against human nature? (p. 173)

And the writer contends that Swift's nature was always devoid of tenderness.[3]

One note, at least, is lacking in all the reviews--the Macaulayesque or the Thackerayesque; no longer do

---

[1]Forster, *op. cit.*, 336-37.

[2]See also the *Spectator*, January 8, 1876: the reviewer insists that Stella's was a sorrowful destiny; and *Temple Bar*, February, 1876.

[3]Forster has, of course, answered this charge in his gentle interpretation of the famous "When I come to be old" Resolutions. (*op. cit.*, *p.* 116)

writers pour vitriol upon the recumbent body of the Dean. They are more likely, in fact, to speak contemptuously of his earlier biographers! In the British Quarterly Review for April, 1876, we find an account of Forster's book, in which the writer chides Jeffrey for his complacent prejudices and calls the observations of Macaulay, Thackeray, and Taine nothing short of libelous. The critic believes, in contradistinction to Hannay, that Swift was a purely literary spirit drawn only by force of circumstance into political controversy. No one, he says, can rightfully call him an apostate without a careful examination of all the evidence--and this Forster alone has attempted to do, thus giving us a picture of Swift as he actually was, not as a figment of lurid imagination. And the writer sees the Dean, finally, as a man neither genial nor easy, yet not utterly compounded of melancholy; a man so thoughtful that, though truly religious, his mind stood above doctrinal forms; a man of literary temperament, who considered party a sham in which, to his misfortune, he had acquiesced, and who simply refused to fetter himself to either Whig or Tory; a man whose grimly despairing cynicism arose from a hatred of mankind which was bitter "only because he felt what love for his kind might be" (p. 160); a man, lastly, whose life was darkened by some mystery we cannot hope to solve--a something to which we may attribute all his restlessness, his seeming cruelty to women, and, above all, "that utterly loathsome coarseness that stains his works." (p. 161)

Another reviewer, John Paget in Blackwood's (May, 1876), also much in sympathy with Forster's portrait, remarks upon "the acrid animosity of Jeffrey, the reckless vituperation of Lord Macaulay, and the sarcastic flippancy of Thackeray." (p. 530) The main interest of his article, however, lies in its refutation of the marriage story--a refutation based, as the essayist significantly tells us, on a "careful and long-continued examination into the life and writings of Swift." (p. 530) He finds Monck Mason's testimony incontrovertible; the idea of a private marriage between Swift and Miss Johnson grew out of rumor and gossip, but "a story told by A acquires no additional validity by being repeated by B, C, and D." (p. 535) That Vanessa madly loved poor Swift, who, being impotent, was incapable either of satisfying her passion or averting it, is the sole fact of the whole Stella-Vanessa melodrama to which the critic can give his consent.

In James Thomson's Essays and Phantasies (London, 1881) we find the last contemporary review of Forster;[1] and here again we see the Dean's latest biographer praised for his honest and earnest labor, despite the fact that he has obscured the picture of his central figure by "the multitude of subsidiary details," and the

---

[1]"A Note on Forster's Life of Swift," dated May, 1876, 281-88.

most influential earlier commentators, Macaulay and Thackeray, roundly censured for their impressionistic sentimentality. Swift, according to the admiring Thomson, was "a model of sagacious private charity" and a champion of liberty, "with a courage and constancy equalled by few, with a power and effect equalled by none." (p. 286) The English have generally disliked him, and it is doubtful whether they even read him; they are disgusted and alarmed by a man who, as a Dean, should have been sleek and jolly, but instead was eaten to the core by a savage indignation against hypocrisy and dishonesty:

> Too strong and terrible for Thackeray and Macaulay, Swift is much more so for the average middle-class John Bull, who, while among the bravest of the brave in many respects, is one of the most timorous of mortals face to face with disagreeable truths, truths that perturb his eupeptic comfort, truths hostile to his easy old-fashioned way of thinking without thought, expecially if these truths affront his fat inertia in religious, moral, or social questions. (p. 287)

Thus, in the space of a few years a remarkable change has taken place in the conventional attitudes toward Swift; and his famous calumniators have themselves been repudiated--at least as critics of the Dean. His so-called political apostasy, especially, has at last found champions. Besides the articles already mentioned, we find a defense of Swift's politics in an essay in Blackwood's (November, 1876) called "Swift and Lord Macaulay," by a writer who considers the Dean's "most malignant slanderer" to be the man most resembling him in character and genius--a man who never knew the passion of love, who hated with gusto, and whose power of inflicting torture was even greater than that of his vilified predecessor! (p. 528) And William Lecky, in his History of England in the Eighteenth Century, the first two volumes of which were published in 1878, offers another refutation of Macaulay's insinuations in the fact that from first to last "an exclusive Church feeling" was Swift's genuine passion, though it was inevitable that, having been brought up as secretary to Temple, he should have entered public life with Whig prepossessions. (I, 157)

On August 7, 1877, Leslie Stephen wrote to John Morley à propos of the English Men of Letters series:

> Put me down for 'Johnson,' if you please.... I have a kind of sneaking feeling that 'Swift' would have made a better life, and he has had no Boswell. But I suppose that

> you have someone else in your eye, and, after all, it does not much matter.[1]

Morley did, in fact, intend to write the biography himself, but so much other work intervened that by January, 1882, Stephen had accepted the commission and had already begun his task. "If I cannot," he wrote to Edmund Gosse, "make an interesting book out of such a hero I deserve to be excommunicated."[2] Some years before, in a few passages of one of his greatest works, Stephen had given the world an appetizing foretaste of his impression of Swift. He had written of him as one who excites a strange mixture of repulsion and pity, as a shrewd, vigorous cynic, whose bitterness showed that he had "not parted with his illusions without a cruel pang,"[3] as, in short, the most tragic figure in English literature, resembling a deeply cursing victim "tied to the stake and slowly tortured to madness and death." (loc. cit., p. 372)

> He stands in fierce isolation amongst the calmer or shallower intellects of his time, with insight enough to see the hollowness of their beliefs, with moral depth enough to scorn their hypocritical self-seeking, and with an imagination fervid enough to give such forcible utterance to his feelings as has scarcely been rivalled in our literature. But he had not the power or the nobility of nature to become a true poet or philosopher or reformer. (p. 374)

This fierce, tragic figure, with an eternal curse on his lips, reappears in the pages of the finished biography.[4]

Within the limits of this study we cannot hope to summarize in detail Stephen's characterization of the Dean. It is perhaps sufficient to point out that the author adds nothing materially new to what was already known of Swift's life, that he refuses to agree with those who have called the Dean a political apostate, (op. cit., p. 74) and that he reserves judgment on the marriage question and considers it hardly worth discussion, since, whether or not the ceremony was performed, it was nothing but a ceremony. (p. 133) For the rest, despite his admiration for the Dean, the biographer evinces an ill-concealed aversion toward his personality and discourses with little relish upon what have seemed to other critics some of the strongest points in Swift's favor. Actually, I suppose, it is the very strength of

[1] F. W. Maitland, *Life and Letters of Leslie Stephen*, London, 1906, p. 302.

[2] *ibid.*, p. 346.

[3] *History of English Thought in the Eighteenth Century*, 1876. I quote from the second edition, London, 1881, II, 34.

[4] *Swift*, London, 1882. My quotations are from the New York edition, 1898.

Swift's character which most distresses the fastidious mind of Leslie Stephen. We find him making contemptuous remarks like the following, in reference to Swift's humble letter to Temple, requesting a recommendation: "This seems to be the only occasion on which we find Swift confessing to any fault except that of being too virtuous." (p. 24) He seems to think of the Dean as constantly in a furious state of resentment, "whether against the fates or some personal object" (p. 30), as one whose friendships were rather "annexations than alliances" (p. 31), a "consistent egotist" (p. 75) with an "imperious demeanour" (p. 102), who, charitable though he may have been, thought always of himself first--a monomaniac. For his solid scholarship and his appreciative understanding of literature in general, Stephen must be admired. His book utilizes all the known facts and, brief as it is, offers them in thoroughly digested form; it is concise and yet illuminating; its discussions of the greater works are, as we shall see, of the first order. But he had one failing: an over-concentration on the serious and moral side of life; and thus Swift, a sufficiently tragic figure from any point of view, becomes completely tragic. Swift as a man of tender sentiments, of a gay and light humor--Swift, indeed, as James Hannay had been perspicacious enough to see him--never appears in Stephen's book.

To some extent his biography seems to have revived the old antagonism. One reviewer, as contemptuous of Swift as his ancestors, censures the biographer for his willingness to palliate obvious cruelty and selfishness.[1] Another, speaking of Swift as "one of the standard authors whose books are not read," finds him honest in purpose but dishonest in method, cruel to women though constant in his friendships with men, and, like Pope, having an "unrivalled capacity for debasing" his genius.[2] Edward Dowden, in the Academy (September 30, 1882), tempers his admiration of Stephen's work with the remark that the biographer has tried to be too just; he even hints at a need for a certain obscurantism in the field of scholarship:

> When a man effuses a legend about himself, much of the real man's virtue lives in the legend; we need be in no hurry to disengage the prosaic figure from the mist which magnifies it. (p. 233)

And, insisting that the perfect biographer of the Dean must be both attracted and repelled, he makes much of the old paradoxes: Swift's vices were inverted virtues, his foulness "cleanliness grown rabid"; he was "a patriot who hated his country" and "a philanthropist who scorned his species." His ideals of moral excellence were, finally,

---

[1] *Athenaeum*, September 30, 1882, 425-26.

[2] *Spectator*, September 23, 1882, 1228-29.

contradicted by his own limited nature:

> The Houyhnhyms (sic)...are calm, rational, benevolent creatures, devoid of passions: and he himself is devoured by scorn and hate. They have not learnt to say the thing that is not: and Swift does not scruple to print monstrous falsehoods for a party purpose. They are modest and cleanly: and Swift flings ordure in the faces of women and of little children. They have tranquil deaths, towards which they move with resignation: and he makes his exit in a rage. (ibid.)

Swift, no longer a monster but still a raging giant--this, it seems, was the impression produced by Leslie Stephen's attempt to portray the Dean impartially. Only one critic, keener than the rest, noted the unfortunate defect of the Life. A true lover of Swift, said a writer in the Saturday Review (September 30, 1882), would hardly have chosen Leslie Stephen as his biographer:

> Mr. Stephen cannot taste intellectual cakes and ale; he thinks Saturday night and high jinks childish. The quick alternation of laughter and tears, the change from savage invective to humorous trifling, vexes him and throws him out. (p. 443)

It is the reviewer's interesting contention, in fact, that Swift was primarily a humorist and only incidentally the tragic figure of deep earnestness.

Interesting though it was, Stephen's book, primarily a popular one, could hardly satisfy thoroughgoing students of Swift. It had barely reached the public, however, when a new Life of Jonathan Swift appeared, the work of Henry Craik, who gave the world in completed form what John Forster had been unable to finish--an authoritative, well-documented biography. Published in London in 1882, it immediately became the standard authority and has not even yet been entirely superseded. Craik's accomplishment cannot be over-estimated. His book is as scholarly as Forster's without the top-heavy treatment of minor details. It adds much to knowledge of Swift's life, yet reads easily; for, as far as possible, it relegates discussions of controversial matters to appendices. It utilizes much new material[1] and reprints the interesting Holyhead Journal, discovered by Forster and originally edited by Collins in the Gentleman's Magazine (June, 1882). From a careful consideration of newly discovered letters it carries on Forster's work of clarification and of making Swift's motives and actions more comprehensible. And, in so far as such a thing is possible, the

---

[1]See *Preface*, xii-xiv.

author sacrifices his prejudices to an impartial consideration of every biographical fact which throws light upon the personality of the Dean as he really must have been. His object, as he tells us, was not to attempt to paint Swift as a man of conventional virtue in the manner of most of his early champions. Scott, for instance, had admired Swift in spite of his politics, in spite of his misanthropy, and, in part, because of his sincere belief in the truths of Christianity:

> But before we begin to make allowances for Swift's politics, as antiquated and unpopular, we must be sure that we have found out the true key to their adoption by one very considerably in advance of the current opinion of his own or of any other time. If we look upon his misanthropy as only an occasional blemish which mars his genius, and which we must endeavor either to forgive or to forget, the chances are that, in our apology, we may miss an essential trait in Swift's character, whose origin we should rather seek to explain, and whose influence in his work it is our business to trace. As to his acceptance of religious dogma, without denying or doubting its sincerity, may we not doubt whether we have described it rightly, in labelling it with the mark of conventional and respectable orthodoxy? (p. x)

This attitude, to be sure, which seeks not to extenuate but to explain and understand, was by no means a new one. Lesser men than Craik had seen that only in such a method lay the solution to the problem of Swift criticism. But the transcendent importance of Craik's work rested in the fact of its thoroughness.

His conception of Swift is above all that of a magnificent genius, whose very powers were a source of uneasiness to him, because, always great, they were often "restless, morbid, and undisciplined." (p. 43) Keenly sensitive and fiercely indignant, he was doomed from the beginning to loneliness, for he could not help seeing what was hidden to more conveniently "healthy" men--the "infinite littleness of humanity; the endless and hopeless reign of disorder and injustice: the ludicrous incongruity between principle and practice." (500-01) Thus his religion was bound to be unconventional; of an intensely earnest nature himself, he could not help treating irreverently what he saw in others as sheer cant. For himself he never attempted to follow "the mazes of metaphysical speculation" (p. 502); his conception of religion, neither profound nor elevated, was none the less clear and masculine:

> His formal creed touched only the surface of the real religious feeling that

> underlay, and gave meaning to, his cynicism, no less than his tenderness. But he held that formal creed with what we may call a stern rigidity, and with no mere semblance of belief. (p. 162)

In the same way his politics were based upon a hatred of abstract reasoning; while others laboriously theorized, he pierced "straight to the heart of a question" (p. 503) and "never ceased to judge his party, not by their professed principles, but by their acts." (p. 504) Thus his change from Whig to Tory "involved no surrender of principle." (p. 201)

Craik concurs in the traditional belief in Swift's marriage to Esther Johnson,[1] unconsummated, however, not because of sexual impotence, but because of a certain world-weariness, forebodings as to the future state of his health, and a morbid intellectualism which left little room for "feelings that with most men are so strong." (p. 331) He refuses to grow sentimental about the fate of Stella, since, he says, she made her own choice and, so far as we know, accepted it without question. There is, he avers, little connection between the stories of Stella and Vanessa. Former biographers have wrongly linked the names together; for the two women stood in totally different relations to Swift, and there should be no question in his conduct of "a vulgar and thoughtless infidelity" to either. (p. 313) Vanessa flattered Swift's weaker side, but she never succeeded in gaining a real hold on his heart; their friendship continued, once it had begun, on a very "limited" footing--it "played only on the outside of Swift's life." (p. 317)

> Without the story of Vanessa, Swift's life would have stood out, more clear, more complete, and less ambiguous: without the story of Stella, it would have been a maimed and lopped fragment, with one half of the man's nature wanting. (p. 324)

As he grew older Swift became more and more the lonely, despairing misanthrope, haughty and domineering; but in his prime--and it is this quality that makes Craik's a finished portrait--he was tender, he was bright, he could be sweet-natured, he had a quick and subtle humor which lacked only calmness to give it warmth. (179-80)

In this picture of Swift, then, no more true in its essentials than that of some lesser men, but painted upon a broader canvas with more attention to detail, we see the man as he appeared to his most successful biographer--great and good and clear-sighted, and with such depths of unfulfilled power that happiness was inevitably denied to him in this little world of ours. And with that picture--

---

[1]See Craik, *op. cit.*, Appendix IV.

so understanding and yet so impartial--we have reached the last phase in our study of the development of the reputation of Swift in the nineteenth century. Much has happened since; opinions have changed and knowledge increased. But it is hard to believe that any new information will ever arise necessitating marked changes in the general outlines of Craik's portrait. There has been impressionistic criticism since 1882, and there always will be, doubtless, critics with facile pens and novel points of view; but the painstaking scholar with a merely normal imagination will seldom, I believe, come to essentially different conclusions from those of Henry Craik.[1]

---

[1]I have not discussed John Churton Collins' biography of Swift, although its first section appeared in the *Quarterly Review* for April, 1882, since the work was not completed until the following year; and when it was published as *Jonathan Swift* in 1893, the whole thing was revised and enlarged. After all, Craik's book marks a significant point at which to conclude our study. The great accomplishments of later scholars can, indeed, be considered as carrying on the traditional methods so excellently exemplified by the work of Forster and Craik. For contemporary reviews of Craik's biography, see *The Saturday Review*, January 13, 1883; George Saintsbury in *Academy*, February 17, 1883; and *Blackwood's*, March, 1883. These are in the main extremely favorable. The *Spectator*, January 20, 1883, is not; it accuses Craik of too much leniency toward Swift's faults.

II

The Works

1

Personal Papers and Political Writings

The Journal to Stella had been originally published in two sections. Hawkesworth brought out Letters 1 and 41 to 65 in 1766; and in 1768 Letters 2 to 40 were first edited by Deane Swift. The originals of those published by Deane Swift have disappeared, but those printed by Hawkesworth were deposited in the British Museum; and there it was that John Forster discovered them and made a careful collation of the first and twenty-four out of twenty-five of the last of the series. Needless to say, he found that both the original editors had been unscrupulous in their treatment of the Journal; in their regard for Swift's reputation, they had omitted or changed much of the "little language" and "polished" the phrasing throughout. With characteristic energy, Forster made a point of restoring and deciphering the original language of the letters, in so far as he could, in order that posterity might have some idea of what Swift had really written. This was certainly a praiseworthy object: Swift must be seen as he really was, no matter how puerile and nonsensical he might appear to the more serious-minded. And so, besides a long chapter which summarizes the general trend of the Journal (op. cit., 306-28), Forster included an even longer appendix (420-73), printing all the restored passages with explanatory notes wherever possible.

A renewed interest in the Journal was thus aroused. Before 1875 most critics had found the prospect of Swift in undress a rather charming one. His most brutal detractors had enjoyed the racy picture of the last years of Queen Anne's reign, with its utter lack of self-consciousness and its incontestably tender concern with the affairs of Mistress Johnson. They had welcomed the privilege of looking at the Dean through a key-hole; but the absence of restraint which they admired was not really absence of restraint at all. The Swift they saw was clothed in flimsy garments constructed for him by his cautious editors. D. Laing Purves, in his introduction to the work, praises Swift for his ability to stand the trying test of appearing, metaphorically, a hero to his valet. The Journal, he says, shows Swift in night gown and cap, unreservedly testifying to his every picayune mood and indulging in the childish nonsensicality of "playful condescensions" to Stella. (op. cit., p. 226)

The nonsensicality as Forster gives it, however, seems less like a playful condescension to Stella than an integral part of the Dean's very thought. It pervades the work in a way that earlier readers could hardly have suspected. It is Swift really living a life of "stealth"; and there is in its whimsy--one cannot avoid the feeling--a something almost morbid, as though one has blushingly come upon the Colossus of Rhodes playing at jacks. Some of Forster's early readers were grateful to him for helping to humanize Swift to this unprecedented extent. In his Essays and Phantasies James Thomson expressed his gratitude in especially warm terms:

> Here for the first time we read, just as they were written, the "little language" and the caressing diminutives and abbreviations Swift used with his darling; the delightful, fantastic, secret, childish, infinitely tender babblement, never weary of repeating itself, welling up amidst and around the records of the ruggedest affairs of State, like perennial springs of pure sweet water in a region of savage rocks....The sternest cynics have such soft places in their heart of hearts! incomparably softer than the softness of unctuous sentimentalists; liquid with living fountains where these are boggy with ooze. (p. 284)[1]

But others were repelled rather than attracted by the newly discovered extravagant littleness of the "little language." The Cornhill (February, 1876), which finds "something anomalous and not exclusively edifying in this queer billing and cooing, this fondling and petting--rather maudlin, we would say, than manly," (p. 181) calls upon "Mr. Foster" to explain why Swift's tenderness evaporated in such hyper-sentimentality. "Why did Swift's love, like his patriotism, and his friendship, and his genius, become a source of suffering!" (ibid.) Burton finds in the Journal weakness of character, vanity, and other defects "of a nature not to be palpably discussed in an age of decorum like the present."[2] To Leslie Stephen the Journal is a fascinating document; though Swift has failed to touch upon much that might be of great historical interest to us today, and though his letters contain no seriously introspective passages which might give them the interest of a confession, the Journal is singularly delightful. The reader is like a man waiting in a parliamentary lobby during an exciting debate, the recipient of hasty bulletins poured out with an unconscious betrayal of hopes and fears by one of the chief actors. (op. cit., p. 81) But there is one drawback: the tender

---

[1]See also *Quarterly Rev.*, January, 1876; and *Blackwood's*, May, 1876.

[2]*Hist. Reign of Anne*, p. 274.

playfulness is charming, but it is addressed to a mature woman of thirty:

> Macaulay imitates some of this prattle in his charming letters to his younger sister, and there we can accept it without difficulty. But Stella was not Swift's younger sister. (p. 125)

And Craik, appreciative as he is of the Journal, says of Forster's work of collation and interpretation: "Not a few may deem that such secrets lose in charm more than they yield of biographical interest, by a too painful nicety of interpretation." (op. cit., p. 530)

As a writer of political pamphlets Swift receives more justice from the critics of this period than from those of any earlier age. The English and Irish tracts are alike praised by most writers for their clever arguments and nervous forcefulness of style, and especially for the fact that often, as the North British Review (January, 1870) puts it, "unconsciously to himself, he was aiming beyond the abuse at which he struck." (p. 169) And the same writer, not always friendly to the Dean's memory, yet points with admiration to his work in the Irish conflict: whatever his faults and limitations, his thoughts "constantly dwelt upon Irish grievances" and "his vision was all the clearer to see the transparent iniquities of foreign government." (p. 181)[1]

Charles Cowden Clarke was one of Swift's most outspoken supporters. His essay in the Gentleman's Magazine for September, 1871,[2] which is not very solid from the biographical point of view, concerns itself primarily with literary criticism. He makes his attitude toward Swift the writer apparent in the following lines:

> HAD Swift written no other verses than those on his own death, he would have deserved honourable mention among our national poets; had he written no other history than the "Tale of a Tub," he must have ranked among our greatest wits; had he produced no other work of imagination than "Gulliver's Travels," he would have been great among the greatest satirists; had he put forth no other tracts than the "Drapier Letters," he would have deserved a votive offering from the nation whose interests he had undertaken to protect; and had he projected no other scheme than the plan of an Academy for the correcting and enlarging, polishing and fixing of his native language,

[1]See also Froude, *The English in Ireland*, pages 503 and 530: in "colours which will never fade" his genius condemned the Wood transaction to "an infamous immortality."

[2]"On the Comic Writers of England," VI.--"Swift."

> he might have claimed the gratitude and reverence of the whole British people. (p. 436)

His satires, says Clarke, castigate such universal human weaknesses that they will never lose their freshness; and the greatest of these in the purely political realm are the Irish pamphlets!

> His arguments are so naturally adduced, and his principles are so clear and homely, that perusal and conviction are simultaneous.... And yet, plain and simple as these compositions appear at first sight, and such as any ordinary writer might imagine he himself could produce, as he would a letter of ceremony; yet, inspect them critically, and they will be found to have been constructed with consummate art and skill. (443-44)

And much is said of something left virtually unnoticed by former critics of the tracts--their homely, quiet humor, which helps to make them "so interesting that the reader must indeed be inert who can quit them." (p. 445)

Personal prejudice as a criterion of literary value has, to be sure, not yet breathed its last. In his Manual of English Prose Literature (Edinburgh, 1872) William Minto, for example, who was a Scotchman, expressed his disapproval of the Drapier's Letters in no uncertain terms. In this work, he said, the Dean pictured unreasonable consequences of the Wood measure, and appealed with his groundless charges to naive passion instead of to reason. His ludicrous exaggerations in the name of liberty would have been laughed at, except for "the strong feeling existing against England, which blinded the Irish to every consideration of reason." (p. 432) Yet, except in the case of the Irish tracts, Minto accorded Swift a full measure of praise as a pamphleteer. The Conduct of the Allies, with its skilful and calm presentation of fact, demonstrates Swift's consummate ability to pick out and to show in a strong light "facts that were escaping general notice," thus relieving the public "from the fascination of military success, and fixing their eyes on the other side of the picture." (p. 431) What, in fine, he possessed more than any other political satirist of his time were unexampled powers of persuasion.

And with this last judgment few men disagree. Swift is an unrivaled master of political satire; "when he bites, he bites to the bone," and "when he shows his teeth, he scares his antagonists" and strikes them dumb.[1] He was, says Lecky in his History of eighteenth-century England, "the most effective political writer in England

[1] *Spectator*, January 8, 1876, p. 46. See also *Spectator*, September 23, 1882, p. 1229; and *Athenaeum*, September 30, 1882, p. 425.

at a time when political writing was of transcendent importance." (I, 158) But though Lecky, who was not, as I have said, a notably original critic of the Dean, considers the Drapier's Letters perfect models of "popular political eloquence and argument," (II, 424) animated in great part by a generous hatred of injustice, he speaks of Swift's patriotism as "of a very mingled order" and of his indignation as an outgrowth of "personal disappointment acting on a nature singularly fierce, gloomy, and diseased." Swift united the Irish by his energy and intellect--but also by rather questionable means; and, Lecky remarks, it should not be forgotten that, despite his criticism of Wood's contempt for the Irish parliament, he himself did everything in his power to discredit that same governing body when it touched the interests of his religious order, by writing an invective "which is perhaps the most savage in English literature." (II, 425-26)[1]

A better judgment of the Dean's work in Ireland comes from the pen of Stanley Lane-Poole, whose long essay in Fraser's of September, 1881, on "Swift and Ireland" consists of quotations from the tracts with critical, historical, and biographical comments; the gist of what Lane-Poole has to say is contained in the following lines:

> His work in Ireland ought to have given him more satisfaction than any other phase of his varied life.... He was not always right in his judgments; he was very seldom pleasant in his counsel; he told the people unpalatable truths in the roughest tones he could command; he spared no man, still less a woman, in the cause of justice; he scrupled no virulence of abuse when he had oppression and fraud to chastise. And in spite of his rude manner and contemptuous tone, the people worshipped him. He taught them that their opinion was a power, that the passive resistance of men's minds could withstand a bad law and turn aside the purpose of a government. He created a public opinion in Ireland, and he guided it. (p. 400)

We turn now to the three great biographers of the period, Forster, Stephen, and Craik. What did they have to offer either new or stimulating in criticism of Swift as a political writer? The work of Forster on this score is, of course, negligible. His book closes with Swift's change to the Tory party, mony months before the publication of The Conduct of the Allies, when his only important published tracts were the early and not too interesting Contests and Dissensions of the Nobles and Commons in Athens and Rome, in which the biographer can find little worth noting beyond the statesmanlike qualities of its

[1]He means, of course, *The Legion Club*.

arguments (op. cit., p. 142), and several of the Examiner papers. To these latter Forster gives high praise: their unshrinking confidence, their grave humor, their "short telling sentences" and eminently suitable illustrations, their style and wit and simplicity of manner--all these qualities told. Nor were they over-vitriolic in tone; "Swift was not so clumsy at his own craft"; savage invective came only later in the heat of hard-fought battle. (p. 345)

It is to be regretted that Forster was not permitted to deal with Swift's later political work. The first of his successors, Leslie Stephen, was hardly suited for the job in taste or temperament. To him the Dean's political writings are "acts" rather than words; their merit lay primarily in the effect they caused; Swift cared only to hit his mark, at the cost of eloquence, logic, even veracity; and so, despite their vigor, they make decidedly "heavy" reading. (op. cit., p. 88) The intensity of Swift's absorption in the immediate end partly deprives the Irish pamphlets of literary merit; "and we, to whom the sophistries are palpable enough, are apt to resent them. Anybody can be effective in a way, if he chooses to lie boldly." (p. 158) In general Stephen's remarks about Swift's genius, frequent as they are, cannot overcome our opinion of his inability to appreciate the true power of the Dean. We may agree with him that the economics of the Drapier's Letters are faulty; but we lose patience with his studiously serious discussion of the speciousness of Swift's half-humorous arguments against Wood's halfpence.[1]

Henry Craik is more capable of following and appreciating the strength and range of Swift's magnificent sarcasms; he begins, for example, by accepting the fact that it was not in the Dean's nature "to treat with elaborate minuteness the details of statistical facts." As he puts it in his significant account of the Conduct:

> They have no fascination for himself, and he knows they will be worthless for the purposes he has in view. But although details are never allowed to be cumbrous, it is perfectly evident that Swift, in preparing the pamphlet, has sifted evidence, examined treaties, made himself master of official documents, to an extent never equalled in any other of his works. And yet to the rapid composition of the book is due much of its sustained and telling force. He writes under the impulse of one strong mood of indignation, which has no time to vary or calm down; and it is his special strength to infect his hearers

[1] See, for instance, pp. 153-54, where Swift's certainly rash, but delectably sustained, arguments in Letter II are refuted with solemn dignity.

> with the same heat of anger. (op. cit., 235-36)

Thus, says Craik, it is a mistake to suppose that the Dean himself believed in the truth of much of what he declared would be the consequences of Wood's halfpence. "His object was simply to put a scandalous transaction in the grossest aspect possible." (p. 349) But even from the time of the first of the Drapier's Letters Swift saw the question as a greater one than that of the simple matter of coinage; and in the fourth letter, "instinct with life, and thrilling with sarcastic force," he asserted with consummate vigor what the first pamphlets had been leading up to: a cry for the independence of Ireland. Boldly he tore to pieces the flimsy technicalities of debate and came straight to the point, to defy all the sickening cant of his opponents. This straightforwardness of expression and this swiftness of movement make the political tracts enduring monuments of controversial literature.[1]

2

Bagatelles and Miscellaneous Works

Thackeray and others had almost totally neglected Swift's lighter side; when they had touched upon his fun-making, they had either taken it seriously or deprecated it, in pathetic misunderstanding of the man and of the age in which he lived. Toward this attitude a reaction begins to set in with the broadening tastes of the latter part of the century. An unwillingness to accept Swift as a pleasant humorist perseveres in some minds, to be sure. Charles Cowden Clarke, though ranking him among England's comic writers, repeats the old statement that he wrote too much "trumpery," which should never have been printed (loc. cit., p. 452) Burton finds the Directions to Servants irresistibly attractive, yet so filthy that it haunts him with the horror of a "nightmare-dream." (loc. cit., p. 275) And Leslie Stephen, who considered Swift's the only readable eighteenth-century sermons, because he "has a real go in him which cannot be quenched even by theology,"[2] could not appreciate that "go" in its lighter manifestations; he found, as we learn from the biography of Swift, the Directions to Servants unpleasant in its details, though a masterpiece of trivial satire--"admitting such satire to be legitimate" (p. 199)--the Polite Conversations "perversely" amusing (p. 197), and the Partridge Papers of a not very "exquisite flavour" (p. 59)!

But this refusal whole-heartedly to accept Swift as a humorist is not concurred in by other critics. Hannay, for example, finds him equally great in both serious and

[1] See also Craik's discussion of the *Examiner* papers, pp. 204-09.
[2] *Life and Letters*, p. 248.

playful composition. His Sentiments of a Church of England Man, his Letter to a Young Clergyman, and his other completely serious works are masterpieces of exposition and reasoning, but "if at other times he brought in his marvellous humour to assist these qualities, that ought not to have detracted from their merit since it added so much to their effect."[1] According to Hannay, Defoe's Shortest Way with the Dissenters is clumsy as compared with that specimen of murderous irony, the Argument against Abolishing Christianity; and this is also the opinion of William Minto, who singles out the Argument and the Modest Proposal less for their serious intent than for their subtle and surprising turns of wit. "Swift had real humour," wrote Carlyle in a letter to William Allingham; he "could really banter and enjoy a joke, the grimmest real humourist I know of."[2] James Friswell, whose admiration for Swift stops only this side idolatry, commends him for having "introduced into literature a great deal of humour, and what is now known as fun."[3] And both Forster and Craik treat the more trivial pieces respectfully, though, as biographers, both men evince more interest in their biographical backgrounds than in their literary value. That Forster even enjoys Swift's puns is evident from his extensive treatment of the subject; and of course he finds the Partridge Papers "exquisite." (op. cit., p. 235) To Craik, however, we owe the most illuminating appreciation of this little-understood side of Swift's nature. In speaking of the Directions to Servants and of the coarseness which clings to almost every part of the Dean's genius, he says:

> Without the keen insight, without the deliberate and relentless dissection, without the plain and homely humour, without the contempt for conventional grades of dignity, which are so distinctive of the Directions to Servants, that genius could not exist. (op. cit., p. 475)

The critic of the Saturday Review (September 30, 1882) whom I have already cited as regretting Leslie Stephen's inability to enjoy "intellectual cakes and ale" takes violent exception to Stephen's frigid remarks on the Polite Conversations. Stephen, he insists, has completely missed the "exquisite flavour" of the work and "the wonderful skill with which Swift has outlined his various characters, the wealth of social satire, the way in which, under a merely 'modish' guise, perennial distinctions of temper and manners are indicated, the positive personal interest in the speakers which this book excites." (p. 443)

The same writer, with his interesting theory that Swift was pre-eminently a humorist, refuses to believe in the Modest Proposal as a diatribe against oppression.

[1] *Temple Bar*, October, 1867, p. 325.

[2] From Allingham's *Diary*, ed. H. Allingham and D. Radford, London, 1908. The letter dates from October 13, 1874.

[3] *Essays*, p. 219.

Swift was not the fiercely indignant warrior his biographers have painted him, says the critic:

> He was from first to last a misanthropic pessimist, and his misanthropic pessimism was always genuine. He was from first to last a political gladiator who fought not for pay, but partly for love and partly for conviction, and his political animus was always genuine likewise. But the immediate occasions of the exercise of his genius were for the most part accidental, and we no more believe that he seriously considered English government of Ireland as per se oppressive than we believe that he really thought the ancients superior to the moderns. In saying this, we are bringing no charge of insincerity against him, but merely deprecating the ascription of an excessive sincerity. (443-44)

This is a thought-provoking point of view, but its limitations are obvious. At any rate, we find no other such denial of the Dean's earnestness of emotion. Certainly "that ghastly piece of irony,"[1] A Modest Proposal, is taken as a heartbreaking cry against Irish extremities by all who comment upon it.[2]

Most of Swift's lesser works, both humorous and serious, are mentioned by Stephen and Craik, and by Forster as far as he has gone; but really stimulating criticism is, after all, reserved for the more famous masterpieces. Beyond a few remarks on the sweep of Swift's irony and the straightforward good sense of his serious style our critics do not, in general, choose to go, preferring rather to give the context of the pamphlets and to examine them simply for such light as they throw upon Swift's thought. With this attitude the modern reader can hardly quarrel. Swift's reputation has developed along lines marked clearly by three all-important criteria: first, his life and personality; secondly, his art as expressed in the Tale, the Battle, Gulliver, and, to an extent, the poetry; and lastly, the general impression of his ability as a writer created by a survey of both his life and work, as each illuminates, supplements, or belies the other. Comments upon his minor works have never been lacking; but even had those minor works remained unwritten, his critical reputation would, as I think this study has shown, have been but slightly affected.

---

[1]Lecky, *History of England*, II, 217.

[2]See, for example, *North Brit. Rev.*, January, 1870, p. 184; Stephen, *op. cit.*, 162-63; and Craik, *op. cit.*, 414-15.

3

The Battle of the Books and A Tale of a Tub

James Thomson was tempted at first to blame Forster for occupying space in a book not intended for "the uneducated vulgar" with extended accounts of such classics as the Battle and the Tale. But on reflection he decided that the "so-called educated classes" actually needed "formal introductions to these works." (loc. cit., p. 286). It is certainly true, as we have seen, that, though both masterpieces had been read and at least touched upon by most critics in their discussions of Swift, very little careful thought had been wasted upon them prior to the last part of the nineteenth century. Neither the Tale nor the Battle lends itself easily to critical analysis; and the commonest approach to both has been historical. In the case of the Tale attention has centered upon its allegory and its religious sincerity or lack of it; and critics have been content to discuss the Battle of the Books as the high point of the quarrel about ancients and moderns, or as an example of Swift's originality or lack of it--depending on whether or not the critic has seen the French book upon which it was supposed to have been based.

We find a typical sample of pre-Forster criticism of the Battle in Allingham's casual remarks in Fraser's (November, 1867) upon its quiet irony, its happy descriptions, its coarse jestings--and its intrinsically worthless arguments (p. 644). This is, naturally, all true, with the truth inherent in most vulgar estimates of great works of art; that the Battle was, as a later writer puts it, "so purely popular that it lost nothing by being whetted on the wrong edge"[1] can hardly be gainsaid. The fault of the statement lies in the fact that it does not go far enough: there is much more to be said about this, the most exquisite of Swift's shorter pieces. The spider and bee episode, for instance, had never, from Orrery to Forster, been singled out for the praise it deserves as a spirited and meaningful piece of prose. It is Matthew Arnold perhaps to whom we should credit the re-discovery of what has become the most famous passage in the work. His Culture and Anarchy, published in 1869, must have sent readers scurrying to their editions of Swift to see the source of an expression which runs like a leit-motif through Arnold's book: "the two noblest of things, sweetness and light." It is, therefore, of little moment that, in the very act of making Swift's words his own, Matthew Arnold gratuitously remarks upon the fact that the Dean "of one of the two, at any rate, had himself all too little" (p. 23).

Forster seems to have thought himself the first to refute with any degree of certainty Wotton's charges of plagiarism in the Battle, though he must have known that

---

[1]R. C. Jebb, *Bentley*, London, 1882, p. 77.

Monck Mason had done so back in 1820. His chief contribution to criticism of "this triumphant piece of humour" (op. cit., p. 104), however, lay in his appreciative summary of its incidents (106-08) and in his pointing to the episode of the spider and the bee as a noteworthy one. There is, he says, not a line in this extraordinary piece of "concentrated" humor which does not run over with sense and meaning.

> If a single word were to be employed in describing it, applicable alike to its wit and its extravagance, intensity should be chosen...; not an episode or allusion being introduced merely for itself, but every minutest point not only harmonizing or consisting with the whole, but expressly supporting and strengthening it. The apologue of the Spider and the Bee is so marvelously good as almost to cheat one into the belief that there is a question to fight over. (p. 108)

But Forster's remarks are as nothing to those of one of his reviewers--an anonymous writer whose insight into the value of the Battle provides us with probably the best criticism of the work to appear during the nineteenth century. To the British Quarterly Review (April, 1876), with its unusual conception of Swift as a standard example of the literary spirit, the temporary controversial matter of the piece was as nothing compared with its eternal truth. Swift, with his finely tempered weapons of ridicule, placed the contest between ancients and moderns in a new light. He was not merely a dependant of Temple, assuming the defense of his master:

> To us it seems quite evident that, however his advocacy is marred by his personalities and distorted by the necessities of his position, his place was naturally on the side of the Ancients in the dispute. Stript of its accessories, that side represented the protest against the anarchical element in literature. It maintained the standard of classic taste, as opposed to the erratic flights of over-strained originality.... That, with all its varieties, a certain adherence to some classical standard, be it ancient or modern, is necessary, was the first principle of his creed, as it is of that of every man impressed with the literary spirit. If we fix upon the finest passages in the book, which are those where there is least of personal reference, we shall find that this is precisely the point upon which Swift insists. (p. 148)

And the writer, finding the gist of the dispute in the spider-bee episode, speaks of the bee's words to the spider as extending the range of the quarrel "far beyond the merits or defects of this or that Ancient or Modern."

> They apply not merely to the fray between Temple and Wotton, or Bentley and Boyle; they express the very marrow of the truth which literature must always maintain, that excellence depends not on accidental coincidence with the taste of a day or a clique, but upon permanence of duration, upon harmony with the calmest judgment, and, at the same time, the most 'serious emotion' which even the Edinburgh reviewer could not achieve. (p. 149)

This, it seems to me, is literary criticism of a high type; it shines still more luminously when contrasted with other contemporary opinions. The Battle is, to the Quarterly (January, 1876), "a piece which we confess we have never had much pleasure in reading" (p. 51); and to the Cornhill (February, 1876), it "has ceased to be very amusing." (p. 181) Leslie Stephen, too, makes, as usual, a point of damning with faint praise:

> Swift probably knew and cared little for the merits of the controversy. He expresses his contempt with characteristic vigour and coarseness; and our pleasure in his display of exuberant satirical power is not injured by his obvious misconception of the merits of the case. The unflagging spirit of the writing, the fertility and ingenuity of the illustrations, do as much as can be done to give lasting vitality to what is radically (to my taste at least) a rather dreary form of wit. (op. cit., 35-6)

It would seem, then, that to the typical nineteenth-century mind the Battle of the Books appealed only as a rather dreary form of wit, well-executed but dull. Our admiration for the greater insight of the British Quarterly increases when we find Craik, the best of the critics, repeating its sentiments in different words. Swift's preference for the ancients, he says, went deeper than literary criticism:

> He preferred them because of their opposition to all the undiscipline of incompetent assumption, because of their freedom from all that moved his satire in ages nearer to his own. His abhorrence of that self-assertion which piques itself on originality because it knows no rule, lay at the very root of Swift's literary, as it did of his religious and moral, judgment. (op. cit., p. 72)

Thus the Battle has in a way come at last into its own; and the same thing is also true of A Tale of a Tub. I do not mean that the Tale attains to universal acclaim. It does not. Its coarseness and its flippancy help to restrain the encomiums of Swift's most sympathetic Victorian critics. Those critics do, however, see values in the work not apparent to their predecessors.

The most interesting discussion of the Tale prior to Forster's is that of William Allingham (loc. cit., 643-44). Others, greatly appreciative of the piece, judge it according to established standards: Hannay, for example, argues for it as a satire against the corruptions of Christianity, not against Christianity itself (loc. cit., p. 325); Charles Cowden Clarke showers upon its allegory adjectives like "fine," "delightful," "masterly," and calls it "the highest order of satire" (loc. cit., p. 441); and Minto praises its constructive skill (loc. cit., p. 422). But Allingham denies its greatness, "wonderfully clever as it is"; and the originality of his strictures lies in the fact that he approaches it primarily from the point of view of its structure and literary meaning, with no reference to its Christianity or lack of it, and with only one incidental remark about its "foul smell." His chief quarrel with the book is that it is "amorphous" and not eminently readable.

> The abundant images and illustrations, often ingenious and pithy, are at best the product of a whimsical fancy, not of a humorous or witty imagination; they are clever but not truthful and delightful, not exhilarating, nor satisfying.... The broad Rabelaisian jesting on Peter and Jack threw no kind of light upon Catholicism or Calvinism. (loc. cit., 643-44)

This is interesting, not because it is true, but because it at least tries to judge the Tale as a work of art.

To Forster the Tale of a Tub was "the earliest of the two greatest prose satires[1] in the English language," (op. cit., p. 157) for which, admitting the one objection of "its insufferable coarseness," hardly any praise could be deemed excessive. To the corruptions of religion and learning it applied an "astonishing and never-ceasing play of wit and raillery." (p. 165) Forster's chief contribution to criticism of the Tale, however, was his pointing out what had never before been given proper significance: "that the corruptions of religion and the abuses of learning handled in the Tale of a Tub are but the continued pursuit, in another form, of the controversy between the claims of ancients and moderns." (p. 109)

With Forster's opinion the reviewers in general agreed, with both the Quarterly and Cornhill elaborating

[1]The other was, of course, *Gulliver*.

upon the inexcusable indecencies of the work. The writer in Cornhill goes so far as to say that, vigorous and excellent a performance as it is, "no man could enjoy The Tale of a Tub, and certainly no man could write it, in whom reverence, tenderness, and love formed the most essential element of religious feeling." (p. 182) And Leslie Stephen, testing the work by the imaginative process of giving it to Bishop Butler and Voltaire to read, asks:

> Can any one doubt that the believer would be scandalized and the scoffer find himself in a thoroughly congenial element? Would not any believer shrink from the use of such weapons even though directed against his enemies? (op. cit., p. 43)

We cannot help thinking that Stephen, so much out of sympathy with the very essence of Swift's being, was less well-qualified to write his biography than the anonymous British Quarterly reviewer of Forster, who once more comes to our rescue with the sensible observation that it is not necessary to accept Swift's allegory in order to appreciate the marvelous genius of the Tale. What commands our admiration is, he says, "the ease with which the allegory succeeds for the time in achieving its object, be that what it may, and in making all but its own standpoint seem utterly ridiculous." (p. 149)

It is in Craik's long discussion of the work, however, that we find the most compelling criticism of the century. Craik emphasizes the forgotten truth that the allegory of Peter, Martin, and Jack includes only about one-third of the book; and he finds this portion the poorest part of the whole, strained in metaphor, irregular in proportion, and limited in satirical appeal. (op. cit., p. 109) To such a judgment few readers would whole-heartedly subscribe; but as a corrective to traditional opinion its value cannot be over-estimated. Since Craik few men have dared to discuss the Tale simply as a religious allegory. He opened our eyes, so to speak, to its wider application:

> It is because it expresses with such absolute and even reckless freedom, the whole range of the author's mind, because it plays so easily round all subjects of human interest, that the elasticity of its humour has moved each generation, and retains its hold upon us now with all the freshness and vivacity of youth. It has abundance of faults. It is digressive, and occasionally diffuse: it has many mannerisms, and its humorous dress is of an antiquated, to some, it may seem, even an artificial, fashion. There is no graphic or dramatic interest to sustain the reader. It is often obscure, and some of its effects are due to

> topics which to us have no more than antiquarian interest. But all these are only new proofs of the central interest of the book. It is not only by its flashes of wit, by its bursts of eloquence, by the steady and relentless beat of its satire, that it is redeemed: but still more by the marvellous strength and grasp with which the whole of human nature is seized, bound to the dissecting table, and made to yield to his pitiless scalpel, the tale of its subterfuges, and pretences, and tricks. Other satires have their special application. Who is it that can limit the range of the satire in the Tale of a Tub? (p. 102)

In the dedication to Prince Posterity, Craik finds a perfect example of a power peculiarly Swift's--that of covering with dignified and eloquent argument what is underneath "nothing but arrant inconsistency and nonsense in a solemn dress" (p. 104). This, he says, is an unexcelled method for a superior kind of sarcasm, which resembles only in its tone of irony the Hudibrastic stream to which it might be compared; for Butler only occasionally glances at some larger truth of human nature, whereas Swift begins with a wide view of humanity and works downwards and inwards. (107-08) It is this universality of application which makes of the Tale so telling a work of satirical genius. And in his realization of that fact, Henry Craik cleared the way for the fuller appreciation of what some consider Swift's greatest and most representative work--an appreciation which has increased with the passing of the years.

4

Gulliver's Travels

It would be a gross libel on the critical species to say that after the middle of the nineteenth century there was nothing left for the critic to talk about, where Gulliver's Travels was concerned. But it is none the less true, as we have seen in the course of our study, that the field had been very largely canvassed by earlier commentators. From the moment of its publication--and even before--Gulliver was talked about at length by all who read it. It fascinated its readers; it mystified them; it called forth all their faculties for perception and interpretation. So it was that by 1865 the critic could hardly hope to add a great deal to pure literary criticism of the work. We need only glance at D. Laing Purves's introduction to Gulliver (op. cit., 110-12) to see how opinion of it had crystallized to a point where individual thought on the subject must have seemed unnecessary. All the old critical dicta, all the old catch-phrases, fall glibly and with categorical finality from the pen of the writer: the charm of the story, its verisimilitude, the force of the satire, the reversal of the telescope in the first two voyages, the observance of exact proportions, the inferiority of the third voyage, and the libelous quality of the fourth. To one or more of these elements each critic who mentions the book pays his respects. Allingham loves the story, "not profound, but simple, striking, unforgettable, new to every generation." (loc. cit., p. 651) Clarke finds the moral of the book admirable in its implied reverence for true honor and worth and praises its machinery as not nearly so easy of achievement as Dr. Johnson had thought it. (loc. cit., 446-48) J. Nichol, in his article on Swift in Ward's English Poets, remarks upon "the hideous immortal mockery" of the fourth voyage and terms it, as we should expect, a "terrible libel."[1] The only stimulating discussion of the work before Leslie Stephen's comes from the pen of the critic in the North British Review (January, 1870), who offers an unusual apology for it.

He begins by calling its personalities and political satire relatively unimportant. The more the narrative advances, he says, the more Swift rises to general principles of state polity. His plan throughout was to show what a country should be rather than to ridicule its defects; and, being an Englishman to the core, "he detested as visionary and dangerous whatever could not be measured by plumb and line." It is this feeling, continues the writer, which explains the voyage to the Houyhnhnms. Instead of being merely the spleen of a misanthrope, it is in actuality a refutation of Mandeville's cynical and indecent philosophy:

> The natural man, whom Mandeville, like Rousseau at a later date, believed to be simple, veracious and temperate, Swift saw as the savage or the Yahoo.....On the other hand, destroy thought and literature, restrain natural affection within the narrowest limits, and reduce the science of life to the provision by simple instinct for common wants, and the most perfect exemplar of polity will be among beasts. Voltaire's remark after reading Rousseau, that "he did not wish to walk upon all-fours," is in fact the spirit of Swift's answer to Mandeville. It is a satire upon the Englishman of his time, "the reasoning, governing animal of his country;" but it is emphatically a vindication of humanity. (182-83)

But the writer of those words, despite his laudable effort to look beneath the surface of the book, can be accused of reading into Gulliver what Swift had no intention of putting there. Curiously enough, it is Leslie Stephen who provides the best discussion of the work

[1] I quote from the 1922 London edition, III, 35.

before Craik. He makes, of course, the obvious remarks: the book is almost the most delightful child's story ever written and at the same time an unrivaled satire (op. cit., p. 168);[1] its charm lies partially in its "sobriety of fancy, " which leads to its apparent realism (p. 169); and its success in simulating plausibility gives the lie to Johnson's words about the rest being easy once you have thought of big and little men (170-71). But beyond all this, Stephen sees--what few men have noticed--Swift's creation of delightful characters, Glumdalclitch in particular; and he insists upon the evident good humor of the first two voyages, in which Swift really "seems to be amused, as well as amusing." (p. 171) And in his treatment of the allegorical intent of the work, the critic analyzes it with thoroughness and perspicuity. We may not, to be sure, agree with his conclusions; but that fact will not invalidate his criticism.

Hazlitt's contention had been that Gulliver strips the mask of imposture from the world, that it hits at nothing of true worth; but Stephen, considering the matter coldly, cannot agree. There is no question, he says, of right or wrong in the war between Lilliput and Blefuscu. Swift's real sentiment was not that of a moralist, but of a superior being, who looked down upon mankind and found it contemptible. He created the machinery of size in his first two voyages merely to bring his readers into a frame of mind congenial to his own:

> We despise the petty quarrels of beings six inches high; and therefore we are prepared to despise the wars carried on by a Marlborough and a Eugene. We transfer the contempt based upon mere size to the motives, which are the same in big men and little. (p. 175)

What Stephen is saying is, in short, that Gulliver is Swift's allegorical method of showing the world how much he despised it; the Dean has proved nothing and has attempted to prove nothing; he has simply provided for himself, and for every man who despises his species, "a number of exceedingly effective symbols for the utterance of his contempt." (p. 176) If this is true of the first part of the book, how much truer is it of the last! In the voyage to the Houyhnhnms and in his hideous picture of the Struldbrugs, Swift has carried his wrath against mankind and life itself to its highest pitch, and these portions of Gulliver are oppressive in their misanthropy. Yet we must rather pity than condemn the tortured and perverted spirit which engendered these lamentable "caricatures." (p. 182) It was not, as Edward Dowden put it in his review of Stephen's biography (Academy, September 30, 1882), that Swift expected "infinite things" from

[1]See, however, the *Spectator*, September 23, 1882, which says that *Gulliver*, although it can never be a dead book ("revised for family reading"), is eagerly sought after by neither children nor adults!

life, but that he thought men might at least be clean, temperate, and rational; and he found them nasty and diseased--"creatures by so much more hateful than the Yahoo as corrupted reason is worse than brutality itself." (p. 233)

No longer did apologists try to explain away Swift's misanthropy. It was there; it was obviously the burning inspiration of Gulliver's Travels; all the impartial critic could do was to attempt to understand it. Like Stephen, Craik finds more good humor than bitter satire in the first voyage, and much contempt for the pettiness and triviality of human nature in the second--though, "bitter as is the drift of the satire in Brobdingnag, it is not without relief." (op. cit., p. 391) In both Lilliput and Brobdingnag we are carried along by the amusing story and forget that we are laughing at ourselves;[1] but in the last two parts the allegory becomes charged with bitterness: Swift concerns himself less with careful construction and nicely adjusted proportions than with a direct expression of sheer hatred.

> It is not without purpose, that Gulliver is made to return from Lilliput and Brobdingnag, by vaguely described and almost miraculous means; while from Laputa he sails to the allied empire of Japan, and from the Houyhnhnms prepares for his voyage as he would have done in starting from Rotherhithe. In the latter region, we are no longer in realms of pure fancy, but only in places where the ordinary laws of nature are confounded in a bewildering jumble. Fancy and reality are constantly intermingled. As the Academy of Lagado comes nearer to the type of human crotchet-mongers, and as the Yahoo typifies more closely humanity, so the construction of the allegory fails, but so also the directness of the satire is increased. (p. 391)

The fourth voyage, clumsy in fable, coarse, and with "no great depth of satiric force" (p. 392) in its fancy of horses ruling men, is none the less a powerful sentence of despair. Scathingly it "strips off the trappings and disguises with which we deceive ourselves, and leaves us face to face with the stern realities of our nature and our lot." (ibid.) But, Craik asks, was it possible that Swift satisfied himself with his picture of the ideal Houyhnhnm--a creature so lacking in emotion and affection? And as an answer to that question he offers a startling theory: might not the portrait of the Houyhnhnms be but "another ply of the satire on humanity, whose best ideals could be attained only be eliminating all

---

[1]Compare *Brit. Quart. Rev.*, April, 1876: *Gulliver* is the most intense tragedy ever penned; yet the world "must laugh at its own pitiful discomfiture." (p. 159)

that made life worth living, but whose passions and emotions, when ripened to full maturity, ended only in the loathsomeness of the Yahoo?" (ibid.)

This, if really Swift's purpose, would be misanthropy carried to its logical extreme. But one cannot feel that the Dean, even in his tragic later days, entirely lacked sympathy with his fellow-men. If his picture of the ideal horses seems insipid, the fault may equally well be due to the fact that his interests were concentrated upon the negative rather than the positive side of his argument. With all Craik's exhaustive analysis of Swift's mind and art, one wonders whether he has come any closer to the truth here than some of his quick-sighted--if less thorough--predecessors.

5

The Poetry

Dryden's unforgiven criticism of Swift as a poet referred to the Pindarics. These early efforts of the Dean have never been considered good poetry, even by his least severe critics. In general, however, we read his octosyllabics today with pleasure--and we call them poems.[1] The latter years of the nineteenth century witnessed a movement in this direction, but the romantic idea of poetry survives in the strictures of two works published in 1880. Nichol, in his introduction to the selection of Swift printed in Ward's English Poets, says of the Dean's genius that, though powerful, it was not refined enough to be poetic. With an undeniable talent for rhyme, he nevertheless wrote verse merely because it was the fashion. It is careless, harsh, frigidly complimentary or coarsely vituperative; its sole merits are those of his prose: "condensation, pith, always the effect, generally the reality, of sincere purpose, and, with few exceptions, simplicity and directness." (loc. cit., p. 37) This is not poetry. The society verses are like those of a man writing with his feet, for Swift, despising art, delighted in trampling upon what others caress, and rode rough-shod "through bad double rhyme and halting rhythm, to his end. War with the cold steel of prose was his business"--his poems "mere side-lights." (p. 38) And Burton, shocked by the Dean's indelicacies, poses the rhetorical question, "Why, to use a plebeian metaphor--why continually rub our nose in it?" (loc. cit., p. 277) Continuing by contrasting Swift with Byron, who, though he could be as sarcastic as Swift, was "endowed with a sense of the sublime and beautiful," the critic does justice to the true worth of neither. There is something almost prurient in the manner in which, utterly neglecting some of Swift's better-known poems, he dwells upon the "vile insinuation" of the notoriously equivocal lines

[1]See, for example, Quintana's discussions of the verse, especially *op. cit.*, 358-62.

in Cadenus and Vanessa and upon the verses famous for their scatology--verses which, if uttered today, would be deemed a "stinging insult" by "every gentleman who had wife, daughter, or sister to cherish and protect." (p. 280) It was, after all, the historian's smug theory that his own age could be "witty and censorious with scarce a particle of the depravity of the age of Pope and Swift." (p. 283)

But these remarks are reactionary rather than representative. In general, critics have become less arbitrary in their impression of the true function of poetry, and Swift is praised for what he has done, instead of being censured for not doing what Milton had done. Friswell, who thought him "a wonderful genius, who did every thing he did do as no other man of the time could do it," (loc. cit., p. 217) called the verses on his death "some of the noblest, wisest, deepest, and saddest verses ever written." (p. 218) Clarke found the "austere drollery" and the "most pure vein of irony" in some of the poems "extremely amusing"; and he called attention to the "golden thread of pathos" running unaffectedly through certain passages. It is not without significance, either, that with no hint of fault-finding he simply states the fact that "Swift was the poet of sterling, downright sense, and not of speculative fancy, or of excursive imagination." (loc. cit., p. 448) And one writer, commenting upon Dryden's prophecy, establishes the case for Swift as a poet in clearer terms than those of any previous apologist:

> One can imagine Rubens saying to his pupil, the elder Teniers, ere the latter deserted 'high art,' and devoted himself to 'Dutch drolleries:' 'Pupil David, you will never be a painter!' But David made himself and his son into most effective painters, though neither of them painted fleshy Flemish Madonnas or fleshy Flemish chivalry. Swift could not have written 'Alexander's Feast;'--granted. Could Dryden have written 'Cadenus and Vanessa,' or the 'Humble Petition of Frances Harris'? Had Swift stuck to Pindaric odes...it may be admitted that he never would have been a poet. When he struck into his own peculiar vein of fancy and humour, he became one. It is not the choice of subjects familiar or elevated that confers the title of poet; it is the inspiration of the poetical breath of life into the subjects chosen, whatsoever they may be.[1]

Most of the Dean's best poetry was written after the period of which Forster writes, but the most congenial of Swift's biographers undoubtedly admired his verse. In his long discussion of Baucis and Philemon he makes

[1] *Quarterly Rev.*, January, 1876, 76-7.

evident his belief that the changes in the poem made at Addison's suggestion weakened instead of improving it. (op. cit., 171-87) There is no question in Forster's mind as to Swift's poetical judgment. And even Leslie Stephen concedes poetic merit to the verse. Though it is in essence merely Hudibrastic rhymed prose, and though Swift was never a poet in the sense in which Milton or Wordsworth or "even" Dryden was a poet, yet, says Stephen in somewhat muddle-headed fashion, the Dean's verse "differs from prose, not simply in being rhymed, but in that the metrical form seems to be the natural and appropriate mode of utterance." (op. cit., p. 202)

I have used the adjective "muddle-headed" advisedly. In the words just quoted, it seems to me, Stephen has granted to the poetry the very element which distinguishes poetry from other forms of literature. Elsewhere he has called it, even in its earliest and worst manifestations, thoroughly sincere (p. 54); he has claimed originality for it (p. 202); he has felt a suppressed passion, a "glow and force of feeling" in the verses On the Death of Dr. Swift, which "affect us with a sentiment which may be called poetical in substance more forcibly than far more dignified and in some sense imaginative performances." (202-03) Yet, with all this, he hesitates to give it the name of poetry. It is the name alone at which he stops, frustrate!

In Craik's biography we find a novel point of view, which marks a vital departure from former attitudes--not toward the poetry of Swift perhaps, but toward Swift as a poet. The Dean, says Craik, may be said never to have found fully congenial work into which to throw his unreserved energies. From the very beginning, with his unsuccessful Pindarics, he was fighting a battle for expression, with an almost "passionate eagerness to find an utterance for his own strained feelings." (p. 73) And though he never attempted to rise to great heights of poetry, though he studiously avoided the passionate and, once rebuffed in his effort to achieve conventional sublimity, consciously kept to his unique note of humorous irony, there was in the original bent of his genius something which his accomplished work does not contain. In his verse there are no flights of imagination and no grandeur of emotion or form:

> But when we search through the tangled mazes of the Pindaric odes: when we watch their tensity and earnestness in the light of these early confidences[1]; when we place side by side with them the fierce energy of the later verses,--evident as is the severe repression therein of any poetic fancy,--we feel that Swift, though he never attained to true poetic utterance, had a temperament,

[1]Craik refers here to the recently discovered letters to Thomas Swift, in which the young poet hesitatingly confides his aspirations.

> which in his own words, was "blasted with poetic fire."... But how much of Swift's cynicism, how much of his waste of power, how much of his apparent indifference to fame, was due to the withering of those early aspirations, and to the repression of a temperament of surpassing keenness, forced to utter itself only in the language of satire, and not of poetry? (498-99)

The verse itself is lucid, brilliant, broad in range; but it is merely the repressed effluence of an essentially poetic nature compelled through external factors and through its own limitations to write prose! This is Craik's stimulating theory.

III

Swift the Writer

Where, then, did Swift stand in the literary hierarchy in the days of Forster and Craik? Today we grant him a place high in the list of Britain's natural geniuses, but that fact hardly distinguishes our age from former periods. Our study has proved, I think, that at no time has there been any question in the public mind as to the Dean's genius. Seldom indeed has anyone seriously dissented from the general opinion of the power and intensity of his art. But the periods of greatest antagonism toward him have differed from our own in their unwillingness to understand and accept that art for what it is. They have sought in him more than he had to give--or, at any rate, they have censured him for giving what they did not care to take. Men of keen mind have never been wanting, and they have sprung to his defense; but today--and herein lies the uniqueness of the present age--he requires no defenders. His life and personality apart, he is accepted unquestioningly as the author of some of the most telling works in the language. We read him for his own sake and enjoy him accordingly. We should count that man lost who might deny merit to Milton and Wordsworth because neither of them could have written A Tale of a Tub. And so it is with Swift. He wrote A Tale of a Tub, and we thank the gods for it, with no reservations on the ground that he was not also responsible for Paradise Lost.

In the days of Forster and Craik the modern spirit was already emerging from the chrysalis of the past. The picture we have seen of men like Jeffrey and Macaulay and Thackeray recoiling from Swift's genius at the very moment of admitting its excellence has begun to fade. The scene has changed; the gloom has risen. Only off in the corner stands an occasional solitary figure, still deploring with his fathers the Dean's lonely earthiness. Leslie Stephen is one of these, in spite of himself; for he obviously cares little, though he avoids a definite statement of his distaste, for the Dean's way of thinking, for his preoccupation with things temporal, for, in short, his indifference to the mystical aspects of life.[1] And Burton, entirely out of sympathy with his subject, compares Swift unfavorably with those who were infinitely greater in the breadth and beauty of their genius--Shakespeare, Scott, and Milton--and calls the Dean's art a poisonous one; he may at times have administered the lash where it was needed, but who could envy him such a "hangman's duty"? (loc. cit., p. 280) And, with the History of the Four Last Years as an example, he suggests

[1]See, for example, his discussion of Swift's religious beliefs, *op. cit.*, 47-50.

that Swift could write only very dreary, commonplace English "when he had to restrain himself, and has been able to lay his demon for a time." (p. 281) Which is, indeed, as much as to say that the Dean could write well only when inspired--an amazingly brilliant observation, of amazingly slight critical value.

William Allingham states another point of view in his essay in Fraser's (November, 1867), in which, perhaps, there is a kernel of truth. It is his idea that Swift's fame apart from Gulliver does not rest upon his literary works at all, excellent as they were, but upon his striking life-story. His works afford "but poor nourishment for the soul"; the critic finds in them, as he finds in all literature of the "thin" Augustan age, only practical sense, vigorous realism, and ironic humor. Swift was, to be sure, stronger and more sincere than most of his contemporaries, but his satire, while it forcibly smites vice and folly, too often "attacks human nature itself." (p. 652) Allingham despises the coarseness so characteristic of the Dean. In this respect he speaks for his age. Without exception, critics of the period are repelled by the foul odor exhaled from so many of Swift's pages.[1]

But aside from his scatology, Swift the writer has in general come to be appreciated as never before. Critics have more and more begun to realize that the truths he tells, though often "nasty," are essentially strong and valuable, and that they are expressed with unparalleled art-concealing art. Young people, says James Friswell, can neither read nor enjoy Swift's works, with the exception of Gulliver's Travels; "but when men and women are grown up and know the world, then indeed no deeper nor wiser guide can be taken." (loc. cit., p. 219) And the critics of Friswell's time seem to have attained somehow to the maturity requisite for a full appreciation of the Dean. Their objective is a completer understanding of his genius; their method, a reading of his works with as few preconceptions as possible. Why, asks Mackay, in the New Monthly (September, 1870), have so many commentators kept in the background, as it were, "those whole pages of genial and sunny humour, of innocent joke, and quaintly perpetrated pun?" (p. 352) And why, in criticizing him both as man and writer, have they tried to see dishonesty and insincerity where the printed

[1]Even Forster, *op. cit.*, p. 164, can find no adequate excuse for this. See also Stephen, *op. cit.*, 177-78; Craik, *op. cit.*, *passim*, but especially p. 501; Minto, *loc. cit.*, p. 419; *Brit. Quart. Rev.*, April, 1876, p. 161: Swift's utterly loathsome coarseness is "the suggestion of his incipient madness, or its cause..."; and others. *Blackwood's*, November, 1876, p. 534, says that it should at least be remembered to his credit that in an age "when 'The New Atalantis' was the fashionable novel, when Congreve and Vanbrugh were the most popular of dramatists, and Prior was read by young ladies as Tennyson is now," Swift never wrote a line really calculated "to arouse licentious passion or to weaken the bonds of morality."

page gives no hint of these; why not judge him according to what he has written, especially where "the printed page and the performed act do not give the lie to each other?" (ibid.)

This idea is echoed by Clarke in the Gentleman's Magazine (September, 1871). He sees no reason why Swift's satire--other than the unfortunate fourth voyage of Gulliver--should be conceived of as a disparagement of human nature. And he finds a reflection of Swift's own straightforward character in the perfect transparency and determination of purpose of his style:

> It will be observed that in his writings we rarely meet with a superfluous word, and never with a superfluous epithet....Swift is the most English, the most thoroughly national in his diction of all our classic writers...; and, moreover, he is master of the idiomatic peculiarities, and lurking, unapparent resources of the language to a degree of perfection that leaves him almost without a competitor. (p. 437)

It is this idea that the man himself can be best known through what he has written which signifies the new conception of the primary function of Swift criticism. And that the excellence of what he has written depends entirely upon its own merits is equally a postulate set forth by the new critics. Says the British Quarterly (April, 1876): "Literary excellence does not accept the limitations that may fitly be placed upon us in our social responsibilities. If what it expresses be true, it has fulfilled all we can demand of it." Thus, the writer continues, though Swift's satire has been called evil and though we may regret its expression of things better left veiled, "we cannot question its truth because we question its expediency." (p. 149) And he goes on to say that only if we understand the peculiar qualities of the Dean's special type of humor can we appreciate the misanthropy that runs through his writings. His humor was intense and concentrated; it was a temperamental clarity of vision, to which no human deception "could prove a veil."

> And he had the gift besides of unrivalled clearness of language, which served to lay before his reader the whole truth of the vision that he saw, unexaggerated by any false rhetoric, unsoftened by any drapery of words. His style is calm, cold, unimpassioned as a piece of sculpture; with no tawdry ornament, no mannerism, no slovenly ambiguity.... To feel the littleness of the good and the vastness of the evil ever before him, would shake the nerves of the most steadfast martyr, and make the tongue of the most fervid preacher dumb. But upon

> this sight Swift could never close his mind's eye; and, sleepless himself, he could not suffer others' sleep.
>
> The power that could create real humour, which the world would know for such, out of this grim material, was even more marvellous than the clearness of vision itself. And yet it is unquestionably there. (p. 159)

Thus, concludes the critic, for his amazing ability to treat grim tragedy in terms of humor Swift remains "in his own peculiar line...the greatest genius which England ever produced." (p. 161) And others repeat this extreme approbation of the Dean's art as a fact hardly requiring proof![1]

There is, we are told by another commentator, a "masterly and inimitable quality of internal truthfulness" in Swift's writings, and few other authors have achieved results "which seem so easily explicable and yet are so absolutely incontestable and so perfectly secure."[2] To this impression of persistent effectiveness Minto's Manual also lends its authority. With all the palpable faults of the Dean's style--a simplicity which verges on coarseness, an insolent sarcasm, a studied repudiation of the kindly and pathetic, a savage impatience, and an intense egotism--with all these faults, says Minto, Swift's work, taken as a whole, leaves upon the reader's mind an unexampled impression of eloquence, wit, and originality, as compared, for instance, with such common and hasty "performances" as those of Defoe. He combined subtle wit with demoniac perseverance, a notable clarity and correct syntax with a refusal to indulge in any obviously striking peculiarities of style, and an ability to use the English language either unadorned or filled with brilliant metaphor and fanciful imagery:

> The surprising persistence and power of his efforts appears not less in the quantity than in the quality of his analogies. In the 'Tale of a Tub' and in 'Gulliver's Travels,' the multitude as well as the aptness of the parallels between the imaginary

---

[1]See *Sat. Rev.*, September 30, 1882, p. 444: Swift is one "whom some critics do not hesitate to rank as the greatest prose writer of the severer kind in the English language"; *North Brit. Rev.*, January, 1870, p. 185: Swift is our greatest English satirist. There have been skilful mechanics of style in every age, but Swift, when he wrote from the heart, wrote "for eternity"; and *Quarterly Rev.*, January, 1876, p. 44: Swift's works have won a permanent place in the modern mind, "which they will no more lose with any generation of intelligent readers, than the world will 'willingly let die' Pantagruel's history, or the Pilgrim's Progress."

[2]*Sat. Rev.*, December 4, 1875, p. 716.

> narrative and the facts allegorised are absolutely unrivalled among works of that nature, and could have been conceived only by the greatest powers at the maximum of intense concentration. (loc. cit., p. 417)

These words, it must be remembered, were penned by one not always in complete sympathy with everything Swift wrote.[1]

And so the "exiled" Dean of St. Patrick's, who died "like a poisoned rat in a hole," who wrote ostensibly for his day alone, and who became a great author virtually without caring, would have found himself, could he have known it, a living force nearly a century and a half after his death. More than that, he would have seen the light of his works shining brighter and more steadily than ever before. "The questions agitated in his day," says Craik, "are forgotten; its party struggles and its political theories have passed away: but his genius is for us no mere historic memory." (op. cit., p. 506) His art lives; and it will always live--not alone for its purposeful lucidity of style, nor for the commanding calmness of its humor, "with its back-ground of grim earnestness" (ibid.)--not for these, magnificent as they are, but, above and beyond them, for the stern sincerity with which he has forever pinioned within the covers of his books that most universal and hateful of demons, the something called Cant. The mere shams of one generation are, according to Craik, "soon fathomed and exposed" by the next:

> But who can place bounds to the dominion of Cant? Who can say into what specious theories it does not enter, over what sphere it fails to leave its trail? And yet, though the preacher cannot rid us of it, it must still blanch in all time coming, before the calm irony of Swift's humour, before the relentless tragedy of the picture that his genius has drawn. If his pride was boundless, if his anger was consuming, they have at least left to us a rich inheritance, in the discomfiture which that ever-present foe suffered at his hands. (p. 507)

---

[1]See his criticism of *Drapier*, above.

CONCLUSION

Nearly sixty years have passed since the publication of Henry Craik's biography of Swift. The twentieth century has witnessed a remarkable recrudescence of interest in the literature of the Augustan age, and modern scholarship has helped us to take unprecedented strides in the direction of a better understanding of the period. No study of the Dean's reputation since 1882 would dare limit itself geographically to the British Isles; on the European Continent and in America scholars have accomplished so much of essential value that their work can never again be disregarded. Critical biographies and book-length studies of Swift have literally flooded the presses. Factual contributions to the study of his life and works have appeared in learned journals with an almost disconcerting regularity. All his prose, his correspondence, his poetry, have been edited and re-edited, studied and re-studied, during the past half-century. Men have even made new discoveries; they have printed hitherto unpublished letters; they have combed the background of his masterpieces and have searched, not in vain, for sources; they have re-established the known facts of his life upon a firmer foundation.

And yet, how much better do we know Jonathan Swift than did Henry Craik and his contemporaries? Inevitably we must see his picture more finely outlined against the background of his age, but is our vision any clearer, any deeper, than that of those who read and appreciated him with none of our comfortable aids to comprehension? No one has yet solved the mystery of his life and personality. Men still argue about the truth of his marriage to Stella. His life is still open to new interpretations: of late he has been judged a victim of "sexual anaesthesia"[1] and through posthumous psycho-analysis has been found to be a consummate "egoist," with all the concomitant Freudian complexes.[2] Prejudice, controversy, misunderstanding have not died, nor ever will. Scientific research, much as it has accomplished and much as it may yet accomplish, can provide the literary critic with scattered bits of information to bridge the still unfilled _lacunae_ of his factual knowledge, but it cannot breathe an organized life of thought into that knowledge. Without the shaping spirit of his imagination, without keen critical insight, the modern scholar is little better off than were Sheridan, Scott, Hazlitt, and Hannay. For a complete understanding of Jonathan Swift, whose eyes penetrated beyond the veil of surface shams, a like clarity of vision must always be essential; and no amount of pedestrian scholarship can do more than prepare the way for the miracle of apprehension.

---

[1]Gold, *Swift's Marriage to Stella*, p. 128.

[2]M. M. Rossi and J. M. Hone, *Swift; or, the Egoist*, New York, 1934.

Over a period of nearly two centuries the way has been prepared. The reputation of Swift has developed in consonance with the changing ideals of successive ages; and if this study, in following that development, has any reason at all for being, its value lies in its demonstration of what should be an obvious truth--the continuity of human thought, the universality and permanence of some few transcendent ideas. Jonathan Swift is as alive today as he was in 1700, as he was in 1882. We need to hear his message. We need more than ever to listen responsively to the clear, ringing tones of his voice.

BIBLIOGRAPHY

(At one time or another I have consulted most of the books on Swift that have been printed since 1882. Occasionally some of these have been cited in the notes. Those most often cited are:

Pons, Emile. *Swift--Les Années de Jeunesse et Le "Conte du Tonneau,"* Strasbourg, 1925.

Quintana, Ricardo. *The Mind and Art of Jonathan Swift,* New York, 1936.

Teerink, Dr. H. *A Bibliography of the Writings in Prose and Verse of Jonathan Swift, D. D.,* The Hague, 1937.

Good bibliographies of other publications since 1882 can be found in Quintana and Teerink.)

SOURCE MATERIAL

(I have tried to use the earliest British editions of the works cited. When these have not been available, I have made it clear in the notes which editions I have quoted from. In this bibliography I have followed the same procedure. Periodical articles by known authors are included both in the list immediately following and in that of the periodicals.)

Aikin, Dr. *Select Works of the British Poets. With Biographical and Critical Prefaces,* London, 1820.

Allingham, William. "Moor Park and Swift"--*Fraser's* (Nov., 1867) (pseudonym--Patricius Walker, Esq.)
A Diary, ed. H. Allingham and D. Radford, London, 1908.
Letters to William Allingham, ed. H. Allingham and E. B. Williams, London, 1911.

Anderson,. Robert. *The Works of the British Poets. With Prefaces Biographical and Critical,* vol. IX, London, 1795.

Arnold, Matthew. *Culture and Anarchy,* London, 1869.

Barrett, John. *An Essay on the Earlier Part of the Life of Swift,* London, 1808.

Beattie, James. *Essays: On Poetry and Music,* Edinburgh, 1778.
Dissertations Moral and Critical, London, 1783.

Beddoes, Thomas. *Hygeia or Essays Moral and Medical,* vol. III, Bristol, 1803.

Berkeley, George-Monck. *Literary Relics.... To which is prefixed, an Inquiry into the Life of Dean Swift,* London, 1789.

Berwick, Edward. *A Defence of Dr. Jonathan Swift, Dean of St. Patrick's, Dublin; in Answer to certain Observations passed on his Life and Writings, in the fifty-third number of the Edinburgh Review,* London, 1819.

Blackburne, E. Owens. "Dean Swift's Ghost"--*Belgravia* (Jan., 1875).

Blair, Hugh. *Lectures on Rhetoric and Belles Lettres,* London, 1783.

Boswell, James. *Life of Samuel Johnson,* ed. G. B. Hill, Oxford, 1887.
Journal of a Tour to the Hebrides, ed. F. A. Pottle and C. H. Bennett, New York, 1936.

Brougham, Henry Lord. *A Discourse of Natural Theology*, 1835. Revised edition, Edinburgh, 1872.
Historical Sketches of Statesmen who flourished in the Time of George III. Third series, vol. II, London, 1845.

Bulwer-Lytton, Sir Edward. *Poetical and Dramatic Works*, vol. III, London, 1853.

Burton, John Hill. *A History of the Reign of Queen Anne*, vol. III, Edinburgh, 1880.

Byron, George Gordon Lord. *Poetical Works*, ed. E. H. Coleridge.

Carlyle, Thomas. *Lectures on the History of Literature; Delivered in 1838*, ed. J. R. Greene, New York, 1892.

Chalmers, A. *The British Essayists*. "Historical and Biographical Preface to The Tatler," vol. I, 1803. (Boston, 1856)

Chambers, Robert; and Carruthers, Robert. *Chambers's Cyclopaedia of English Literature*, 2 vols., Edinburgh, 1844. (Third edition, London and Edinburgh, 1876.)

Clarke, Charles Cowden. "On the Comic Writers of England," VI.--"Swift"--*Gentleman's Magazine* (Sept., 1871)

Cobbett, William. *The Progress of a Plough-Boy to a Seat in Parliament*, ed. W. Reitzel, London, 1933.

Coleridge, Samuel Taylor. *Works*. (See notes for editions used).

Collier, William Francis. *History of English Literature*, London, 1862. (Revised edition, London, 1898)

Cooke, George Wingrove. *Memoirs of Lord Bolingbroke*, vol. I, London, 1836.

Courtenay, Thomas Peregrine. *Memoirs of the Life, Works, and Correspondence of Sir William Temple, Bart.*, vol. II, London, 1836.

Cowper, William, *Table Talk*, 1782.

Craik, George L. *A Compendious History of English Literature*, 1861. (New York, 1875, vol. II)

Craik, Henry. *The Life of Jonathan Swift*, London, 1882.

Croker, John Wilson. *A Sketch of the State of Ireland, Past and Present*, Dublin, 1808.

Cunningham, George Godfrey. *Lives of Eminent and Illustrious Englishmen*, vol. V, Glasgow, 1838.

Delany, Patrick. *Observations upon Lord Orrery's Remarks on the Life and Writings of Dr. Jonathan Swift*, London, 1754.
A Letter to Dean Swift, Esq; on his Essay upon the Life, Writings, and Character of Dr. J. Swift, London, 1755.

De Quincey, Thomas. *Collected Writings* (vol. XI), ed. D. Masson, Edinburgh, 1890.

Dilke, Charles Wentworth. *Papers of a Critic*, London, 1875.

Dilworth, W. H. *The Life of Dr. Jonathan Swift, Dean of Saint Patrick's, Dublin*, London, 1758.

Dowden, Edward. Review of Leslie Stephen's *Swift*--*Academy* (Sept. 30, 1882)

Drake, Nathan. *Essays, Biographical, Critical, and Historical, Illustrative of the Tatler, Spectator, and Guardian*, vol. III, London, 1805.

Dunlop, John. *The History of Fiction*, 1814. (Second edition, Edinburgh, 1816, vol. III.)

Eagles, John. "Thackeray's Lectures--Swift"--*Blackwood's* (Oct., 1853)

Fielding, Henry. *The Covent-Garden Journal*, ed. G. E. Jensen, New Haven, 1915.

Forster, John. *The Life of Jonathan Swift*, 1875. (New York, 1876.)

Forsyth, William. *Novels and Novelists of the Eighteenth Century*, London, 1871. (New York, 1871)

Friswell, James Hain. *Essays on English Writers*, London, 1869.

Froude, James Anthony. *The English in Ireland in the Eighteenth Century*, vol. I, London, 1872.

Gilfillan, George. *A Third Gallery of Portraits*, 1854. (New York, Sheldon & Company, n. d.)
"Satire and Satirists"--*Scottish Review* (Jan., 1856). Reprinted in *A Gallery of Literary Portraits*, London, 1909.

Godwin, William. *The Enquirer*, London, 1797.

Goldsmith, Oliver. *Works*, ed. J. W. M. Gibbs, London, 1886.

Hallam, Henry. *Introduction to the Literature of Europe*, vol. IV, London, 1839.

Hannay, James. *Satire and Satirists*, London, 1854. (New York, 1855)
"Thackeray on Swift"--*Temple Bar* (Oct., 1867)

Harris, James. *Philological Inquiries in Three Parts*, London, 1781.

Hawkesworth, John. *An Account of the Life of the Reverend Jonathan Swift, D. D. Dean of St. Patrick's, Dublin.* In the *Works of Jonathan Swift*, vol. I, London, 1755.

Hayley, William. *The Triumphs of Temper*, London, 1781.

Hazlitt, William. *Lectures on the English Poets.* Lecture VI, 1818. In the *Collected Works*, ed. A. R. Waller and A. Glover, vol. V, London, 1902.

Howitt, William. *Homes and Haunts of the Most Eminent British Poets*, Vol. I, London, 1847.

Hume, David. *Letters*, ed. J. Y. T. Greig, Oxford, 1932.

Hunt, Leigh, *Wit and Humour*, London, 1846.

Irwin, Thomas, *Versicles*, Dublin, 1856.

Jameson, Anna. *Memoirs of the Loves of the Poets*, 1829. (Boston, 1857)

Jebb, R. C. *Bentley (English Men of Letters* series), New York, 1882.

Jeffrey, Francis. Review of Scott's *Edition of Swift--Edinburgh Review* (Sept., 1816)

Johnson, Samuel. *Lives of the English Poets*, ed. G. B. Hill, vol. III, Oxford, 1905.

Landor, Walter Savage. *Works*, London, 1876.

Lane-Poole, Stanley. "Swift and Ireland"--*Fraser's* (Sept., 1881)

Lawrence, Frederick. "Private Life and Personal Character of Dean Swift"--*Sharpe's London Journal* (XI, 303-10)

Lecky, W. E. H. *Leaders of Public Opinion in Ireland*, London, 1861.
A History of England in the Eighteenth Century, vols. I and II, London, 1878.

Macaulay, Thomas Babington. Review of Lord Mahon's *History of the War of the Succession in Spain*--*Edinburgh Review* (Jan., 1833)
"Life and Writings of Addison"--*Edinburgh Review* (July, 1843)
"Life and Writings of Sir William Temple"--*Edinburgh Review* (Oct., 1838)
History of England, 1855. (*Works*, vol. VIII, New York, 1898)

Mackay, William. "The Mad Dean"--*New Monthly Magazine* (Sept., 1870)

Mackintosh, Sir James. *Memoirs*, ed. R. J. Mackintosh. (Boston, 1853. From the second London edition)

Macknight, Thomas. *The Life of Henry St. John, Viscount Bolingbroke*, London, 1863.

Mahon, Lord (Philip Henry Stanhope). *History of England From the Peace of Utrecht to the Peace of Aix-La-Chapelle*, vols. I and II, London, 1836-37.
History of England Comprising the Reign of Queen Anne until the Peace of Utrecht, London, 1870.

Mahony, Francis. "Dean Swift's Madness. A Tale of a Churn."--*Fraser's* (July, 1834)

Maitland, F. W. *Life and Letters of Leslie Stephen*, London, 1906.

Mason, William Monck. *The History and Antiquities of the Collegiate and Cathedral Church of St. Patrick, near Dublin, from its Foundation in 1190, to the Year 1819*, Dublin, 1820.

Masson, David, Review of Thackeray's *English Humourists*--*British Quarterly Review* (Oct., 1854)
British Novelists and their Styles, London, 1859.

Minto, William. *A Manual of English Literature*, Edinburgh, 1872.

Mitford, John. *Life of Swift*. In *Poetical Works of Jonathan Swift*, vol. I, London, 1833.

Monk, James Henry. *The Life of Richard Bentley, D. D.*, London, 1830.

Nichol, J. *Jonathan Swift*. In Ward's *English Poets*, 1880. (London, 1922, vol. III)

Noble, Mark. *A Biographical History of England, from the Revolution to the End of George I's Reign; Being a Continuation of the Rev. J. Granger's Work*, London, 1806.

Orrery, John Earl of. *Remarks on the Life and Writings of Dr. Jonathan Swift*, London, 1752.

Paget, John. "Swift"--*Blackwood's* (May, 1876)
"Swift and Lord Macaulay"--*Blackwood's* (Nov., 1876)

Phillips, Samuel. "Dean Swift"--London *Times* (Oct. 3, 1850), p. 3.

Pilkington, Letitia. *Memoirs*, ed. Iris Barry, London, 1928.

Purves, D. Laing. *The Works of Jonathan Swift, D. D.*, Edinburgh, 1869.

Richardson, Samuel. *Correspondence*, London, 1804.

Robinson, Henry Crabb. *Diary, Reminiscences, and Correspondence*, ed. T. Sadler, London, 1869.

Roscoe, Thomas. *Life and Works of Jonathan Swift*. In the *Works of Jonathan Swift*, vol. 1, London, 1841.

Scott, Sir Walter. *Memoirs of Jonathan Swift, D. D. Dean of St. Patrick's, Dublin*. In the *Works of Jonathan Swift*, vol. I, Edinburgh, 1814.

Shaw, Thomas B. *Outlines of English Literature*, 1848. (Philadelphia, 1849)

Sheridan, Thomas. *Life of Dr. Swift*. In *The Works of the Rev. Jonathan Swift, D. D.*, ed. J. Nichols, vol. I, London, 1801.

Stephen, Leslie. *History of English Thought in the Eighteenth Century*, vol. II, London, 1876. (Second edition, 1881)
Swift (English Men of Letters series), London, 1882. (New York, 1898)

Swift, Deane. *An Essay upon the Life, Writings, and Character, of Dr. Jonathan Swift*, London, 1755.

Thackeray, William Makepeace. *The English Humourists of the Eighteenth Century*. In *Works*, vol. VII, New York, 1899.

Taine, H. A. *History of English Literature*, tr. H. Van Laun, vol. II, Edinburgh, 1871.

Taylor, W. C. Introduction to *Gulliver's Travels*, London, 1840.

Thomson, James. *Essays and Phantasies*, London, 1881.

Thomson, Katharine (pseudonym Grace Wharton). *The Literature of Society*, vol. II, London, 1862.

Trollope, Anthony. *Thackeray (English Men of Letters* series), New York, 1879.

Vandam, A. D. *Amours of Great Men* ("A Bachelor from Conviction"), London, 1878.

Waller, John Francis. Introduction to *Gulliver's Travels*, Dublin, 1864.

Walpole, Horace. *Letters*, ed. Paget Toynbee, Oxford, 1904.

Ward, A. W. "Swift's Love-Story in German Literature"--*Macmillan's* (Feb., 1877)

Warton, Joseph. *An Essay on the Genius and Writings of Pope*, vol. II, London, 1782.

Weber, Henry. Introductory Dissertation to *Popular Romances*, Edinburgh, 1812.

Wilberforce, William. *The Life*, by Robert and Samuel Wilberforce, vol. V, London, 1838.

Wilde, W. R. *The Closing Years of Dean Swift's Life...*, Dublin, 1849.

Wilson, *Swiftiana*, London, 1804.

Wyon, Frederick William. *The History of Great Britain During the Reign of Queen Anne*, London, 1876.

Young, Edward. *Conjectures on Original Composition*, ed. E. J. Morley, Manchester, 1918.

PERIODICALS

(All articles, unless otherwise designated, deal specifically with Swift. American editions of English periodicals are marked (1).)

The Academy:

XXII, 233-34. Sept. 30, 1882. (Dowden)

Analytical Review:

IV, 77-8. May, 1789. In a review of *Mammuth.*

The Athenaeum:

Sept. 30, 1882; p. 426.

Belgravia:

II, 173-81. April, 1867.
XXV, 398-403. Jan., 1875. (Blackburne)

Blackwood's Magazine:

XVIII, 719-23. Dec., 1825.
XVIII, 724-29. Dec., 1825.
XIX, p. 583. May, 1826. In "Prodigality of Words."
LXXIV, 494-518. Oct., 1853. (Eagles)[1]
CXIX, 527-44. May, 1876. (Paget)[1]
CXX, 521-36. Nov., 1876. (Paget)[1]

British Quarterly Review:

XX, 528-60. Oct., 1854. (Masson)
LXIII, 145-61. April, 1876.[1]

Chambers's Edinburgh Journal:

VIII, p. 302. Nov. 6, 1847.

The Cornhill Magazine:

XXXIII, 172-83. Feb., 1876.

The Critic:

XII, 374-76. July 15, 1853.

The Critical Review:

LVIII, 349-55. Nov., 1784.
XVIII (series the third), 151-59. Oct., 1809.

Dublin Review:

XXVI, p. 125. March, 1849. In an article on the Duke of Marlborough.

Dublin University Magazine:

XII, 269ff. Sept., 1838.
XV--(pt. 1) 131-44. Feb., 1840.
(pt. 2) 333-44. March, 1840.
(pt. 3) 538-56. May, 1840.
(pt. 4) 634-61. June, 1840.
XXXIII, 374-81. March, 1849.

Edinburgh Monthly Review:

IV, 1-37. July, 1820.

Edinburgh Review:

XXVII, 1-58. Sept., 1816. (Jeffrey)
LVI, p. 538. Jan., 1833. In a review of Mahon's *History of the War of the Succession in Spain.* (Macaulay)
LXVIII, 113-87. Oct., 1838. "Life and Writings of Sir William Temple." (Macaulay)
LXXVIII, 193-260. July, 1843. "Life and Writings of Addison." (Macaulay)
CII, p. 273. July, 1855. In an account of Sydney Smith.

English Review:

XVII, 209-18. March, 1791. In a review of Berkeley's *Literary Relics.*

The Englishwoman's Domestic Magazine:

XVI--(pt. 1) 6-8. Jan., 1874.
(pt. 2) 63-5. Feb., 1874.

European Magazine:

VI, 282-86. Oct., 1784.
XVIII, 182-85. Sept., 1790.
XVIII, 329-35. Nov., 1790.
LII, p. 278. Oct., 1807.
LII, p. 443. Dec., 1807.

Fraser's Magazine:

X, 18-32. July, 1834. (Mahony)
LXXVI, 638-53. Nov., 1867. (Allingham)
XXIV (new series), 385-400. Sept., 1881. (Lane-Poole)

Gentleman's Magazine:

LII, p. 470. Oct., 1782.
LIII, p. 24. Jan., 1783.
LXXXIX (pt. 1), 156-57. Feb., 1819.
XCII (pt. 1), 247-51. March, 1822. In a review of Masons's *History of St. Patrick.*
XCVI. 3-6. Jan., 1826.
XLIII (new series), 146-52. Feb., 1855.
XLIII (new series), 258-61. March, 1855.
XLIV (new series), 34-6. July, 1855.
VII (entirely new series), 436-56. Sept., 1871. (Clarke)

Hogg's Instructor:

I (third series), 74-9. July, 1853.

London Medical Gazette:

XVII, 115-19. Oct. 24, 1835.

Macmillan's Magazine:

XXXV, 308-17. Feb., 1877. (Ward)

Monthly Review:

V, 407-24 and 475-87. Nov. and Dec., 1751.
XI, 56-77. July, 1754.
LXI, 356-65. Nov., 1779.
LXXII, 321-37. May, 1785.
I (new series), 1-9. Jan., 1789.
III (new series), 241-44. Nov., 1790. In a review of Berkeley's *Literary Relics.*

National Review:

I, 280-81. Oct., 1855. In "The First Edinburgh Reviewers."

The New Monthly Magazine:

XVII, p. 140. July, 1826. In "Specimens of a Dictionary of Love and Beauty."
LXIV, 110-22. Jan., 1842.
CXLVII, 342-53. Sept., 1870. (Mackay)

North British Review:

XI, 180-98. Aug., 1849.[1]
LI, 169-98. Jan., 1870.[1]

Quarterly Review:

I, 162-77. Feb., 1809.
CI, 410-14. April, 1857. In an essay on political satire in England.
CXXIX, p. 25. July, 1870. In a review of Mahon's *History of England Comprising the Reign of Queen Anne...*
CXLI, 42-80. Jan., 1876.

Saturday Review:

XL, 714-16. Dec. 4, 1875.
LIV, 443-44. Sept. 30, 1882.

The Scots Magazine:

LXXVI (pt. 2), 847-54. Nov., 1814.

Sharpe's London Journal:

XI, 303-10. 1850(?) (Lawrence)

Spectator:

XLIX, 46-8. Jan. 8, 1876.
LV, 1228-29. Sept. 23, 1882.

Temple Bar:

XXI, 322-30. Oct., 1867. (Hannay)
XLVI, 255-67. Feb., 1876.

London *Times:*

Oct. 3, 1850, p. 3. (Phillips)